The Ultimate Guide to the vi and ex Text Editors

Hewlett-Packard Company

The Benjamin/Cummings Publishing Company, Inc.

Redwood City, California • Fort Collins, Colorado • Menlo Park, California
Reading, Massachusetts • New York • Don Mills, Ontario • Wokingham, U.K.
Amsterdam • Bonn • Sydney • Singapore • Tokyo • Madrid • San Juan

Sponsoring Editors: Mark McCormick, Alan Apt
Production Editor: Eleanor Renner Brown
Copyeditors: Rhoda Simmons, Bob Klingensmith
Cover Designer: Juan Vargas

Library of Congress Cataloging-in-Publication Data

The Ultimate guide to the vi and ex text editors / Hewlett Packard.
    p.   cm.
    ISBN 0-8053-4460-8
      1. UNIX (Computer operating system) 2. vi (Computer program)
3. ex (Computer program)   4. Text editors (Computer programs)
I. Hewlett Packard Company.
  QA76.76.063U48   1990
  652.5'53--dc20   89-18318
                                         CIP

8910 -DO- 95 94

The Benjamin/Cummings Publishing Company, Inc.
390 Bridge Parkway
Redwood City, California 94065

Preface

Hewlett-Packard has shipped a form of this book to over 50,000 UNIX users in the past few years. Feedback from these users suggested that others would benefit from our experience. This motivated us to make this book available to a wider audience through commercial publication.

This book was written for the broad range of new and experienced UNIX users who want to take advantage of the power of the vi or ex editors. The vi and ex editors are shipped as part of the standard implementation by nearly every UNIX supplier. This book describes vi as it is implemented on systems such as Apple, DEC, Hewlett-Packard (including Apollo systems), IBM, Sun, Xenix, and even personal computers. vi is an integral part of the UNIX system. This book takes a comprehensive look at these two editors.

Since other editors such as ed, edit, view, and sed are also available to UNIX users, the choice of an editor can be confusing and difficult. We help you make that decision easy by describing these different editors.

New users can be productive using the vi editor within minutes of reading Chapter 1. The proficient user will appreciate the coverage of many of vi's advanced features and the coverage of the ex editor that can be accessed directly from vi. Since vi is derived from ex, we describe the capabilities of the ex editor accessible from vi.

If you are familiar with other text editors and are making the transition to the vi editor on UNIX, you will find the task orientation of this book helpful. **Task oriented** means that we explain how to do specific tasks that you want to do instead of explaining the functionality of the editor. For example, the section called "Merging Another File into Text" explains how to insert a file into the current file being edited. Even the index contains entries for user tasks.

This book describes some of the **unique and obscure capabilities** of the vi editor. Some of these capabilities have only shown up as references without explaining how to apply them until now (such as the -t tags option). These powerful capabilities are rarely discussed in other texts. Some of these obscure capabilities are targeted at programmers (such as the ctags command and the lisp option). Some of the power of the vi editor is evident in its ability to interact with other UNIX commands outside of the editor. This feature makes it possible, for example, to sort a list while you are editing it, then convert the list to multiple columns.

We have provided many useful **examples** that show how to use the power of this editor. Examples that will provide you with a better understanding of the power of `vi` and `ex`.

The book also contains **tutorials** for the `vi` and `ex` editors that include tips to speed the learning process.

For those who are still trying to figure out how to configure `vi` with correct settings in the *.exrc* file, we have included a chapter that describes the setting of the different **configuration options.** For many users, this information alone makes this a valuable book to have.

We include an appendix on **regular expressions,** the wildcard characters of UNIX, because much of the power of `vi` is related to its searching and text substitution capabilities.

Contents

4. Cursor and Display Control

5. Manipulating Text

6. Copying and Moving Text Using Buffers and Text Objects

Figures

Tables

1

All You Need to Know

It has been said that vi is hard to learn. Not so. Everything you need to know is on this and the next page.

vi the Lazy Way

If you thumb quickly through this book, you will discover that several hundred pages were needed to detail vi's many capabilities and show how to use them properly. If you want to become a proficient vi user, you will find a thorough study of its contents very rewarding.

If you are too busy to take time now, you can get by using just 12 basic commands. They are summarized here for those who insist on doing it the "quick and dirty" way. You'll be much less efficient, but you will be able to get simple jobs done. Then, when the pressing matters of the moment are less urgent, you can study this book in detail and discover how much time you could have saved by using better methods. Here are the basic commands:

Command Mode Access Commands

(ESC)   Return to command mode. Used to terminate adding new text after i, a, o, and O commands. If you press (ESC) and get a beep, you are already in command mode.

:   Start ex mode command at bottom of screen. A few commands are listed on the next page.

vi Editor Commands

i   Insert new text in front of current character. (ESC) ends insertion.

a   Append new text after current character. (ESC) ends appending.

x   Delete current cursor character.

dd   Delete entire current cursor line.

h   Move cursor left one position.

l   Move cursor right one position.

j   Move cursor down one line.

k   Move cursor up one line.

More vi Editor Commands

o   Open a new line after current line and start inserting new text until (ESC) is pressed.

O   Open a new line before current line and start inserting new text until (ESC) is pressed.

ZZ   Terminate the editing session after storing the buffer file in permanent storage.

/text   Search file for series of characters that matches *text*.

ex Mode Commands

:w   Write file to *filename*.

:q   Quit if the file has been preserved in permanent storage.

:q!   Quit after discarding edited file. Do not store it permanently.

Easier Ways

r   Replace current cursor character with a new single character.

R   Replace existing text, one character at a time, until ⌈ESC⌉ is pressed.

u   Cancel the last change and restore to condition before change.

U   Restore current line to original condition before you changed it.

Y   Yank (copy) current line into the unnamed buffer.

p   Put unnamed buffer contents into text after the current cursor position.

P   Put unnamed buffer contents into text before the current cursor position.

/   search foreward

?   search backward

!   pipe (filter)

:   ex commands

2

Introducing the vi/ex Editor

The UNIX[1] operating system contains a powerful text editor program that exhibits several personalities, depending on which command was used to start it. However, of the six possible commands, only two really distinctive personalities exist:

- The `vi`, `view`, and `vedit` commands access the interactive style of operation that maintains a continuously updated screen display that shows changes as they occur.

- The `ex` and `edit` commands access the line editor style of operation, which is essentially an extended version of the UNIX line editor program, `ed`.

The Background of vi

The `vi` text-editing program was written by Bill Joy,[2] a graduate student at the time at the University of California at Berkeley. His work was an effort to enhance the `ed` editor, which originated at Bell labs (later AT&T). `ed` is a memory-efficient line editor rarely used (except in shell scripts) today. `sed` is a batch editor that is derived from `ed`.

---

[1] UNIX is a registered trademark of AT&T in the U.S.A. and other countries.
[2] Bill Joy wrote about the `vi` editor in *An Introduction to Display Editing with Vi*. He also wrote a related document, *Ex Reference Manual*.

UNIX Command Names for the vi Editor

vi   Full-capability visually interactive editor that maintains a continuously updated display screen showing the changes made by the editor as they occur.

view   Equivalent to vi except that the original file is marked as "read only" to the editor so that it is reasonably safe from being casually or accidentally overwritten or destroyed[3] by the user or the editor during the session. However, the edited file can be stored elsewhere in a new file. This command is commonly used when original source files must be carefully preserved.

vedit   Same capabilities as vi, but special flags are set, indicating to the editor program that the user is a beginner who wants special treatment. Various releases of vi have differing default options for vedit, making the behavior of this command somewhat unpredictable. Most users, including casual and inexperienced, use the standard vi and view commands. Few UNIX users ever use vedit.

UNIX Command Names for the ex Editor

The following UNIX commands access editors that are functionally similar:

ex   Extended form of the ed editor. Not as popular as the vi editor because it does not maintain an updated display of edited text as the session progresses and most ex features are readily accessible from vi.

edit   Counterpart of vedit for the ex editor. Editor behavior is altered to accommodate the needs of casual or inexperienced users. This form of ex holds little or no interest for most UNIX users.

---

[3] The original file can be overwritten by a forced write command if you have the necessary access permissions on the file.

vi and view are by far the most commonly used editors among UNIX users equipped with CRT display terminals because of their interactive nature. Although not truly **WYSIWYG** (What You See Is What You Get), vi and view are close, showing a full screen of information at a time.

ex is used much less frequently, usually in situations where commands cannot work correctly in the standard vi environment. vedit and edit are rarely used on most systems, mainly because vi is reasonably straightforward and as easy to learn and use, despite its powerful capabilities.

Switching Between vi and ex

There are times when it is necessary or desirable to switch from vi to ex editor personalities and vice versa without leaving the session. This is easily accomplished by pressing Q (SHIFT-Q) when in vi to change to ex or typing vi Return after the colon prompt when in ex. This situation most commonly arises when performing intermediate and advanced editing tasks as described in later chapters that deal with more advanced topics.

For ex Users

If you are using ex exclusively instead of vi (perhaps because you have an electro-mechanical printing terminal instead of a CRT display terminal), most of the mechanics of using ex are explained in Chapter 9 and Chapter 11, with some topics of interest scattered elsewhere, such as in Chapter 6 and Chapter 7. However, this book is intended for those who have access to CRT terminals or bit-mapped displays (almost all UNIX users).

International Language Support

On many UNIX systems, vi and ex support 8-bit character codes necessary for editing text files in various languages. These UNIX systems may support several 8-bit character sets such as Katakana and Roman. This means that these editors do not strip the eighth bit from ASCII text. Many vi and ex implementations strip the eighth bit. For 8-bit character sets to be correctly displayed on a terminal, system terminal support must be correctly configured for the language and character set being used.

Some computer systems also support a 16-bit version of vi for Asian character sets.[4]

Why vi?

The vi editor provides a powerful, visually interactive text editor that provides a continuously updated text display as editing progresses. The close interaction between user and text editor includes the ability to recover from mistakes by using the editor's undo command.

Since vi is an extension of the ex editor, it also supports many ex capabilities that simplify repetitive operations such as search-and-replace and global changes on all or part of a file from a simple command, provide typing aids with the abbreviate command, and support file manipulation and other capabilities. These conveniences, coupled with several safeguards to aid in recovery from user errors, provide a flexible tool that meets the needs of beginning and experienced users alike.

The ex command accesses a useful, but much less commonly used, editor that does not provide the high level of visual interaction with the user that is available from vi. ex is an extended form of the early UNIX editor ed that receives only limited use on most systems (other than in shell scripts and programs). Both ex and vi are really only a single program that behaves differently depending on the command used to access it. However, where, when, and how each command is used varies significantly.

---

[4] For example, Hewlett-Packard Series 9000 computers support 16-bit character sets based, in part, on software developed by the Toshiba Corporation.

Audience Definition and Learning Suggestions

This book is designed so that anyone who has a rudimentary understanding of the UNIX file system and text editors in general, but little experience with UNIX, can quickly begin performing useful work using vi, then progress with study and experience to an expert level. Because of the broad range of skill and knowledge that is addressed, this book is, of necessity, rather lengthy. However, few users will have a need to read it entirely from start to finish.

Use the table of contents to grasp the general outline and structure of the book, then select those areas you need to understand and proceed accordingly. Beginning users should read the first four chapters and try the examples before proceeding.

If you are a more experienced user, you will likely discover that time spent perusing topics you are already familiar with will yield useful techniques that you had previously overlooked, making the effort worthwhile. Considerable effort has been invested in providing various unusual shortcuts to editing by bringing some of vi's largely undiscovered capabilities out of obscurity.

Organization of This Book

The bulk of this book explains how to use the vi editor and access and use the ex commands from vi. A separate chapter explains how to access and use the ex editor, then refers to other chapters for detailed information about ex editing commands. The chapters that form the body of this text are tutorial in nature. An appendix at the end contains abbreviated reference material on regular expressions for experienced users. The table of contents provides a useful list of the topics covered, and the index is more comprehensive than is typical in most UNIX-like systems documentation.

User Interaction

vi has three main operating modes and a few related behavior traits that may be somewhat confusing to beginning users. They are presented here for reference. You may prefer to skim this section so that you know what it contains, then come back later when understanding it becomes important.

Operating Modes

The three primary operating modes are as follows:

■ vi command mode

■ text input mode

■ ex command mode, sometimes referred to as external mode

Associated with the ex command, or external, mode is the shell escape command that is used to access UNIX system commands as well as the external capabilities in the ex editor that are used by vi for such tasks as global changes, search-and-replace, and other operations.

vi Command Mode

When vi is started and ready for use, command mode is active. The editor stays in command mode until a valid text input command is seen. There are two classes of commands: non-printing and printing.

■ Most vi user commands are non-printing, which means that they are not printed on the terminal as they are received by vi because they would disrupt the visible text display. Such commands are usually related to inserting, deleting, or altering text relative to the current cursor position, or they pertain to cursor movement or changing text position on the display screen. Processing these commands without printing them on the display screen is not a problem because other visible terminal or display behavior indicates that the command was received correctly. If you make a mistake, the undo command quickly repairs the damage and you can try again.

- vi has only four printing commands. They are:

  / The forward search command

  ? The backward search command

  ! The shell pipe (or filter) command

  : The prefix for ex commands being executed from vi

These commands and the ensuing command text (search string and/or UNIX command) are printed on the bottom line of the display screen below the displayed text. These commands are used for such editor tasks as searching forward or backward for a text pattern or piping all or parts of the **buffer**[5] through a UNIX command (such as sort, adjust, or pr).

vi always uses the bottom line of the screen to display printing commands, error messages, and echoed command lines. Look there to verify your commands or find other information about errors and command completion.

Text Input Mode

vi enters text input mode whenever an insert text, append text, or change text command is given. In text input mode, characters are added to the text file as they are typed from the terminal keyboard until you press (ESC), at which time vi returns to command mode. Text input mode is described in detail in later chapters.

If you press (ESC) while in command mode, the terminal vi ignores the command and causes the terminal to beep or flash the screen.

New vi users often find it difficult to determine whether they are in input mode or command mode. The editor can be reconfigured quite easily to display the mode by typing the following command from the keyboard after the editing session is started, as described later:

> :set showmode (Return)

Once this command has been typed, vi displays the message INPUT MODE in the lower right-hand corner of the editor display screen when in input mode. If not in input mode, no message is present. This command can

---

[5] The **buffer** is the temporary storage location holding the most recent deleted or yanked text. See Chapter 6 for more information.

also be placed in your *.exrc* file, as explained in Chapter 11 under the topic "Automating Editor Configuration."

External Mode or ex Command Mode

External mode is accessed by typing : while in command mode. The colon, the first character in a printing external command, is displayed on the bottom line of the screen and tells vi that the command is to be executed by ex. If the colon is followed by an exclamation point, the exclamation point tells ex that the remainder of the command is to be passed to a UNIX shell for execution instead of being processed by ex.

Upon completion of any external mode operation, control is returned to vi. When an ex command results in a shell escape, the return from the UNIX shell requires that you press a key telling vi to update the display screen and resume operation. This provides an opportunity for you to review any displayed information on the screen (such as the results from a file-listing command, for example) before it is destroyed when vi overwrites the screen. Whenever vi suspends operation for a shell escape, it provides a prompt indicating the proper recovery procedure.

If an open file was modified prior to the external mode command, vi may issue the following message:

```
[No write since last change]
```

This message occurs when the command that produces the message results in a shell escape from the editor. It has two purposes. First, it is a warning telling you that the current workfile (that is, the text that is currently being edited with the editor) has not been written back to permanent storage and the changes you have made will be lost if no write operation occurs before terminating vi upon return from the shell escape.

Second, it also tells you that if a UNIX program such as a compiler is run by the external mode command, the source file cannot be used because it is not up to date. Since most shell escape commands result in a return to vi, loss of the edited file is not usually a concern unless something happens that causes vi to be aborted. However, if you run a compiler such as cc on an older version of the file, you will probably not get the desired result. If you need to abort such a command, press the interrupt key[6] (usually (BREAK) or (CTRL)-(C)) to return to the editor.

When UNIX completes the shell escape and returns to vi, vi usually displays the message

```
[Hit return to continue]
```

Press any typing key such as (Return) or the space bar to resume editing. vi then updates the screen and places the cursor where it was before vi was interrupted by the external command.

What Are All Those Tildes (˜) on My Screen?

If you are editing a new file (see Figure 2-1) or if text is positioned on the display screen such that the·end of the file occurs before the bottom line of the screen, vi displays tilde (˜) characters down the left-hand column of the display screen. These characters are placed there by vi as part of its normal display-screen–handling processes to mark lines on the display that have no corresponding line of text in the file being displayed.

---

[6] The interrupt key can be set using the stty command in *.profile* (Bourne or Korn shell) or *.login* (C shell).

```
        ~
        ~
        ~
        ~
        ~
        ~
        ~
        ~
        ~
        ~
        ~
        ~
        ~
        ~
        ~
        ~
        ~
        ~
        ~
        ~
        ~
        ~
"vi_example" [New file]
```

Figure 2-1. The vi screen at startup

vi does not place any visible characters in the text file stored on disk other
than those that were intentionally placed there by someone using vi at the
time the file was created or during a subsequent editing session, so relax —
those tildes are *not* part of your file, but they can help you recognize blank
lines at the end of a text file.

If you see empty lines between the last line of visible text in the file and the
first line with a tilde in the left column on the display screen, those empty
lines are blank lines in the file (or a long string of spaces and/or tabs on the
last line that forced the line to wrap to the succeeding line(s) — not likely,
but possible).

You may also occasionally see a ~ at the end of the last line in the file. The
tilde indicates that the last line in the file is not terminated by a newline
character. Normally, this can happen only when the original file being edited

had no trailing newline at the start of the session. When the file is written back out at the end of the editing session, `vi` places a newline after the last line.

What About Long Text Lines at the Bottom of My Screen?

Occasionally, you may encounter files where a single line contains more characters than can be displayed on a single line of the terminal's CRT display. When such a line is encountered, `vi` wraps the line at the right screen margin onto the next line without regard for word boundaries. The line is still a single line in the stored file too, but it is displayed as two or more lines on the CRT.

Occasionally, as when scrolling text, a displayed line preceding a long line may occupy the next to the last line of the CRT display window (excluding the command line at the bottom of the screen). Since `vi` cannot display the following line on the single available line at the bottom of the screen because it is too long, `vi` omits the line from the display and, instead, places a single character (@) in the left column of the blank display line. If the undisplayed line requires two or more lines on the CRT display, an @ character is placed at the beginning of each blanked display line until sufficient lines are available to display the entire line of text as it exists in the buffer file.

If a long line is scrolled off the top of the screen, it disappears one display line at a time as the lines roll up. If the screen is scrolled down, the display jumps downward by enough display lines to bring the long line fully into view.

Program Limits

`vi` and `ex` impose several limits that must be considered when you depart from the range of typical applications. However, these limits rarely affect most users. They are grouped here for your convenience should you need to know what they are. The commands and other conditions that these limits affect are described throughout the later chapters in this book.

File Types

vi can only be used to edit text files, not binary files (such as compiled programs) nor directories.

Maximum Line Length

vi allows line lengths up to 1024 characters, including a small number of characters (about 2 or 3) used for overhead. In general, unless your line lengths exceed 1020 characters, you should not have difficulty.

If you load in a text file with lines longer than the maximum allowed, they will be truncated to the maximum. Be careful not to store such an editor file away if the information was important; all the additional text will be lost.

Trying to create lines with vi greater than the allowable length will cause a Line too long error message.

Maximum File Size

On some UNIX systems, memory constraints may limit maximum file size. However, generally the system capacity is such that file size is rarely, if ever, of concern since the silently enforced maximum file length is 250,000 lines. Consult system manuals for more information about this limit if it is important.

vi copies the source file being edited into a separate buffer area (temporary storage location) during the editing session and puts it back at the end of a session. The time required to perform the copying can become disconcerting if extremely large files are being edited. This can also be a problem when performing searches and other global operations on large files.

Other Limitations

Other limits you are likely to encounter as you reach more advanced levels include:

- 256 characters per global command list

- 128 characters in a filename in `vi` or `ex` *open* mode. (AT&T System V-based UNIX systems usually allow a maximum filename length of 14 characters. Berkeley 4.x-based UNIX systems usually support longer filenames up to 256 characters. Some systems can be configured for either limit.)

- 128 characters in the previous insert/delete buffer

- 100 characters in a shell escape command

- 63 characters in a string-valued option (`:set` command)

- 30 characters in a program tag name

- 32 or fewer macros defined by `map` command

- 512 or fewer characters total in combined existing `map` macros

Basic Editing

Editing consists of various related tasks that include:

- Creating new text; called text entry or text input

- Deleting existing text

- Altering existing text

- Inserting or appending new text into an existing line

- Inserting new lines between existing lines

- Rearranging blocks of existing text

The next few chapters describe relatively simple editor tasks that are commonly used by a majority of users. More advanced topics are discussed in later chapters. A summary of commands, key functions, and other information is located in an appendix at the end of this book for easy reference.

Chapter Summary

These are highlights of topics detailed in this chapter:

Modes

Command mode
> Initial startup mode when vi is executed; waiting for text input command.

Text input mode
> Entered by text input command such as insert (i), append (a), or change (c) command.

External mode or ex command mode
> Entered by typing a colon (:), which precedes all ex commands.

Program Limits

File type
> ASCII text only. No binary or object code files can be edited.

Line length
> About 1020 characters maximum per line.

File size
> Determined by file system and implementation (never exceeding 250,000 lines).

Global command list
> 256 characters maximum.

Filename length
> 128 characters maximum (AT&T System V allows only 14-character filenames).

Insert/delete buffer
> 128 characters maximum.

Shell escape command length
> 100 characters maximum.

:set command string length
> 63 characters maximum.

Program tag name length
> 30 characters maximum.

Combined map macro length
> 512 characters total maximum.

3

Starting and Ending a Session

An editing session begins when you invoke vi from a UNIX user shell (or program). The session can be terminated normally by a write-and-quit command, or it can be aborted by using only the quit command (in which case the results of the editing session are discarded unless they were previously saved by a separate write command). This chapter describes each of these possibilities in greater detail.

What's in This Chapter

This chapter covers the following topics in detail:

- Starting vi with a new or existing file
- Protecting files against overwriting
- Ending an edit session, with or without saving text
- Saving an edited text file
- Recovering from problems
- Entering text
- Setting end-of-line word wrap
- Recovering from a system crash

File Usage During an Editing Session

When vi starts operation, it creates a temporary file (in the system directory /tmp) that is used to hold the text being edited. If you are editing an existing file, the existing file is copied into the temporary file for editing. If you specify a new file to edit, new text from the terminal keyboard is copied into the temporary file and edited according to the editing commands you provide. At the end of the session, unless you specify otherwise, the contents of the temporary file are copied back into the existing file or a new file is created to hold the temporary file contents if you are editing a new file.

Starting an Edit Session

The editing session begins by invoking vi with an optional filename. If no filename is specified when you start the session, you must end the session by using a write or write-and-quit command with a filename provided at that time. Thus, it is usually preferred (and easier) to provide the filename when vi is invoked. If you want to edit an existing file, it is much easier to provide a filename at the beginning than to use read commands to retrieve the file after vi has started.

Selecting the File

vi can be used to edit an existing file or to create a new file. In either case, the name of the existing file or the name of the new file to be created is usually specified when invoking vi, as follows:

vi *filename* (Return)

If you intentionally or inadvertently invoke vi without including the filename, vi opens a temporary file that is maintained for the duration of the editing session. Upon completion of (or at any time during) the session, you can save the contents of the temporary file in a specified *filename* by using the write command, described later in this chapter. If you prefer, you can abort the session at any time and destroy the contents of the temporary file without disturbing the original contents of the source text file by using the quit command, as explained later in this chapter under "Ending an Edit Session."

File Must Be a Text File

Only text files consisting of ASCII (or other supported) characters can be edited using vi. If you attempt to edit a non-text file, an error will probably result. Non-text files can also wreak havoc with terminal configuration.

Existing or New File?

During startup, vi checks to see if *filename* exists. If the file is present in the current (or specified other directory), it is copied to a temporary file, then the beginning part of the temporary file is printed on the display screen. (If the file is smaller than the available screen size, the entire file is displayed and any unused display lines are marked by tildes in the left-most column.)

When vi opens an existing file for editing, pertinent information concerning the filename and number of lines and characters in the file is displayed at the bottom of the screen. During the edit, unless you issue a write command, only the temporary file is used. The original file is preserved in its original, undisturbed form. Depending on which options you use when terminating the edit session, the temporary file is usually written back to the original file, at which time the original file is destroyed and replaced by the new edited file.

If *filename* does not exist, vi opens a temporary file and displays a blank screen with tilde (~) characters down the left side, one on each line. vi then awaits your first command. At the end of the session, again depending on which options you select and what commands you use to terminate the edit, vi usually writes the contents of the temporary file to a new file, giving it the filename you specified when invoking vi at the beginning of the session.

Note the message at the bottom of the screen when the file is opened. If the specified file does not exist, vi displays the filename enclosed between double quote marks followed by

```
[New file]
```

What If *filename* Is a Directory?

If the specified file is a directory, the filename between quotes is followed by

```
Directory
```

This means that you must take alternative action now or later becase vi cannot be used to alter the contents of a directory. To allow otherwise would create catastrophic confusion in the UNIX file system. If this situation arises, refer to "Common Difficulties" later in this chapter for further instructions.

Editing an Existing File

If *filename* already exists, vi copies the file into a temporary file, then displays the first few lines of the file on the terminal screen. You can now edit the file as discussed in later chapters. When you have finished editing, terminate the session using ZZ or :w.

Protecting an Existing File

Most users occasionally need to edit an existing file but need a guarantee that they cannot accidentally overwrite it during or at the end of an editing session. As usual, UNIX and vi provide several ways for doing this. You can use the UNIX cp command to copy the original file to a new file and then edit the new file, or you can use the readonly option to the command, which, again, can be handled in one of several ways:

- Start the session by using a -R option between the vi command and the filename.

- Use the view command, which is equivalent to using the -R option with vi.

- Start the session with the usual vi command, then use the :set readonly command to the editor to prevent overwriting the file.

These techniques are equivalent. Obviously, the easiest of the three is simply to use the view command instead of vi, then proceed with the edit. When you are ready to save the file in permanent storage, use the :w command and a different filename before terminating vi. Exact procedures for saving the edited file are explained in detail later in this and subsequent chapters.

Note	Be careful when using the `:set readonly` or `view` commands to protect your source file. You can still destroy it by using a `:w!` command (no space between w and !) if you have proper access permissions to the file. This is especially hazardous if you start editing another file while in the current editing session by using a `:vi` *filename* command from `vi` or `view`. The best way to protect a file is by setting the file access permissions to read-only (mode 400, 440, or 444) by using the UNIX `chmod` command.

Ending an Edit Session

Upon completion of an editing session, you have several options:

- Terminate normally by writing the temporary file contents to the file specified when `vi` was invoked.

- Abort the edit and destroy the contents of the temporary file.

- Write all or part of the temporary file to one or more alternate filenames, then continue editing.

- Write all or part of the temporary file to one or more alternate filenames, then abort.

- Write all or part of the temporary file to one or more alternate filenames, then write it to the file specified when `vi` was invoked and terminate normally.

- Any combination of the above as well as other options.

Normal Termination

`vi` editing sessions are nearly always terminated normally by a write-and-quit command that can be given in either of two forms. With `vi` in command mode (if you are not sure, press (ESC) once or twice until you hear a beep from the terminal), type either of the following:

ZZ

or

: wq (Return)

Obviously the first is easier because it is a shorthand form of the second and does not require use of the (Return) key.

The second form is an ex command that is executed from vi. The w tells UNIX to write the temporary file to the current file that was (usually) specified when vi was invoked. The q command tells vi to abort after the file is written to permanent storage.

Other forms of the write (:w) command are useful for splitting files, saving parts of a file in other locations, and other related tasks. The write command is described in greater detail in the section "Using the Write Command" later in this chapter as well as in Chapter 8.

Note   The ZZ command must be used with care when using the :w or :w! command to copy the working file to other files. If the original file is modified and then written to another file, typing ZZ terminates the edit without updating the original file.

Aborting an Editing Session

You may occasionally want to abort an editing session for any of various reasons. Sometimes a complex operation can be disastrously misdirected due to a typographical error or accidental keystroke, making it easier to start over than to repair the damage. At other times, you may simply decide to abort the edit and go back to the original version. You also may use vi at times to scan a file, then want to abort the session to ensure that the source file is not altered.

You can easily exit gracefully without disturbing existing file structures by using the quit (:q) command. If you execute any editing command before quitting, vi will not accept :q as a valid quit command (this is to keep you from abandoning a long editing session if you accidentally give a wrong command). If you want to quit, even though you may have already executed an editing operation, use :q! instead to override the protection barrier.

If you send vi an ordinary quit (:q) command and an override is needed because one or more editing commands were executed before the quit command was received, vi sends the error message

```
No write since last change (:quit! overrides)
```

To force vi to quit, repeat the quit command with the exclamation point. If you want to continue editing, just give vi your next command. No recovery is necessary. Note that :q and :quit are equivalent, but most users prefer :q because it is easier to type.

Common Difficulties

Typographical errors, oversights, slips of the finger, or brief mental lapses can lead to mistakes, however minor, when invoking vi. The consequences are seldom serious, but they can be disconcerting if you don't know how to recover. Here are a few examples of typical problems that cover most situations.

Oops! I Got the Wrong File. Now What?

The most common error is usually accidentally striking the wrong key when specifying a filename. This causes vi to look for an incorrect filename that may or may not exist. If vi cannot find the file, it opens a new file. If a file exists whose name matches the mistyped one, the wrong file is opened for editing.

Another common error occurs when you forget to include a complete directory pathname and the file does not reside in the current working directory. Again, vi opens a new file if the name is not present in the current directory, or it opens a wrong file if a file having the same name is present.

When such accidents happen, you usually do not want to modify an existing file, nor do you want to create a new one. To exit gracefully without disturbing existing file structures, use the quit (:q or :q!) command discussed earlier in this chapter under the topic "Aborting an Editing Session."

Time-Saving Tip

When you abort an editing session and restart with a new file, the vi program must be reloaded into memory by UNIX. You can avoid the time required to reload the editor when you switch to a new file by using the command

> :e *new_filename* (Return)

This ex mode command causes vi to abandon the current temporary file contents and immediately open a new file and reload the temporary file without terminating the editor program, usually saving several seconds. If you have modified a file and want to abort and change files without updating the original file and reloading the editor program, use

> :e! *new_filename* (Return)

Either of these commands can be used after the write command (:w or :w!), described in the section "Using the Write Command" of this chapter, if you need to edit another file and don't want to reload the editor.

What If I Try to Edit a Directory?

It is easy to absent-mindedly type the name of a directory when invoking vi. When *filename* is a directory, you obviously cannot store the temporary file under that filename when you finish. You have three options:

- Change the filename being edited (the easiest option) by typing

  > :e *filename* (Return)

- Abort the edit immediately (least confusing) by typing

  > :q! (Return)

- Continue editing the new file, then write it to a file when finished by using the write command:

:w *filename* Return

and follow it with an abort (:q or :q!) command.

Starting a New File

If you specify a filename that does not exist when invoking vi, after vi completes its startup initialization, including creation of a temporary file, your terminal will show an empty screen with the cursor in the upper-left corner and a row of tilde (˜) characters down the left side. The new filename, followed by the message [new file], appears on the bottom line of the screen, indicating that vi is ready for your first command:

```
~
 ~
 ~
 ~
my_file [new file]
```

Entering Text

To enter text in a new file, type i (insert text in front of the character identified by the current cursor position) or a (append text following the character identified by the current cursor position). At the time you type i or a, the editor is in command input mode, so the command character is not printed when typed and no visible change in the screen display is evident. However, as soon as you type i or a, vi changes immediately to text input mode so you can start typing in new text. Other methods for adding new text are discussed in Chapter 5 which discusses text manipulation techniques.

To quit entering text and return to command mode at any time, simply press ESC.

Backing Up Over Typographical Errors

When occasional typographical errors occur during text input, an important convenience is being able to backspace, overstrike the error, then continue. vi handles the need with only minor inconvenience. Simply use the BACKSPACE key or CTRL-H to back up to the (first) mistyped character, retype it, then retype the text that you backspaced over.

The restrictions to this technique are that you can only back up on the current cursor line, and you cannot backspace beyond the point where you started inserting new text. If the error occurred on an earlier line, you must press ESC to return to command mode, move the cursor to the error, then make the needed corrections using the techniques described in Chapter 4 and Chapter 5.

If the line is long and the error is early in the line, it may be easier to press ESC, back up to the error(s), and replace with new character(s) than to backspace and retype the rest of the line. Again, methods for changing errors in a line are discussed in detail in Chapter 5.

Line Lengths

vi can accept line lengths longer than the width of the terminal CRT screen (up to about 1020 characters). If the line length exceeds the maximum screen width, vi breaks the line at the right-hand screen boundary (often in the middle of a word) and continues it on the next physical line on the display, even though the line is treated as a single line in the text file. This feature is helpful for some situations where long lines are necessary, but for ordinary text, shorter lines are much easier to deal with. A good rule of thumb to use for standard text is:

- Keep lines shorter than the width of the narrowest terminal that will be using the file (usually about 70 to 75 characters is appropriate for standard 80-character screen widths).

- End each line by pressing Return (you can also use the wrapmargin option, which is discussed later in this chapter under "Continuous Text Input," to eliminate the need to use Return after each line).

Limiting line length to a single display line keeps text from confusing other users when they must edit it, especially when moving the cursor up or down through text. For example, suppose a given long line of text in a file occupies three lines on the CRT display while the next line in the file occupies only one line on the CRT.

As you move the cursor down the screen, it reaches the first displayed line of the long line in the file. As the cursor moves down to the next line in the file, it suddenly jumps three lines at once on the screen, creating the illusion that it skipped two lines. However, vi recognized only the long line *in the file,* which happened to require three lines *on the display.* It moved the cursor to the same column of the next line *in the file,* which was being displayed on the third lower line on the display. There is no easy way to move the cursor to the beginning of the middle line on the screen given the above conditions. Cursor commands operate on file lines, not screen lines.

Continuous Text Input

You can use the ex editor's :set command to create an automatic right margin located a specified number of columns from the right-hand side of the terminal screen. Then, whenever the cursor reaches the column that has been defined as the right-hand margin, the cursor is immediately moved to the left margin of the next line. If a word has been only partly typed when the margin is crossed, the first part of the word is also moved to the next line and the cursor advanced accordingly. To set the margin, type

```
:set wrapmargin=8
```

This establishes a margin 8 characters in from the right-hand edge of the screen (column 72 on an 80-column display). To select a different margin, simply replace the number 8 in the command with some other value that does not exceed the width of the screen in columns.

Once wrapmargin has been set, inserted words will automatically move to the new line if the line exceeds the margin. This feature is especially useful to typists who are transcribing large amounts of text or users who want to save a few keystrokes. wrapmargin can also be automatically set each time vi is used by placing a set wrapmargin command in a *.exrc* configuration file in your home directory. Using the *.exrc* file is discussed at length in Chapter 11.

I Have Typed My Text ... Now What?

Once you have placed the editor in insert or append mode by typing i or
a, all incoming characters are treated as new text until an escape character
is received from the keyboard. To terminate text entry, press (ESC) ((ALT) on
some terminals) or (CTRL)-(]). vi then returns to command mode and awaits
your next command.

Saving Text During an Edit

As described earlier in this chapter, vi maintains a temporary file that is
used to hold the text being edited for the duration of the editing session. At
the end of the session, the temporary file is usually copied to a permanent
storage file. It is easy, particularly when performing complex edits, to
make a mistake that can have disastrous effects on the temporary file.
These mistakes are usually corrected without difficulty by using the undo
command. However, a mistake is sometimes not discovered until it is no
longer recoverable by undo, making it necessary to abort the edit and start
over. Much of the lost work can be recovered if the user was cautious and
saved the temporary file in permanent storage periodically during the editing
session, especially before any complicated changes.

Prudent computer users usually update the stored version of the file they
are editing several times during a long editing session using the ex command

> : w (Return)

By keeping the permanent file up to date, an operator error, system crash,
power failure, or other interruption will cause only a minor setback. UNIX
provides extensive protective features that help prevent loss of data due
to system crashes and power failures. However, these mechanisms do not
protect against operator errors.

This command copies the current workfile onto permanent disk storage
in the filename specified when vi was invoked. It does not change your
current location in the file being edited, and it returns you to vi so you
can conveniently continue with your next command as soon as the write
operation is complete. This simple operation can be especially useful when

you are about to try a complex search-and-replace operation and want to make sure you don't lose the work you have already done on the file.

Repeating the :w command periodically keeps your permanent file up to date. This means that you have little opportunity to destroy your work if you make an incorrect keyboard entry in a moment of inattention. The risk of lost work is particularly important to fast typists who occasionally forget to enter input mode before typing new text, especially when the text happens to coincide with a command sequence that destroys part of the file beyond easy recovery.

Using the Write Command

The write command

:w *filename* (Return)

can be used at any time to store the current temporary file in a file identified by *filename* (include the full or relative directory pathname if the file is not being stored in the current directory). This is a convenient way to store slightly different versions of the same file in more than one location. This version of the write command should be used when you want to prevent accidentally overwriting an existing file.

Overwriting Files

You can overwrite the contents of an existing file with the contents of the temporary file by using the overwrite command:

:w! *existing_filename* (Return)

Note	Using the overwrite command, :w!, overwrites the existing file with the specified filename. If you intend to keep the existing file, be sure to use the :w command.

If you use :w! and the file does not exist, the command is treated in the same way as with :w. Remember that no space is allowed between the w and the ! when writing the temporary file to a permanent file.

The exclamation point (usually pronounced "bang" by UNIX users) tells vi one of two things:

- You want the edited version of the file to completely replace the unedited file that you are working on. The previous contents are lost.

- You want the file being edited to be written to the specified filename even if an existing file already has the same name. That existing file will be lost.

If you use the :w command and a file having the specified filename already exists, vi displays the warning message

"*filename*" File exists - use "w! *filename*" to overwrite

You can continue editing, select a different filename, or use the :w! command (no space before the !) to overwrite the existing file. You can also abort the edit by using the command

:q! [Return]

When you have finished editing and are ready to store the file on the previously specified disk file, send a write (:w or :w!) or exit (ZZ) command to vi. The write command copies the temporary file to the specified (or current, if not specified) filename, then returns to vi. To end the session after a write command, use the quit command. ZZ copies the temporary file to the current *filename*, destroys the temporary file, then terminates vi (equivalent to :wq).

When invoking vi with an existing filename, the file must reside in the current working directory. If the file is located in a different directory, the appropriate directory pathname must also be provided with the filename. Any legitimate pathname can be used, including the substitution characters . and .. for the current directory and parent of the current directory, respectively.

Creating Multiple Versions of a File

Occasionally, you may need to create several files that are similar in some respects but different in others. Or, you may want to split a long file into several smaller files. The :w command can be used to accomplish this with little difficulty by copying all or part of the file being edited to another file or files. The use of this and other commands to copy or split files and perform other useful tasks is described in greater detail in Chapter 8.

After using the write command, you can end the vi session or continue editing until you are ready to record another file or end the session. Generally, when you choose a normal termination by pressing ZZ, the current temporary file, as edited, is rewritten over the file originally specified when vi was invoked. However, this is not the case if the contents are written to a file with :w or :w!, as is explained later.

An Important Note Concerning w! and w !:

The previous paragraphs describe the use of :w! without any space between the w and ! to overwrite existing files. This command is radically different from :w ! with a space between w and !, which writes (all or part of) the temporary file out as standard input to a UNIX command. This second form (:w !) is discussed near the end of Chapter 10, which deals with shell operations.

Using Saved Text

Once a new file contains text and has been written to permanent storage, it is treated as an existing file from that time on. Most of the topics discussed in this book can be tried on a text file that contains two or more paragraphs. Use the previous discussion to create a sample text file containing two or more paragraphs, then type ZZ to store the file. Restart the editor, specifying the stored filename, and wait until the text appears on the terminal display screen.

For example, if you start by using the command

```
vi junk (Return)
```

add several lines of text, then type

```
ZZ
```

to terminate the session, a new file named *junk* is created in the current directory and contains the new text you just typed. You can now edit the file by using the same command you used before:

```
vi junk (Return)
```

But instead of the [New File] message at the bottom of the screen, you see "junk" followed by the number of lines and characters in the file. For example:

```
"junk" 21 lines, 382 characters
```

The cursor is located at the beginning of the file, and vi is waiting for your first command. You are ready to proceed as described in later chapters.

Recovering from a System Crash

UNIX provides for most system crashes and shutdowns caused by power failures, software failures, or someone accidentally bumping a power cord loose. The design of UNIX provides high immunity to problems related to power failures and both software and hardware crashes. There is little need for concern other than knowing how to recover when power is restored.

Power Failure and System Crash Protection

Most system disk drives used with UNIX have automatic power-fail detection. If a power failure occurs, they immediately write any data being held by the drive controller onto the correct disk location and withdraw the heads to prevent a head crash. However, the computer may be holding additional data in memory buffers (temporary storage in the computer's memory) that have not been stored to disk. During a power failure, the disk controller does not accept attempted output from the computer because it is busy shutting down the disk drive.

To protect against the loss of data being held in memory by the computer when power fails, most UNIX systems periodically (every 30 seconds or so) empty output buffers to system disk storage. This means that you will not lose more than the last 30 seconds of work if the power goes off.

Recovery Procedure

When a system shutdown occurs, the file being edited is still in its original location and contains the same data it contained at the start of the session or after the last write command that updated it from the temporary file. The preserved temporary file, on the other hand, contains the last memory buffer update by vi. If your system has periodic backup, the computer's buffer memory was saved to disk just before the crash.

Recovering the temporary file from the previous session is easy because vi provides a convenient means for recovering from power failures and system shutdowns. The recovery procedure described below conveniently resumes your interrupted session. It is important to note, however, that this protection against power failure does not reduce the value of periodically updating permanent storage by writing the temporary file to a permanent file, as described earlier in this chapter.

vi temporary files are maintained in temporary storage (usually in the directory */tmp*). When the system is restarted after a failure, you will receive mail from the system indicating that your vi/ex temporary file has been preserved along with instructions on how to recover it. To continue editing that file, use the cd command to change your current working directory to the same directory you were in during the edit, then invoke the vi command exactly as you did for the previous interrupted session *except* use the -r option as follows:

> vi -r *filename* (Return)

The file will be restored to the terminal screen and will contain exactly the data it contained at the time the disk drive shut down or the system crashed. You can then use the :w or ZZ command to update the original file, or you can continue editing—whichever you prefer. In the vast majority of cases, your file will be missing the last line typed or the last few keystrokes, but rarely will there be extensive damage unless the editor was in the midst of a complex undo operation or some similar condition when the power failure occurred.

If you are using another editor such as `view`, `ex`, or `edit`, use the same command form with the appropriate command as follows:

> `view -r` *filename* (Return)

> `ex -r` *filename* (Return)

> `edit -r` *filename* (Return)

Do not wait several days before recovering the preserved file. Temporary editor files are stored in the directory */tmp*. Efficient system administrators usually discard files in */tmp* on a regular basis to conserve disk space and keep the file system clean. If you cannot be available when the system is restored to operation, it is recommended that you arrange for someone to copy the file into another directory from which you can recover it later. You can usually identify your temporary file by the owner name. Use the UNIX command

> `ls -l /tmp` (Return)

The filename listed in the right-hand column will start with Ex, followed by a (usually five-digit) process ID number. The file owner column normally contains your login ID unless you had changed to another user name while logged in. If you need assistance, contact your system administrator.

Chapter Summary

Below are highlights of topics covered in detail in this chapter:

vi *filename*	Create the file and give it the name represented by *filename*.
~ (tilde)	Indicate blank lines on the screen as seen when vi starts up (not a command).
ZZ or :wq	Write contents to file and exit the editor.
:q or :q!	Quit the editing session without storing the edited text.
:e *filename*	Abandon current edit file and bring up text from the file named *filename*.
:set wrapmargin=8	Automatically move words to a new line when the line exceeds the right margin (column 72 for wrapmargin=8).
:w	Save text without exiting vi. This updates the current file.
vi -r *filename*	Recover editor file after a system crash.

4

Cursor and Display Control

Once you have an existing file to edit, you are ready to alter existing text. However, editing is much easier when you know how to control cursor movement, scrolling, and other CRT display features provided by vi.

What's in This Chapter

This chapter addresses two general topics:

- How to use common screen control operations for moving quickly to a location of interest before making desired changes in text.

- Cursor movement commands that are commonly used to alter text objects and blocks of text and accomplish other useful tasks.

Editor Window Operation

Most terminals display 20 to 24 lines of text (excluding the line at the bottom for commands and messages) with 80 characters horizontally in each line. These lines are your access window into the file you are editing. When vi starts up, the window displays the first part of the file, with line 1 of the window being in the same position as line 1 of the file. Figure 4-1 shows how vi provides a window to the file being edited.

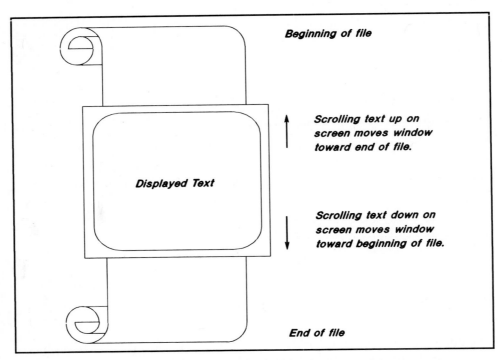

Figure 4-1. `vi` **provides a viewing window into a file.**

You can use cursor control keys to move the cursor to any position in the visible screen area and use scrolling control keys to move the text up or down on the screen. As text scrolls up, the viewing window moves toward the end of the file. To get a good feel for using `vi`'s screen control features, you need a file that is much longer than two full screens (about 50 lines).

Finding a Sample File to Edit

Let's be creatively lazy. Rather than typing a long file just to try a few cursor control exercises, let's use a text file that already exists. An easy place to find relatively large text files to experiment with is the on-line manual page file set. Manual page files are part of most UNIX operating systems and make a good source of material for experimenting.

Be sure you are logged in to your home directory by typing

```
cd $HOME [Return]
```

Then, to capture the text of the vi manual page, type

```
man vi | col -bx > junk [Return]
```

This line takes the output of the man command from the vi reference page and pipes (|) it through the col command (in UNIX parlance, a **filter**). The result is stored or redirected (>) to the file named *junk*. The file *junk* is now ready for use if no errors occur. Now, to start an editing session, type

```
vi junk [Return]
```

This provide a nice long file to play with while learning to use the editor.

Notice that the first line on your screen looks similar to that in Figure 4-2. The next several topics in this chapter help you quickly learn how to move around in the file.

```
Reformatting entry.  Wait...


   VI(1)                            HP-UX                          VI(1)



   NAME
        vi - screen-oriented (visual) display editor

   SYNOPSIS
        vi [ - ] [ -v ] [ -r ] [ -R ] [ +command ] [ -l ] [ -t tag ]
        [ -V ] [ -wsize ] [ -x ] [ file ... ]
        view [ - ] [ -v ] [ -r ] [ -R ] [ +command ] [ -l ] [ -t tag
        ] [ -V ] [ -wsize ] [ -x ] [ file ... ]
        vedit [ - ] [ -v ] [ -r ] [ -R ] [ +command ] [ -l ] [ -t
        tag ] [ -V ] [ -wsize ] [ -x ] [ file ... ]

   REMARKS
        The decryption facilities provided by this software are
        under the control of the United States Government and cannot
        be exported without special licenses.  These capabilities
"junk" 1056 lines, 42204 characters
```

Figure 4-2. vi **Reference Page Ready for Editing**

Determining File Size

When vi first displays the file on the screen, it prints some information about
the file on the bottom line, including the number of lines and characters in
the file. You can recover this and other information about the file during an
edit by using the (CTRL)-(G) or :f command, discussed later.

Positioning the Cursor on the Current Line

The cursor is easily moved back and forth within the current line while the editor is in command mode by using the space bar (or l key) and (BACKSPACE) (or h) key (use of h and l is explained later in the section "Positioning the Cursor on the Screen"). Use the commands in Table 4-1 to move conveniently to specific locations at the beginning or end of the line.

Table 4-1.
Beginning/End-of-Line Cursor Positioning Commands

Command	New Cursor Position
0 or |	Move cursor to column 0 (left edge) of screen on current line.
n|	Move cursor to column n on current line.
^	Move cursor to first non-blank character on current line.
$	Move cursor to last character (blank or otherwise) on current line.

Arrow Keys

vi works correctly with the arrow keys (up, down, left, right, home) on most terminals but not all. How well the keys work depends on your $TERM setting and how the terminal characteristics have been defined in the *terminfo* database, among other things. If the arrow keys are not supported on your terminal, use the "home row" keys h (or (BACKSPACE)), j (for down), k (for up), and l (or space bar for right).

If you are a frequent user of vi and take the trouble to learn to use the home row keys, you will likely find the effort rewarding. Once you become accustomed to them, your fingers will not have to move from the home row position to use them.

Positioning the Cursor on the Screen

Cursor-positioning commands are used to manipulate the cursor's current location on the screen and to control the position of the screen window in the file being edited. The cursor control commands shown here are for general moving around in the file. Other methods for moving the cursor to a specific position in the text file by searching for text patterns and character location on a current line, word, paragraph, or section are covered later in this chapter and elsewhere in the book.

Table 4-2 shows the most commonly used cursor-positioning commands. The *n* represents a numerical value that is typed before the command. (Return) is not used after these commands unless specifically shown. Some of these commands can also be used when deleting or changing several lines or large blocks of text.

In Table 4-2, the beginning of a line is the first visible character in the line or end-of-line, whichever occurs first. For example, if a line contains five blanks (tabs or spaces), the cursor is placed at the last blank character in the line. If the line contains no characters, the cursor is placed at the left margin of the display screen.

Table 4-2. Screen/File Cursor Movement Commands

Command	Cursor Motion
h or [◄] nh	(or [BACKSPACE]) Move cursor left one character. (or [BACKSPACE]) Move cursor left n characters.
j or [▼]	Move cursor down one line; stop at bottom of screen and scroll if necessary.
nj	Move cursor down n lines; stop at bottom of screen and scroll if necessary.
k or [▲] nk	Move cursor up one line; stop at top of screen and scroll if necessary. Move cursor up n lines; stop at top of screen and scroll if necessary.
l or [►] nl	(or space bar) Move cursor right one character (lowercase l). (or space bar) Move cursor right n characters (lowercase l).
[Return] n [Return]	Move cursor to beginning of next line. Move cursor to beginning of the nth line after current line.
+ or n+	Same as [Return] and n [Return].
− or n−	Move to the first visible character in the preceding line or n preceding lines.
G 1G nG	Move cursor to first visible character in last line of file. Move cursor to first visible character in first line of file. Move cursor to first visible character in line n of file.
[CTRL]-G or :f [Return]	Display line number of cursor line and other information about the file on the bottom (command) line of the terminal display.
0 or | ^ $ n|	Move cursor to absolute beginning of line (left column of screen). Move cursor to first visible character in current line. Move cursor to last character in current line. Move cursor to column n in current line.
H or [HOME] nH M L nL	Move cursor to beginning of line at top of screen. Move cursor to beginning of nth line from top of screen. Move cursor to beginning of line at middle of screen. Move cursor to beginning of line at bottom of screen. Move cursor to beginning of nth line from bottom of screen.

Note   When using j, k, or up/down arrow keys to move the cursor up or down, if a vertical cursor movement would place the cursor beyond the last character of the new cursor line, the cursor is placed at the end of the new line. However, vi remembers the column where the cursor began its vertical movements, so if you move the cursor to an equal or longer line than the original cursor line, the cursor is placed it its original column on the terminal screen.

The exception to this rule is when a $ command moves the cursor to the end of the line. Any subsequent j, k, or up/down arrow commands move the cursor to the end of the target new cursor line, independent of line length.

What Is That Beep I Hear?

In the preceding list of cursor-positioning commands, n is any positive integer numerical value (obviously, it must not be preceded by $+$ or $-$), but it cannot exceed the number of lines between the current line and the end or beginning of the file if movement is vertical. For example, if you are editing a 100-line file and the cursor is on line 55, you cannot use the command

    58 (Return)

or

    58+

because $55 + 58$ is more than 100 lines. The same is true if you attempt to use the command

    62-

because you cannot back up beyond line 1. Whenever you try to move beyond the beginning or end of the file, vi responds with a beep and ignores the command.

On the other hand, if you are moving horizontally, vi always tries to meet your requirements. For example if the cursor is located in column 45 of the current line and the line contains 68 characters, the commands

    100 l

or

    100 (space bar)

and

    100 h

or

    100 (BACKSPACE)

move the cursor to the last character or first character, respectively (including tabs and spaces), in the current line without complaint.

Exercise Time

Using the *junk* file you created earlier, try a few combinations of these commands until you feel comfortable with their behavior. Here are some suggestions; try others on your own.

Move the cursor to the end of the 25th line following the current line ($25j or 25j$). Now move to the first visible character of the 10th line preceding (10−).

Go to the end of the last line in the file (G$). Why doesn't $G give the same result when the last line has more than one visible character?

Scrolling Text

Once you have reasonable mastery of cursor movement, you are ready to learn scrolling techniques. Table 4-3 shows the most common scrolling commands. The commands in Table 4-3 are simple and straight forward, especially if you have mastered the cursor control commands. The most unexpected characteristic in these commands is the numbered half-screen scroll.

Table 4-3. Text Scrolling Commands

Command[1]	Resulting Text Motion
[CTRL]-[B]	Scroll backward to the previous screen.
n [CTRL]-[B]	Scroll backward to the nth previous screen.
[CTRL]-[U]	Scroll backward one half screen.
n [CTRL]-[U]	Set half-screen scroll to n lines, then scroll backward one half screen.
[CTRL]-[D]	Scroll forward one half screen.
n [CTRL]-[D]	Set half-screen scroll to n lines, then scroll forward one half screen.
[CTRL]-[F]	Scroll forward to the next following screen.
n [CTRL]-[F]	Scroll forward to the nth following screen.
[CTRL]-[Y]	Scroll backward one line.
n [CTRL]-[Y]	Scroll backward n lines (cursor movement explained below).
[CTRL]-[E]	Scroll forward one line.
n [CTRL]-[E]	Scroll forward n lines (cursor movement explained below).

[1] [CTRL] and the following character are pressed simultaneously. n is a numeric value that is typed before the command.

Half-Screen Scrolls

The numbered half-screen scroll sets the number of lines to be scrolled to n, then scrolls up or down that many lines. From that time on, any half-screen scrolls, whether up or down, will use the same number of lines (unless you specify a new value for n). The default (no n specified) is about 10–12 lines, but you can select any number (within reason). However, values greater than 20 would probably not be very useful.

Cursor Movement During Scrolling

If scrolling moves the current (cursor) line beyond the screen boundary, vi usually positions the cursor at the first visible character or end-of-line (whichever occurs first) at the top (forward scroll) or bottom (backward scroll) of the display screen.

If you are using (CTRL)-(Y) or (CTRL)-(E), vi leaves the cursor at its current location *in the file* until the cursor is forced off the screen, at which time it remains on the top or bottom line and usually moves to the first visible character in the line.

Positioning the Cursor Line in the Display Window

Sometimes you may want to move the line that the cursor is in to a different position in the display window. One example is when forward scrolling leaves the cursor at the last line in the file and at the bottom of the screen. Table 4-4 shows how to move the cursor line to the top, middle, or bottom the screen.

Table 4-4. Commands to Reposition Cursor Line on Screen

Command	Resulting Text Position
z (Return)	Move cursor line to the top of the screen. Scroll surrounding text accordingly. z+ cannot be used for the same purpose.
z.	Move cursor line to the middle of the screen. Scroll surrounding text accordingly.
z-	Move cursor line to the bottom of the screen. Scroll surrounding text accordingly.

If you are familiar with vi, do not confuse the z commands with the H, M, and L commands, which position the cursor and do *not* change the location of text lines on the screen. The H, M, and L commands are described in the section "Positioning the Cursor in a Line."

Where Am I in the File?

vi is a visually oriented rather than a line-oriented editor, so you usually have no need to know line numbers. However, there are occasions when it is helpful to know the current line number. A common instance is the need to specify a line number or range of line numbers when using an escape to the ex editor for global search-and-replace operations.

The G or nG command is used to move to a specific line in the file. To determine the number of the current cursor line at any time, place the editor in command mode, then use the command

(CTRL)(G)

or

:f (Return)

vi lists several items of information at the bottom of the screen on the command line using a format similar to the following:

```
"junk" line 788 of 870 --90%--
```

or

```
"junk" [Modified] line 788 of 870 --90%--
```

The first example shows the cursor is currently located on line 788 in an 870-line file named *junk,* and about 90% of the file precedes the current cursor line (the file has not been modified). The second example is the same line in the same file, but the file has been modified since the editing session began or since the last :w command.

Note   vi can be configured to display line numbers along the left side of the display screen (they are not added to the file being edited) with some loss of available text display space. To display line numbers, use the :set number command, discussed in Chapter 11.

Practice Time

Try some scrolling sequences on the *junk* file on your screen until you feel comfortable with their behavior.

Searching for Text

The / and ? commands are used mainly for two purposes:

- Positioning the text being searched for within the range of the current viewing window, as described in this section.

- Establishing boundaries for text-object modifications, as described later in this chapter.

Text pattern searches scan forward or backward in a text file for a text pattern specified by a **regular expression** included in the command preceding the (Return). Regular expressions are explained in Appendix A. The command format is as follows:

> /*regular_expression* (Return)

for forward searches or

> ?*regular_expression* (Return)

for backward searches.

In its simplest and most commonly used form, *regular_expression* is a simple string of characters identical to the text being searched for. For example:

> /thimk (Return)

searches the file for the characters `thimk` either as a stand-alone full word or as part of a larger word. As you can see, this is a useful means of quickly locating a misspelled word so that it can be corrected.

Other much more elaborate constructions can be used, such as

/the.*wooly.*superstar$ (Return)

which searches the file for the first encountered single line, if any, that contains all of the elements shown in Table 4-5.

Table 4-5. Pattern-Matching Example

Expression	Matching Pattern Result
the	The word `the` anywhere in the line followed by
.*	Zero or more arbitrary characters followed by
wooly	The word `wooly` followed by
.*	Zero or more arbitrary characters followed by
superstar	The word `superstar`
$	End of line immediately after the word `superstar`.

Regular expressions provide a powerful means for specifying text patterns used by many UNIX commands and programs such as `grep`, `awk`, and various editors. Regular expressions and their use is the subject of Appendix A. Refer there for more details and examples.

Repeating the Search

You will frequently need to search for a pattern, then repeatedly search for the same pattern in the same file. Once the search pattern has been specified with a / or ? command, to repeat the search for the *same* search expression in the *same* direction, type n. To repeat the search for the same search expression, but in the opposite direction, type N.

When you type / followed by a text pattern or regular expression (regular expressions are treated in greater detail in Appendix A), `vi` searches the file for the first occurrence of the pattern beginning at the current cursor location, then displays the surrounding text if the pattern is found. The search is conducted in the forward direction. If you are not at the beginning of the file and the end of the file is encountered before the pattern is matched, the search wraps to the beginning of the file[1] and continues until the pattern

---

[1] End-of-file wraparound requires that the `wrapscan` option be enabled, which is the normal default condition. Refer to Chapter 11 for more information.

is found or the cursor location is again reached, meaning that the pattern does not exist in the file.

The ? command works in the same way except that the search is conducted in the reverse direction (backward in the file). If the pattern does not appear between the cursor line and the beginning of the file, the search wraps to the end of the file[1] and continues as before.

Repeating the Search

Sometimes an expression appears several times in a file. You can search for the first occurrence by specifying the pattern. To find additional occurrences of the pattern, it is not necessary to repeat the command. Simply use n to repeat the search in the same direction or N to repeat the search in the opposite direction.

Aborting a Long or Incorrect Search

Occasionally, especially when editing extremely large files, you may enter a search string that does not exist or make a typographical error when entering the search string. To abort the search, simply press the interrupt key as defined in the *.profile* (Bourne or Korn shell) or *.login* (C shell) file. The interrupt key is usually either the [BREAK] key or the [CTRL]-[C] key combination. The editor returns the following message on the bottom line of the CRT display:

```
Interrupt
```

You can then proceed with a corrected search command or another command.

In Case of Difficulty

While vi rarely misbehaves, it can present some perplexing problems on occasion. Here are a few CRT display problems you may encounter along with suggested solutions.

I Can't Scroll Forward

Sometimes (CTRL)-(F) does nothing. This is not a bug in vi. (CTRL)-(F) is the ASCII ACK control character used in the ENQ/ACK data communications protocol, and it gets discarded by any terminal or software interface that is set for the ENQ/ACK protocol. If your terminal does not use or need the ENQ/ACK protocol, you can correct the problem by disabling the protocol with the following command:

```
:!stty -ienqak echoe          from vi
stty -ienqak echoe            from UNIX
```

If your terminal uses the ENQ/ACK protocol, you cannot use the (CTRL)-(F) scrolling feature. If you do not use the ENQ/ACK protocol on your terminal, you can add the UNIX version of the stty command above to your *$HOME/.profile* file or *$HOME/.login* file, thus eliminating having to do this each time you use vi.

Restoring a Garbled Display

Occasionally, you may be in the middle of an editing session when the text on your display becomes garbled. This can happen when noise on the line between terminal and computer causes characters to be incorrectly received; someone writes a message on your terminal (sometimes as an annoying prank); you try to display a non-ASCII file using a command such as more, head, or tail; or something else causes the display to be altered so that you cannot use vi correctly. vi provides an easy solution. Press (CTRL)-(L) simultaneously to tell vi to redraw the screen. This usually solves the problem. If the problem persists or data is repeatedly incorrect, contact your system administrator for help in diagnosing the cause.

What If Screen Behavior Becomes Strange?

UNIX and vi use the lowest possible number of characters to produce new text on the user's terminal display. Sometimes the system uses tab characters to accomplish this objective. As a result, you may occasionally be moving the cursor along a line while vi is in command mode only to discover that the display text starts changing as the cursor moves or blocks of text suddenly relocate on the screen. This is usually caused by the tab stops being altered for any of various reasons but most commonly by embedded control characters in text that cause the terminal to interpret text characters as screen configuration commands. To correct the problem, execute the UNIX command

:!tabs (Return)	*from* vi
tabs (Return)	*from UNIX*

then continue. If the problem persists, clear all the tab stops on the terminal. On a Hewlett-Packard terminal, this can be done by using the AIDS keys or by placing your terminal in local mode (REMOTE MODE off), then pressing (ESC) (3). For other brands of terminals, refer to the terminal operating manual for the correct sequence.

Place the terminal back in remote (REMOTE MODE on), then execute the tabs command again as follows:

:!tabs (Return)	*from* vi
tabs (Return)	*from UNIX*

then resume using vi. This sequence of operations should clear up most problems. If this does not work, you can write the file to permanent storage, log off, cycle the terminal power switch off and then on again, then log in again and restart the editor.

Preventing Unwanted Interruptions

Sometimes, in a multi-user system, a co-worker can interrupt your work by writing to your terminal while you are editing. To prevent other users from interrupting your work, use the mesg n command.

Conflicts Between Commands and Terminal Protocol

Some `vi` scrolling commands and any other commands that use (CTRL) key sequences may be identical to characters used in terminal data communications protocol. Thus, if you are using ENQ/ACK protocol for the terminal connection and you send a (CTRL)-(F) (an ACK character) to `vi`, it is consumed by the terminal interface and does not reach its intended destination. This leads to the problem with (CTRL)-(F) not working as described in "In Case of Difficulty." Similar problems occur when you use (CTRL)-(D), and it is being used as an end-of-file character. These problems are discussed at length in Chapter 11.

Characters that most commonly produce difficulties include DC1 ((CTRL)-(Q)), DC3 ((CTRL)-(S)), ENQ ((CTRL)-(I)), and ACK ((CTRL)-(F)) in the handshaking group; DEL, and ETX ((CTRL)-(C)) sometimes used as an interrupt character; and the quit character configured for your terminal by the `stty` command in your login script file.

Positioning the Cursor in a Line

Discussions of cursor movement in the preceding parts of this chapter are related to positioning the cursor on the CRT display screen and moving the screen display window around in the file. The topics discussed in the remainder of this chapter are focused on moving the cursor to specific locations in a file, particularly with regard to how such movements relate to text modification commands discussed in Chapter 5 and elsewhere in this book.

Moving to a Specific Column on a Line

In some situations, you may want to move quickly to a particular column on the current line. Table 4-6 shows the two commands that move the cursor to the left end of the line.

Table 4-6. Commands to Move the Cursor Within a Line

Command	Result
ˆ	Move the cursor to the first visible text character in the line.
| or 0	Move the cursor to the extreme left column on the current line.
n |	Move the cursor to column n in the line.
n (SPACE BAR)	Move the cursor n spaces to the right from current position.
n (BACKSPACE)	Move the cursor n spaces to the left from current position.

Text Objects

A text object, in vi parlance, is an arbitrary collection of text between the current cursor position and some other user-defined location in the file. vi provides various cursor movement commands for identifying words, lines, sentences, paragraphs, sections, or other text blocks as the text object to be acted upon by an editing operation. In general, the boundaries chosen by vi when identifying an object such as a word, sentence, or paragraph closely resemble the interpretation most people would use given the same situation. However, there are some important (and quite useful) differences that are discussed in detail in the next several sections.

Using the delete (d), change (c), and yank (y) editor commands with cursor movement commands that define the text object being acted upon provides a useful means for deleting, altering, copying, or moving small or large blocks of text anywhere in the file being edited. But as you might expect, getting full value from these capabilities requires that you be aware of their availability and how they can be used.

The Find Commands: f, F, t, and T

vi provides four cursor movement commands (see Table 4-7) for searching forward or backward in the current line for the next or nth occurrence of a given character. They do not search beyond beginning- or end-of-line.

Table 4-7.
Find Commands: Search for Character Within Current Line

Command	Action
fc	Forward to next occurrence of character c.
nfc	Forward to nth occurrence of character c.
Fc	Backward to next occurrence of character c.
nFc	Backward to nth occurrence of character c.
tc	Forward to character before next occurrence of character c.
ntc	Forward to character before nth occurrence of character c.
Tc	Backward to character after next occurrence of character c.
nTc	Backward to character after nth occurrence of character c.
;	To next occurrence of character c in same direction as previous search.
n;	To nth occurrence of character c in same direction as previous search.
,	To next occurrence of character c in opposite direction from previous search.
n,	To nth occurrence of character c in opposite direction from previous search.

In Table 4-7, the search directions and character positions are:

■ *forward:* Toward end-of-line from current position.

■ *backward:* Toward beginning-of-line from current position.

■ *after:* Adjacent to target character, but toward end-of-line.

■ *before:* Adjacent to target character, but toward beginning-of-line.

These commands apply only to the current line and cannot be used to move the cursor to another line.

Examples

Consider the following sentence and assume that the cursor is located under the y in `Wiggly`:

```
Willie the Wiggly Worm went to Washington to wander in wonder.
                  ^
```

Table 4-8 provides examples of cursor movement. Be sure to reposition the cursor at the y in `Wiggly` before each command.

Table 4-8. Cursor Movement Commands Example

Command	Cursor Location After Move
fW	W in Worm
2fW	W in Washington
2fw	w in wander
3fW	No movement because character does not exist
tW	Blank space before Worm
2tW	Blank space before Washington
2tw	Blank space before wander
3tW	No movement because character does not exist
FW	W in Wiggly
2FW	W in Willie
2Fw	No movement because character does not exist
3FW	No movement because character does not exist
TW	i in Wiggly
2TW	First i in Willie
2Tw	No movement because character does not exist
3TW	No movement because character does not exist

The Word Commands: w, W, e, E, b, and B

vi provides four cursor movement commands for searching forward or backward in the file by words: w or W for forward moves and b or B for moving backward in the file. Word boundaries are defined as the imaginary zero-width space at the beginning of the next word. Thus any given word includes the whitespace between it and the next word, if any exists. Moving by words is unlimited within the file and is not restricted to the current line.

vi interprets word boundaries in two ways. You must define which interpretation is to be used as part of each command. Using a lowercase word movement command (w or b) treats any non-alphanumeric character except underscore (_) as part of the next word. An uppercase word move command (W or B), on the other hand, uses whitespace (space, tab, or newline character) as a word separator, and the next word begins at the next character past the one or more whitespace characters adjacent to the end (forward moves) or beginning (backward moves) of the current word.

Table 4-9.
Word Commands: Search for Specified Beginning or End of Word

Command	Action
w	Forward to next beginning of word or first non-alphanumeric character.
nw	Forward to nth beginning of word/non-alphanumeric character.
W	Forward to next beginning of word; only whitespace as word separator.
nW	Forward to nth beginning of word; only whitespace as word separator.
e	Forward to next end of word or first non-alphanumeric character.
ne	Forward to nth end of word/non-alphanumeric character.
E	Forward to next end of word; only whitespace as word separator.
nE	Forward to nth end of word; only whitespace as word separator.
b	Backward to next beginning of word or first non-alphanumeric character.
nb	Backward to nth beginning of word/non-alphanumeric character.
B	Backward to next beginning of word; only whitespace as word separator.
nB	Backward to nth beginning of word; only whitespace as word separator.

In Table 4-9, all moves are from current cursor position and are independent of where the cursor is within the current word. For example, if the cursor is currently located in the middle of a word, the b or B command moves the cursor to the beginning of the current word. Likewise, if the cursor is located in the whitespace between two words, a w or W moves the cursor to the beginning of the adjacent word, not to the beginning of the next word after it.

These commands are not restricted to the current line. The cursor is wrapped to preceding or following lines as necessary in order to meet the specified word count.

Examples of Word Moves

Consider the following line of text:

```
This line contains a one,annatwo!anna_three&four$five(six)seven weird word.
                     ^
```

where the cursor is located at the space character position between the words `contains` and `a` as indicated by the `^` character. To move the cursor from the position indicated to the beginning of the word `weird` requires the command `15w` or `3W`. The command `f2w` would accomplish the same (find the second occurrence of the character `w`; skip the `w` in `two`, stopping at the `w` in `weird`). To move the cursor to the end of the word `seven` (cursor underneath the n), use `14e` or `2E`.

When `vi` performs the forward move by 15 words (lowercase command version), text is interpreted as a succession of the following words:

```
a one , annatwo ! anna_three & four $ five ( six ) seven weird
```

counting from the starting cursor position. Using the uppercase form, W, the same text is interpreted as the following three Words:

```
a    one,annatwo!anna_three&four$five(six)seven    weird
```

Note the unvarying treatment of the underscore character in `anna_three`.

Sentence, Paragraph, and Section Commands: ( ) { } [[and]]

`vi` also recognizes sentence, paragraph, and section boundaries, using a technique similar to that used with words.

Sentences

Ends of sentences are detected by the presence of a period (.), question mark (?), or exclamation point (!) followed by *two* or more spaces. A continuum of one or more empty lines (containing no spaces or tabs) is also treated as a separate sentence (a continuum of one or more apparently blank lines, each containing spaces and/or tabs, is treated as part of the preceding sentence).

To move the cursor to the next adjacent beginning-of-sentence, use) for forward moves or (for backward moves. Use n) or n(to move to the nth beginning of sentence in the forward or backward direction, respectively.

Paragraphs

Recognized paragraph boundaries include any paragraph macro defined by the :set paragraphs and :set sections commands as well as *empty* lines (blank lines containing no space or tab characters). Default paragraph macros include .IP, .LP, .PP, .QP, .P, .LI, and .bp. Beginning-of-paragraph is defined as the beginning of the first empty line after a paragraph of text or the beginning of a text line that starts with a paragraph or section macro. The macros shown are found in document-formatting macro packages such as mm or man, which are both used in conjunction with the nroff or troff text-processing programs. They can be redefined as explained in Chapter 11 by using the :set paragraphs command.

To move the cursor to the next adjacent beginning-of-paragraph, use } for forward moves or { for backward moves. Use n} or n{ to move to the nth beginning-of-paragraph in the forward or backward direction, respectively.

To add any other macros to the list of recognized paragraph macros, use the :set paragraphs command as explained in Chapter 11.

Section Boundaries

Recognized section boundaries include any section macro defined by the :set sections command. Default section macros include .NH, .SH, .H, and .HU. The macros shown are found in document-formatting macro packages such as mm or man (used with nroff or troff). They can be redefined as explained in Chapter 11 by using the :set sections command.

To move the cursor to the next adjacent beginning-of-section, use]] for forward moves or [[for backward moves. Use n]] or n[[to move to the nth beginning-of-section in the forward or backward direction, respectively.

To add any other macros to the list of recognized section macros, use the :set sections command as explained in Chapter 11.

What Is the Exact Boundary of a Text Object?

Most users typically have little concern over the exact boundary of a text object because if they guess wrong, the mistake is easily fixed. However, for those isolated cases where it is important, here are the general rules for determining where a text object starts and ends.

In general, a text object is bordered by the current cursor position and another location in the file that is determined by a cursor movement command or a text pattern search. Its text contents are as follows:

- If the cursor position in the file *precedes* the target location resulting from the move or search, the text object contains all text starting at the cursor position and continuing up to, but not including, the new cursor position character after the move or search is completed.

- If the cursor position in the file *follows* the target location resulting from the move or search, the text object contains all text starting at the new cursor position character after the move or search is completed and continuing up to, but not including, the original cursor position character.

In simpler terms, the object begins at the earlier cursor position boundary in the file and ends with the character preceding the second cursor position boundary in the file.

Entire Text Object on Current Line

Here is an example to illustrate. Note the position of the cursor on the second line before the word `particularly` marked by ^ (circumflex).

```
This is example text placed here purely for illustrative
purposes.  It is neither complicated nor particularly long.
                                              ^
```

Let's use the "change text from current position to first previous beginning of sentence" command, `c(`. The cursor immediately moves to the first character in the sentence under the `I` in `It`. A `$` character replaces the last character before the original cursor location (the `r` in `nor`), indicating that all text from the cursor through the position of the `$` symbol will be replaced with whatever text is typed until you press `ESC` (the change command is explained in greater depth in Chapter 5.

```
This is example text placed here purely for illustrative
```

```
purposes.  It is neither complicated no$ particularly long.
            ^
```

On the other hand, if you use the c) command (change text from current position to next following end of sentence), notice that the cursor does not move and the $ symbol is placed at the period's former position at the end of the sentence:

```
This is example text placed here purely for illustrative
purposes.  It is neither complicated nor particularly long$
                                               ^
```

Text Object on Multiple Lines

If the beginning or end of the sentence is not on the current line, the text object is handled somewhat differently. For example, in the following text the cursor is located after the first word in the first sentence:

```
This sentence is longer than the one before, so it does not
    ^

all fit on one line.  It also has a second sentence in the
same paragraph.
```

Typing c) to change the rest of the sentence causes the text being changed to be removed from the display screen. The paragraph now looks like this, with the cursor under the I in It:

```
ThisIt also has a second sentence in the
    ^

same paragraph.
```

Notice that the whitespace after the period at the end of the sentence is treated as part of the sentence being changed, so it has disappeared. New replacement text is then inserted in front of the cursor character as it is typed until (ESC) is pressed.

Now let's change the second sentence by placing the cursor in front of the last word in the second sentence, then use the c(command to change to beginning of current sentence:

```
This sentence is longer than the one before, so it does not
all fit on one line.  It also has a second sentence in the
same paragraph.
    ^
```

As before, the text that is to be replaced is removed from the screen. Notice this time that the whitespace after the previous sentence is preserved as well as the character in the starting cursor position.

```
This sentence is longer than the one before, so it does not
all fit on one line.    paragraph.
                    ^
```

This clearly shows that the whitespace after a sentence is treated as part of the sentence (unless it is an empty line, which is treated as a separate sentence in and of itself), and sentence boundaries are interpreted as the beginning of each sentence. New text will be inserted in front of the cursor as it is typed until you press ESC.

Chapter Summary

Highlights of the cursor and display control keys are listed here.

Cursor-Positioning Commands

0 (zero)	Move cursor to beginning of line
|	Move cursor to end of line
▲ or k	Move cursor up one line
▼ or j	Move cursor down one line
◄ or h or BACKSPACE	Move cursor left one character
► or l or space bar	Move cursor right one character
HOME or H	Move cursor to top-left corner of screen
)	Move cursor forward to beginning of sentence
(	Move cursor backward to beginning of sentence
}	Move cursor forward to beginning of next paragraph
{	Move cursor backward to beginning of next paragraph

Text-Scrolling Commands

CTRL-F	Scroll forward to next screen
CTRL-B	Scroll backward to previous screen
CTRL-E	Scroll forward one line
CTRL-Y	Scroll backward to previous line

Other Important Topics

[BREAK] or [CTRL]-[C]	Abort a search
[CTRL]-[L]	Restore garbled screen (screen rewrite)
:!tabs[Return]	Correct strange screen behavior
:!mesg n	Prevent interruptions

5

Manipulating Text

The primary purpose of a text editor is to alter the contents of a text file. Editing operations can be performed on an existing text file or on a new file that is being created in conjunction with the editing session.

What's in This Chapter

This chapter explains how to:

- Recover from mistakes ((ESC) and undo).
- Add new text to a file (insert, append, and open).
- Include non-printable ASCII control characters in text.
- Delete text.
- Recover deleted text and move or copy text to other locations.
- Change, replace, or substitute text, including changing uppercase to lowercase and vice versa.
- Use buffers to restore deleted text.
- Swap or transpose characters and words.
- Search for matching patterns.
- Shift text lines horizontally right or left.
- Indent text.

Each of these operations can be performed on new as well as existing files. Several examples are used throughout this chapter to introduce each type of operation and demonstrate its use. Learning is much easier if you try them yourself. Before you can try the example exercises, you must terminate any currently active editing session. If you have been using the file *junk* discussed in the previous chapter, quit vi by typing

    :q! `Return`

When you get your UNIX shell prompt (usually a dollar sign), type

    vi dummy `Return`

to open a new file for practice. To create practice text, type **A** to enter append mode, then press `Return` a couple of times to create some blank lines. Type a practice line, then press `Return` another two or three times for more blank lines. Press `ESC` to return to command mode.

To move around while editing, use j and k to move the cursor up or down from line to line and `Return` to move it to the beginning of the next line, as needed.

Escaping from the Sand Traps of vi

Like a bad swing in a golf game, a wrong keystroke when using vi can put you in a difficult situation that you would usually prefer to avoid. The possible errors are numerous, making it impossible to describe every situation and how to get out of it. However, a few simple skills can be easily mastered so you can readily recover and return to the task at hand.

Using the Escape Key

If you find yourself out on a limb, so to speak, press `ESC` a couple of times until you get a beep. The beep acknowledges that you are in command mode so that anything you type will not be placed in the text you are working on. When you get the beep, examine the screen to see if the text near the cursor is as it should be.

If the incorrect keystrokes have deleted, inserted, or changed characters that need to be restored, type u or U (usually the lowercase command is sufficient) to undo the last alteration, as explained in the next section. If you find yourself elsewhere in the file, use the cursor control commands from the preceding chapter to recover your position. To move to the beginning of the file, type 1G. Use G to move to the end of the file. For other moves, use other appropriate commands. The u and U commands are described next.

Recovering from Mistakes: The Undo Command

Relax. If you make a mistake, it is (usually) quite easy to recover, provided, of course, that you do it immediately — not after you have made some other change.

vi has an undo command that reverses the last change made by vi, but the command does have some limitations that you should understand (most mistakes are easy to correct, but habitual carelessness can be dangerous). Table 5-1 shows the two forms of the undo command and their differences. These forms of the undo command need additional explanation.

Table 5-1. The Undo Command

Command	Action Taken
u	Undo the most recent text change. If the most recent change was an undo, undo the preceding undo (u or U).
U	Undo all of the changes made to the current line since the cursor was moved to the current line. Not allowed if cursor is moved from current line, then returned, with or without a subsequent text change.

The u Command

The u command applies to the most recent text change regardless of present cursor location. It can also be used to undo an immediately preceding undo, provided no other changes have been made since. Thus, if you alter line 50 in a file, then move the cursor to line 75 and type u, the cursor returns to line 50 and the last change is reversed to its original form (cursor location in the line after the undo operation may or may not reflect the location where the change was made). Typing u again reverses the undo, restoring the original change and leaving the cursor on the changed line. There is no limit to the number of times u can be used in succession, but it cannot undo more than the last previous change or undo.

The U **Command and Examples of Use**

The U command, on the other hand, applies *only* to changes made on the current line while the cursor was on that line, and it can be used only once on that line (unless you make additional changes to the line). If the cursor is moved to another line, the U command cannot be used, even if it is returned immediately to the correct line before U is attempted. For example, consider the following line of text:

```
This is the original line.
```

Now use two separate insert/append commands to add the two words shown in different locations without allowing the cursor to move to a different line:

```
This is NOT the original UNCHANGED line.
```

Type U to restore the original text:

```
This is the original line.
```

Repeat the previous insert/append commands to get the altered sentence or type u:

```
This is NOT the original UNCHANGED line.
```

Now move the cursor to a different line (press (Return), for example), then move it back to the altered line. Type U again. Note that the cursor may move to the beginning of the line, but the text is not changed. Type U again. As before, you get no change, but you also get a beep because U cannot undo itself, unlike u. The altered sentence is still present:

```
This is NOT the original UNCHANGED line.
```

Adding New Text to a File

Before discussing how to change text, let's spend more time on adding new text to a file. If the file is empty (you are performing a new edit on a file that does not already exist), the cursor is at the beginning of the first line and cannot be moved because there are no additional characters in the file. If you are editing an existing file, the cursor must be moved to the location in the file where the change is to be made before you select an editing command to add new text. Table 5-2 shows the commands used to add text to a file.

Table 5-2. Commands for Adding Text to a File

Command	Result
i	Insert new text in front of current cursor character until (ESC) is pressed.
I	Insert new text in front of the first visible character in the current line until (ESC) is pressed.
a	Append new text after the current cursor character until (ESC) is pressed.
A	Append new text following the last character on the current line until (ESC) is pressed.
o	Open a new line after the current line and add new text until (ESC) is pressed.
O	Open a new line above the current line and add new text until (ESC) is pressed.

When any of these commands is used, there is no limit on the number of characters that can be added. You can add zero characters by pressing (ESC) immediately, add a few or several characters, or add many lines of new text. Here are some examples that demonstrate the effect of each command. Consider the following sample line of text, where the circumflex (^) character represents the current cursor location:

```
This is the starting sentence.
              ^
```

In each example that follows, the text being added does not vary; only the command changes between examples. Only the characters shown are typed; there are no leading or trailing blanks (spaces) before or after the new text.

```
ADDED TEXT (ESC)
```

Using the i command:

```
This is theADDED TEXT starting sentence.
```

Using the I command:

```
ADDED TEXTThis is the starting sentence.
```

Using the a command:

```
This is the ADDED TEXTstarting sentence.
```

Using the A command:

```
This is the starting sentence.ADDED TEXT
```

Using the o command:

```
This is the starting sentence.
ADDED TEXT
```

Using the O command:

```
ADDED TEXT
This is the starting sentence.
```

ASCII Control Characters in Text

Many common situations require the ability to insert or deal with ASCII control characters as part of the normal text body. The need may arise in a computer program, or be as simple as the insertion of a form feed or other character being used to control devices or programs that interact with the file when it is used or processed in the future.

Control Characters Defined

ASCII is an acronym that stands for *American Standard Code for Information Interchange*. A particular pattern of binary digits (bits) establishes a code pattern that defines a corresponding character. Thus a code value equivalent to 106 decimal represents lowercase j and the code value equivalent to decimal 82 represents uppercase R. Most ASCII character codes produce visible text when printing or editing. However, certain characters called **control characters** such as form feed (FF), carriage return (CR), and end of transmission (EOT) do not produce a visible printed character because their functions are related to data handling and formatting instead of forming words.

Obtaining Control Characters

Control characters are usually typed from the terminal keyboard by pressing a normal typing character key while holding the [CTRL] key down, thus producing a control character. However, many control characters represent vi editor commands, making it impossible to enter them directly into text.

For example, [CTRL]-[H] and the [BACKSPACE] key both generate a backspace character, which is used as a backspace command while in insert/append mode. If you needed to include an ASCII backspace character in the text file being edited, the editor would interpret the character as a backspace command and act accordingly instead of placing it in the text file. Other control characters are also interpreted as editor commands, either during insert/append mode or while in command mode. For example, [CTRL]-[D] and [CTRL]-[F] are used for screen manipulation in command mode.

Displaying Control Characters

When vi or UNIX displays control characters, each control character is displayed as a combination of two characters: a circumflex (^) character representing the [CTRL] key, followed by the typing key that is pressed simultaneously with the [CTRL] key to obtain the control character. For example, [CTRL]-[K], which produces a vertical tab character, is displayed in text on the display screen as ^K. However, the two displayed characters represent only the single control character that exists in the file being edited.

Thus when you move the cursor along a line containing a control character, you will discover that the cursor skips over the circumflex character and stops on the uppercase character that follows it, thus identifying the character as a single control character rather than two ASCII printable characters.

A complete list of control characters and the keypress combinations required to produce them is contained in Table 5-3 later in this chapter.

Entering Control Characters

When adding new text during insert, append, replace, substitute, and similar operations with vi/ex, press (CTRL)-(V) (think "verbatim" to remember the *V*) to tell the editor that the next character is a text character instead of an editor control command (this rule applies both in insert mode and in regular expressions). vi acknowledges the (CTRL)-(V) by placing a circumflex character (^) on the screen at the cursor position. When you type the next control character, the cursor advances one column and the typing character used with the (CTRL) key is displayed.

If the next character is not a control character (the (CTRL) key was not held down while the typing key was pressed), the circumflex character from the (CTRL)-(V) is removed and the typed character is displayed in its stead. Thus you can change your mind after typing ^V and continue typing normal text without any special procedures to abort the control character setup.

Control characters in text are easily differentiated from a circumflex character followed by another character. While in command mode, use the space bar or (L) key to advance the cursor across the character(s). For ordinary text, the cursor stops on the circumflex. For a control character, the cursor skips the circumflex and stops on the following character.

Note   Control characters used in terminal-computer handshaking, such as ENQ, ACK, etc., are consumed by the datacomm interfacing hardware and are not transmitted as part of the text. Thus they cannot be used. This also means that (CTRL)-(F) cannot be used for scrolling on an ENQ/ACK protocol connection because it is an ACK character.

Selecting Control Characters

Understanding how to enter control characters is all well and good, but you cannot conveniently use them without knowing which typing key produces a given control character. Few books document the relationship between a typed key and its corresponding control character (obtained when (CTRL) is pressed at the same time). Table 5-3 lists the 32 ASCII control characters and provides a key sequence to obtain each one. Not all key sequences are available on all systems.

Columns 1, 2, and 3 in the table show octal, decimal, and hexadecimal numerical equivalents for the ASCII character code whose acronym is shown in the fifth column. Column 4 contains the character code as displayed on a terminal screen by vi. Column 6 contains the full name of the character, and the right-hand column lists the keys that must be pressed simultaneously to produce the control character described on that line.

To obtain the DEL character, press (CTRL)-(V), then press (DEL). The displayed tilde character is not stored in the file as a tilde.

For a complete list of ASCII character codes, refer to the *ascii*(5) manual entry in the on-line UNIX reference (using the man command). If your system supports European languages, see *roman8*(5) instead. Control character codes are identical in both character sets.

Table 5-3.
Typical Typing-Key-to-Control-Character Conversions

Oct	Dec	Hex	Display	Symbol	Character Name	Keypress
000	000	00	none	NUL	Null	CTRL-SHIFT-@
001	001	01	^A	SOH	Start of Header	CTRL-A
002	002	02	^B	STX	Start of Text	CTRL-B
003	003	03	^C	ETX	End of Text	CTRL-C
004	004	04	^D	EOT	End of Transmission	CTRL-D
005	005	05	^E	ENQ	Enquire	CTRL-E
006	006	06	^F	ACK	Acknowledge	CTRL-F
007	007	07	^G	BEL	Bell	CTRL-G
010	008	08	^H	BS	Back Space	CTRL-H
011	009	09	^I	HT	Horizontal Tab	CTRL-I
012	010	0A	^J	LF	Line Feed (newline)	CTRL-J
013	011	0B	^K	VT	Vertical Tab	CTRL-K
014	012	0C	^L	FF	Form Feed (newpage)	CTRL-L
015	013	0D	^M	CR	Carriage Return	CTRL-M
016	014	0E	^N	SO	Shift Out	CTRL-N
017	015	0F	^O	SI	Shift In	CTRL-O
020	016	10	^P	DLE	(or DEL) Delete	CTRL-P
021	017	11	^Q	DC1	Device Control 1	CTRL-Q
022	018	12	^R	DC2	Device Control 2	CTRL-R
023	019	13	^S	DC3	Device Control 3	CTRL-S
024	020	14	^T	DC4	Device Control 4	CTRL-T
025	021	15	^U	NAK	Negative Acknowledge	CTRL-U
026	022	16	^V	SYN	Synchronize	CTRL-V
027	023	17	^W	ETB	End Transmission Block	CTRL-W
030	024	18	^X	CAN	Cancel	CTRL-X
031	025	19	^Y	EM	End of Medium	CTRL-Y
032	026	1A	^Z	SUB	Substitute	CTRL-Z
033	027	1B	^[	ESC	Escape Code	CTRL-[
034	028	1C	^\	FS	File Separator	CTRL-\
035	029	1D	^]	GS	Group Separator	CTRL-]
036	030	1E	^^	RS	Record Separator	CTRL-SHIFT-^
037	031	1F	^_	US	Unit Separator	CTRL-SHIFT-_
177	127	7F	~	DEL	Delete	CTRL-V-DEL

8-Bit Control Characters

Table 5-4 shows how 8-bit control characters are displayed on the terminal display screen when you edit files containing 8-bit characters. These control characters cannot be entered directly from the terminal keyboard, but vi does process them correctly if they exist in the file.

Table 5-4.
Display Representation for 8-Bit Control Characters

Oct	Dec	Hex	Display	Oct	Dec	Hex	Display
177	127	7F	^?	220	144	90	^p
200	128	80	^`	221	145	91	^q
201	129	81	^a	222	146	92	^r
202	130	82	^b	223	147	93	^s
203	131	83	^c	224	148	94	^t
204	132	84	^d	225	149	95	^u
205	133	85	^e	226	150	96	^v
206	134	86	^f	227	151	97	^w
207	135	87	^g	230	152	98	^x
210	136	88	^h	231	153	99	^y
211	137	89	^i	232	154	9A	^z
212	138	8A	^j	233	155	9B	^{
213	139	8B	^k	234	156	9C	^|
214	140	8C	^l	235	157	9D	^}
215	141	8D	^m	236	158	9E	^~
216	142	8E	^n	237	159	9F	^>
217	143	8F	^o	377	255	FF	^/

Changing Text: Overview

Most text-change operations involve fairly simple operations such as correcting a typographical error, changing the wording in a sentence, or restructuring a line of computer program source code. vi provides a useful set of tools for performing various combinations of common and not-so-common text alterations. Here are a few topics that are discussed in this chapter:

- Delete text. Deleted text is copied into a buffer so that it can be used elsewhere in the file.

- Replace existing text with new text by using replace, substitute, or change commands.

- Copy (yank) existing text into a buffer so that it can be used elsewhere in the file.

- Copy text from a yank or delete buffer into the current cursor location by using the put command. A delete and put sequence is used to move blocks of text to a different location; a yank and put sequence copies text from one location to another. Under certain conditions, these commands can be used to copy or move text from one file to another, as described in the chapters of this book that cover advanced topics.

Command Format

vi provides several ways for performing similar tasks. This fact will become apparent as you learn more about the editor and its many capabilities. This section shows several commands that are, for most practical purposes, essentially identical or very similar. A significant effort has been invested in making those similarities visible for ease in learning.

All vi commands related to deleting, changing, copying, or moving text objects have a form that, if understood beforehand, makes them much easier to learn and use. Each command is a variation on the following two structures:

    count1 command

or

count1 `command` *count2 text_object*

These two simple structures support a vast selection of editing options, which are described in greater detail in the remainder of this chapter.

Character- and Line-Oriented Commands

Commands that have the form

count1 `command`

are generally commands related to character- or line-oriented operations such as:

- Deleting one or more characters or lines by specifying the number of characters or lines to delete.

- Replacing one or more characters or lines with new text by specifying the number of characters or lines to replace.

- Moving or copying text to another location (however, certain common text copy/move operations require the text object form described next).

Word-, Sentence-, and Text-Object-Oriented Commands

On the other hand, commands that use the form

count1 `command` *count2 text_object*

are generally commands related to specified text objects. Text objects are words, sentences, paragraphs, sections, or all text between two marked or known locations in the file. Editing operations performed on text objects include:

- Deleting one or more text objects such as words, sentences, paragraphs, or all text from the current position to another specified position.

- Replacing one or more text objects with new text by specifying the type and number of text objects to replace.

- Moving or copying one or more text objects to another location by use of buffers.

Note the similarities between this list and the preceding one.

How Text Objects Are Defined

In general, a text object is defined as all text between the current cursor position and another position in the file that is specified by a cursor move command from the current cursor location. Thus, if a delete command is followed by a command to move the cursor forward nine words, the editor deletes nine words starting with the current cursor character, which may or may not be at the beginning of the current word.

Text Object Boundaries

In general, text objects such as words, sentences, paragraphs, and sections are bounded at the start of an object, where the starting point is the boundary between the first character in the object and the preceding character. Thus, in the text string one two three, the word two begins at the boundary between the t and the space preceding it.

Likewise, when the current cursor position is used as a text object boundary, the object boundary is at the boundary between the cursor character and the character preceding it. This means that if a change, deletion, or yank is from the current cursor position in the forward direction, the current cursor character is included in the change because it falls within the object as the first character in the object. On the other hand, if the change, deletion, or yank is in the reverse direction, toward the beginning of the file, the cursor character falls outside the boundary and is not included in the change because the text object starts in the boundary region before the cursor character and progresses away from it toward the beginning of the file.

Text Manipulation Commands and What They Do

This section explains the behavior of individual text manipulation commands based on the type of operation. Detailed examples of how to use many of these commands follow later in this chapter.

Deleting Characters and Lines

When deleting text, the editor performs the deletion as soon as it has sufficient information to determine the operation to be made. Pressing (ESC) is not necessary. Table 5-5 shows the commands used to delete characters, and Table 5-6 shows those used to delete lines.

Table 5-5. Delete Character Commands

Command	Action Taken
x nx	Delete single character at current cursor position. Delete n characters or to end of line, whichever occurs first, starting at current cursor position.
X nX	Delete single character immediately preceding current cursor position. Delete n characters or to beginning of line, whichever occurs first, starting with the character immediately preceding the current cursor position.
D or d$ d0 or d|	Delete all characters from current cursor position to end of line. Delete all characters from left column of screen to character preceding current cursor position on current line.

Table 5-6. Delete Line Commands

Command	Action Taken
dd	Delete current line.
*n*dd or d*n*d	Delete *n* lines beginning at current line.
dG	Delete all lines, starting with current line, through end of file.
d1G	Delete all lines, starting with current line, through beginning of file.
d*n*G	Delete all lines, starting with current line, through line *n* in file (forward or backward, depending on position of line *n* relative to current line).
d-	Delete current and first preceding line.[1]
d+	Delete current and first following line.[1]
*n*d- or d*n*-	Delete current and *n* previous lines.[1]
*n*d+ or d*n*+	Delete current and *n* following lines.[1]

[1] In these commands, k can be used instead of -, and j or (Return) can be used instead of +.

Deleting Text Objects

When lowercase b or w is used, any character other than an alphanumeric or underscore is considered as the beginning of a new word, except whitespace characters that are treated as word separators. When uppercase B or W is used, word boundaries are defined by whitespace word separators. Any other non-alphanumeric characters (including underscore and control characters) are treated as part of the word.

Table 5-7. Delete Word Commands

Command	Action Taken
dw	Delete from cursor position through end of current word.
dW	Delete from cursor position through end of current Word.
d*n*w or *n*dw	Delete from cursor position through *n*th following word ending.
d*n*W or *n*dW	Delete from cursor position through *n*th following Word ending.
db	Delete from nearest preceding beginning of word through character before current cursor position.
dB	Delete from nearest preceding Beginning of word through character before current cursor position.
d*n*b or *n*db	Delete from *n*th preceding beginning of word through through character before current cursor position.
d*n*B or *n*dB	Delete from *n*th preceding Beginning of word through character before current cursor position.

Dealing with Whitespace

When deleting words, any whitespace between the word being deleted (or the last word if multiple words are being deleted) and the word following is also deleted. If the last word being deleted is at the end of the line, the end-of-line remains after the word preceding the deleted text. If one or more words beyond the end of the current line are being deleted, the following line is appended to the current line during the deletion.

If the word count in a multiple-word deletion spans more than two lines, additional lines are appended to the current line prior to the deletion until the deleted word count specification is satisfied. For deletions toward beginning-of-file, the beginning of the removed text block is calculated, then the deletion proceeds from that point toward end-of-file. Table 5-7 lists the commands used to delete words.

Deleting text objects such as words, sentences, paragraphs, and such are not restricted to the current line. If the number of text objects specified exceeds current line contents, the object is extended until the text specification is completely satisfied. Table 5-8 shows the commands used to delete a sentence, paragraph, or section of text.

Word boundaries are defined based on beginning-of-word. Thus in deleting a word in the forward direction (using dw or dW), if any whitespace exists between the current position and the start of the next word, it is deleted. If the deletion is toward the beginning-of-file (db or dB), only whitespace between the current position (not including current character) and the target beginning-of-word is deleted.

Table 5-8. Delete Sentence, Paragraph, or Section Commands

Command	Action Taken
d)	Delete from cursor position through first following end of sentence.
d}	Delete from cursor position through first following end of paragraph.
d]	Delete from cursor position through first following end of section.
dn) or nd)	Delete from cursor position through nth following end of sentence.
dn} or nd}	Delete from cursor position through nth following end of paragraph.
dn] or nd]	Delete from cursor position through nth following end of section.
d(	Delete from closest previous start of sentence through character before cursor.
d{	Delete from closest previous start of paragraph through character before cursor.
d[	Delete from closest previous start of section through character before cursor.
dn(or nd(	Delete from nth preceding start of sentence through character before cursor.
dn{ or nd{	Delete from nth preceding start of paragraph through character before cursor.
dn[or nd[	Delete from nth preceding start of section through character before cursor.

Deleting to a Text Location in Line or File

Text is deleted from the current cursor position to a specified character on the current line or a specified text pattern in the file being edited. The differences between **f** and **t** and between **F** and **T** are subtle, but they are useful in certain situations. Forms of these commands are summarized in Table 5-9 and Table 5-10.

Table 5-9. Delete Through Character on Current Line

Command	Action Taken
df c	Delete text from current position through first occurrence of character c on the current line when scanning toward end of line.
dnf c	Delete text from current position through nth occurrence of character c on the current line when scanning toward end of line.
dF c	Delete text from first occurrence of character c on the current line when scanning toward beginning of line to character preceding cursor.
dnF c	Delete text from nth occurrence of character c on the current line when scanning toward beginning of line to character preceding cursor.

Table 5-10. Delete to a Given Character on the Current Line

Command	Action Taken
dt c	Delete text from current position to first occurrence of character c on the current line when scanning toward end of line.
dnt c	Delete text from current position to nth occurrence of character c on the current line when scanning toward end of line.
dT c	Delete text from character following first occurrence of character c on the current line when scanning toward beginning of line to character preceding cursor.
dnT c	Delete text from character following nth occurrence of character c on the current line when scanning toward beginning of line to character preceding cursor.

Deleting Text to a Text Pattern

In Table 5-11, *search_pattern* is any valid UNIX regular expression recognized by standard UNIX editors and other commands. Refer to Appendix A for more information.

Table 5-11.
Delete Text from Current Position to a Specified Text Pattern

Command	Action Taken
d/*search_pattern* (Return)	Delete all text from current location to first occurrence of text matching *search_pattern* when searching in forward direction toward end of file. If *search_pattern* is matched before end of file is reached, deletion is from current cursor character up to, but not including, the matched text pattern. If search wraps to beginning of file before the pattern is matched, deletion begins with text pattern and all text is removed up to, but not including, the current cursor character.
d?*search_pattern* (Return)	Delete all text from current location to first occurrence of text matching *search_pattern* when searching in reverse direction toward beginning of file. If *search_pattern* is matched before beginning of file is reached, deletion is from start of text that matches *search_pattern* up to, but not including, current cursor character. If search wraps to end of file before the pattern is matched, deletion begins with the current cursor character and continues up to, but not including, the matching text pattern.

Note   In general, the current cursor character is included in all changes and deletions in the forward direction. If the change or deletion is in the reverse direction, the current cursor character remains undisturbed.

Text Delete/Change Command Examples

The following examples show various forms of text delete commands. They apply equally to change or yank commands by replacing the d in each command with c or y, respectively.

- 4dd, d4d, 3d+, and d3+ are equivalent. Each removes four lines starting with the current line.

- d5w deletes five words starting at the current cursor position. If there is only one word left on current line, the remaining four words are deleted on the following line or lines until the count of five words is filled. Counts related to sentences, paragraphs, and sections are handled in the same way.

- word1,word2,word3 is one Word or five words (each comma is treated as a separate word). This_is_one_word is treated as a single word.

- If the cursor is in mid-sentence, d) deletes the rest of the sentence. To delete the entire sentence, use (d) where (moves the cursor to the beginning of the sentence. The same technique applies for paragraphs and sections.

- If the cursor is at the beginning of the sentence, d) deletes the entire sentence. On the other hand, (d) deletes the previous sentence because (moves the cursor to the next previous beginning-of-sentence and the d) deletes to the next following end-of-sentence. The same technique applies for paragraphs and sections.

- (d) and)d(are functionally equivalent if the cursor is not at the beginning of the sentence. The former moves the cursor to the beginning of the sentence and removes text to the following end-of-sentence; the latter moves the cursor to the end of the sentence and removes text starting at the previous beginning-of-sentence. The same logic applies when deleting or changing paragraphs or sections.

Recovering Deleted Text

Whenever a change, delete, or yank command is executed on a text object, the object is copied into a buffer where it can be easily recovered. The command used to recover text from the buffer is the put command, which has the two forms p and P shown in Table 5-12.

Table 5-12. Commands to Recover Text from a Buffer

Command	Action Taken
p	Put buffer contents in text *after* current cursor position.
P	Put buffer contents in text *before* current cursor position.

The buffer may contain part of a line or it may contain one or more lines. Consequently, the transfer of buffer text must be handled according to the nature of the text being copied from the buffer. Generally speaking, text is copied from the buffer as follows:

- If the original command that placed text in the buffer was a change, delete, or yank lines command, buffer text is copied into the file immediately before (P) or immediately after (p) the current cursor line.

- For most other changes, deletions, or yanks (characters, words, sentences, paragraphs, sections, etc.), buffer text is copied into the current line in front of (P) or immediately after (p) the current cursor character.

It is this technique that gives rise to the xp command for swapping the positions of the current and next following character on the current line or the ddp command for swapping the position of the current and following line in a file.

Text can be easily copied or moved from one location to another by using a delete or yank command to place text in a buffer, moving the cursor to a new location in the file, then using p or P to place the deleted or yanked text in the new location. The p and P commands only copy the buffer into text, so the buffer contents are not disturbed. This means you can easily move to another location in the file and use another put command to repeat the operation as many times as you choose.

This method is described in greater detail in Chapter 6, which discusses moving and copying text in a file.

Using Named Buffers for Deleted or Yanked Text

In addition to the default buffer, vi provides 36 named buffers that can be used for copying and moving text objects. Again, these buffers and how they are used in conjunction with delete and yank commands are discussed in detail in Chapter 6, which deals with copying and moving blocks of text.

Changing Text

When the editor is given a text change command, it enters replace or insert mode as soon as it can determine the type of operation being performed, then accepts new input text until (ESC) is pressed. The only exception is the r or *n*r command form, which accepts only one character of replacement text and does not require an (ESC) character to terminate the operation. Table 5-13 summarizes the replace commands.

Replace Text and Change Text

When overstriking characters in conjunction with the R or *n*R command, if you encounter a tab character, the tab character is not replaced by a single replacement character, but rather, the tab is expanded on the display screen and the number of characters that replace the tab is determined by the width of the the tab character on the screen.

To abort a character replacement following an r, *n*r, R, or *n*R command, press (ESC) instead of the replacement character. To abort a substitute or change command, press (ESC), then type u to undo the text removal that results from (ESC).

Table 5-13. Replace Commands

Command	Action Taken
~	Change cursor character from lowercase to uppercase or vice versa, and advance the cursor to the next character on the line.
r	Replace single character at current cursor position (no (ESC) needed).
nr	Replace single character at current cursor position with n copies of replacement character (no (ESC) needed).
R	Replace text, character by character, starting at current cursor position.
nR	Change n characters or to end of line, whichever occurs first, starting with character immediately preceding current cursor position.
s	Replace single character at current cursor position with new text.
ns	Replace n characters (or to end of line if it occurs before n characters) starting at current cursor position with new text.

Table 5-14. Change Line Commands

Command	Action Taken
cc	Change current line.
ncc or cnc	Change n lines beginning at current line.
cG	Change all lines, starting with current line, through end of file.
c1G	Change all lines, starting with current line, through beginning of file.
cnG	Change all lines, starting with current line, through line n in file (forward or backward, depending on position of line n relative to current line).
c-	Change current and preceding line.
c+	Change current and following line.
nc- or cn-	Change current and n previous lines.
nc+ or cn+	Change current and n following lines.
C or c$	Change all characters from current cursor position to end of line.
c0 or c|	Change all characters from left column of screen to character preceding current cursor position on current line.

Change Text Objects

Change Word or Part of Word

Table 5-15 shows the commands that are used to change words. When lowercase b or w is used, any character other than alphanumeric or underscore is considered as the beginning of a new word, except whitespace characters that are treated as word separators.

When uppercase B or W is used, word boundaries are defined by whitespace word separators. Any other non-alphanumeric characters (including underscore and control characters) are treated as part of the word.

When changing words, vi assumes that whitespace should not be disturbed. Consequently, the change is from the boundary between the current cursor character and the character preceding it and the destination defined by the number and type of object(s) to be changed (word, sentence, paragraph, etc.). Any whitespace preceding or following the object to be changed remains unaltered.

Table 5-15. Change Word Commands

Command	Action Taken
cw	Change from cursor position through end of current word.
cW	Change from cursor position through end of current Word.
c*n*w or *n*cw	Change from cursor position through *n*th following word ending.
c*n*W or *n*cW	Change from cursor position through *n*th following Word ending.
cb	Change from nearest preceding beginning of word through character before current cursor position.
cB	Change from nearest preceding Beginning of word through character before current cursor position.
c*n*b or *n*cb	Change from *n*th preceding beginning of word through character before current cursor position.
c*n*B or *n*cB	Change from *n*th preceding Beginning of word through character before current cursor position.

Change All or Part of Sentence, Paragraph, or Section

Changing text objects such as words, sentences, paragraphs, and such are not restricted to the current line. If the number of text objects specified exceeds current line contents, the object is extended until the text specification is completely satisfied. Table 5-16 covers the change commands for sentences, paragraphs, or sections of text.

To abort a change command, press (ESC), then type u to undo the text removal that results from the (ESC).

Table 5-16.
Commands to Change a Sentence, Paragraph, or Section

Command	Action Taken
c)	Change from cursor position through next end of sentence.
c}	Change from cursor position through next end of paragraph.
c]]	Change from cursor position through next end of section.
c(	Change from preceding start of sentence through character before cursor.
c{	Change from preceding start of paragraph through character before cursor.
c[[	Change from preceding start of section through character before cursor.

Change Text Between Two Boundaries in Line or File

Text from the current cursor position to a specified character on the current line or a specified text pattern in the file being edited is replaced with new text until (ESC) is pressed. Table 5-17 and Table 5-18 summarize these editing commands.

Table 5-17. Commands to Change Text on Current Line

Command	Action Taken
cf$c$	Change text from current position through first occurrence of character c on the current line when scanning toward end of line.
cnfc	Change text from current position through nth occurrence of character c on the current line when scanning toward end of line.
cFc	Change text from current position through first occurrence of character c on the current line when scanning toward beginning of line.
cnFc	Change text from current position through nth occurrence of character c on the current line when scanning toward beginning of line.
ct$c$	Change text from before current position up to first occurrence of character c on the current line when scanning toward end of line.
cntc	Change text from before current position up to nth occurrence of character c on the current line when scanning toward end of line.
cTc	Change text from before current position up to first occurrence of character c on the current line when scanning toward beginning of line.
cnTc	Change text from before current position up to nth occurrence of character c on the current line when scanning toward beginning of line.

Table 5-18.
Change Text from Current Position to a Specified Text Pattern

Command	Action Taken
c/*search_pattern* [Return]	Change all text from current location to first occurrence of text matching *search_pattern* when searching in forward direction toward end of file. If *search_pattern* is matched before the end of file is reached, text change is from current cursor character up to, but not including, the matched text pattern. If search wraps to beginning of file before the pattern is matched, change begins with text pattern and all text is removed up to, but not including, the current cursor character.
c?*search_pattern* [Return]	Change all text from current location to first occurrence of text matching *search_pattern* when searching in reverse direction toward beginning of file. If *search_pattern* is matched before beginning of file is reached, change is from start of text that matches *search_pattern* up to, but not including, current cursor character. If search wraps to end of file before the pattern is matched, change begins with the current cursor character and continues up to, but not including, the matching text pattern.

Repeating a Text Change Operation

vi provides a dot command (.) that tells the editor to repeat the last operation that resulted in a text change. It can be used after delete, replace, change, yank/put, or any other command that changes text.

It is most commonly used when making a series of identical or very similar changes throughout a file without typing the text more than once. It is especially useful when using the search commands / and ? together with the repeat search commands n and N. To repeat a search for a given text pattern in a file, use n (repeat search in same direction) or N (repeat search in opposite direction). Adjust the cursor position if necessary, then press . (period or dot) to repeat the last change.

For example, suppose you are building a list of filenames preceded by a common pathname for use in a file manipulation script or a system document. Here is a sample of fictitious text:

```
This program block contains the following files:

Be sure all files are present before compiling the package.
```

You now need to add filenames and pathnames to the text from a handwritten list. Placing the cursor anywhere in the line preceding the blank line, type the o command followed by the pathname and filename—/users/prog_mgr/systemA/fileset1—then press (ESC). The result is:

```
This program block contains the following files:
/users/prog_mgr/systemA/fileset1/file1

Be sure all files are present before compiling the package.
```

By pressing . three times after (ESC) is pressed, the result looks like this:

```
This program block contains the following files:
/users/prog_mgr/systemA/fileset1/file1
/users/prog_mgr/systemA/fileset1/file1
/users/prog_mgr/systemA/fileset1/file1
/users/prog_mgr/systemA/fileset1/file1

Be sure all files are present before compiling the package.
```

Now it is a simple matter to move the cursor to the last word on each of the second, third, and fourth lines and edit the filename to obtain the other desired names. You can also get three more copies of the yanked line by typing yy followed by p.. or ppp after pressing (ESC).

With a little experimentation, you can quickly become proficient in the use of this frequently used command.

Using Numbered Buffers to Restore Text

vi maintains a delete/change buffer that can be used to restore the last change by means of the put (p or P) command. However, the put command by itself is only able to restore the most recent changed, yanked, or deleted text.

vi also maintains a history of changes/deletions in a group of numbered buffers, 1 through 9. They contain the preceding deletions and/or changes in a last-in, first-out push-down stack arrangement. This means that buffer 1 contains the most recent text and buffer 9 contains the least recent. To show how they are used, consider the following text:

```
line 1
line 2
line 3
line 4
line 5
line 6
line 7
line 8
line 9
```

Restoring Changes/Deletions in Reverse Order

Place the cursor on the first line, line 1, and type the dd command to delete the line. Now, press . eight times in succession to delete the remaining lines in the series. To restore the most recent deletion, type a double quote (") followed by the buffer number (1), and the lowercase p command (none of the typed characters appear on the display). Notice how the last line deleted now appears on the next line after the cursor and the cursor is moved to that line. Now, press . eight times to get this result:

```
line 9
line 8
line 7
line 6
line 5
line 4
line 3
line 2
line 1
```

This technique shows that the buffer pointer is advanced to the next buffer each time a put command is executed, provided the buffer number is used for the first put and . is used for successive operations. The recovered line is placed *after* the current line, thus producing the reversed order.

But I Don't Want Them in Reverse Order

You can also do the same without reversing the order. After making the last deletion, use the command "1P (note the uppercase P), followed by . eight times to get this:

```
line 1
line 2
line 3
line 4
line 5
line 6
line 7
line 8
line 9
```

In this example, recovered lines are placed before the current line such that the lines are restored in their original order.

You can also specify any buffer as you need it. For example, "6p restores the buffer containing the text line 4 after the current line if you use the previous deletion example. Specifying any number greater than 9 restores the most recent deletion.

Examples of Using Text Manipulation Commands

In this section, examples are used to illustrate how to use many of the commands previously discussed for deleting and altering text. In many cases, several approaches to a given problem are used to demonstrate the flexibility and power of the vi editor.

Examples of Deleting and Swapping Characters

vi's flexibility offers several ways to accomplish a given task. The approach you use will usually depend a great deal on how familiar you are with various methods and techniques as well as your particular interests and preferences. For example, consider the following line of text where spelling errors have been marked by a circumflex on the next line below:

```
For exammple, Consider the follollowing line of txeT.
```

We could tell you that the easiest way to fix the spelling errors is simply to move the cursor to the beginning of the line, then type the following characters:

```
fmx2fl3xfxxp
```

but you probably would wonder what all those characters mean, so let's take some time and learn how to attack a problem of this nature and determine what methods work best.

Four words need to be changed. A fast typist could move the cursor to the first error, clear the rest of the line, and retype it by using a D command followed by an a or A command. A less proficient user would probably prefer other methods requiring fewer keystrokes. Let's look at our options.

Deleting Characters

Assuming that the cursor is located at the beginning of the line and vi is in command mode, use the space bar (or the l key) to move the cursor to either m in exammple. Deleting a single character corrects the misspelling, so type x to remove the character at the current cursor location.

Now let's try a second, faster method. Type u to undo the change, then type 0 (zero) to move the cursor to the beginning of the line. Now, type fm. What happened? Why? Type 0 again. Now type 2fm. What is different? Why? Type x to remove the current cursor character.

The sentence should now look like this:

```
For example, Consider the follollowing line of txeT.
```

Now let's work on that gruesome word `follollowing`. Before we can fix it, the cursor has to be moved to the characters that should be removed (the first or second `llo`). First, an explanation of several ways to do it:

1. We have already learned that using `l` or the space bar is not always the quickest way to move through a line. It is adequate for up to a half-dozen or so characters, but for longer moves it is usually too slow.

2. The word skip command is available to move over words much like `l` moves over characters. Here is how it can be used:

   While observing the cursor, type `w`. The cursor moves to the comma because it is a non-alphanumeric character that is treated as the beginning of the next word. Type `w` again. The cursor moves to the beginning of `Consider` (the comma and space are treated as a single word). Now type `Fp` to move the cursor back to the previously deleted character position. Type `W`. Notice how the cursor skips over the comma this time and moves to the beginning of the next full word.

   `W` tells `vi` to use only whitespace to detect the end of a word and include non-alphanumeric characters as part of the word being skipped over (use of `w` and other similar cursor control commands are discussed in Chapter 4).

   Return the cursor to the previously deleted character (`Fp`), then type `3W`. Note how the cursor moves over three full words (ignoring punctuation) and stops at the beginning of `follollowing`. Now move the cursor back where it was and type `4w`. Notice that you get the same result as using `3W`. Use the space bar or `l` to move the cursor to the first `llo` in `follollowing`, then type `3x` to delete three characters.

3. The easy way, given the characters in the sentence, is to use the find command, `fl`. Note the new cursor position. Now type `FF`. Note that this gives the same result in this case as using `0`. Type `fl` again. Type `0` to return to the left column. Now type `2fl`, then `3x`.

   Here is another way. Type `u` and then `0` to undo the change and return to the left column, then type `fl` to return to the first `l`. Now type `dfo` to delete characters from the cursor position through the first occurrence of `o`. In this situation, `dfo` is equivalent to `d2tl` (delete up to, but not including, the second occurrence of the character `l`). Simple enough?

4. Repeat step 3, but instead of using 3x, type dfo. This time it removes all characters up through the following o to obtain the same result.

The sentence now reads as follows:

```
For example, Consider the following line of txeT.
```

Swapping Characters

Now let us correct the last word in the line. Press $ to move the cursor to the last character position, then use h or (BACKSPACE) to move back to the x in txet (from the beginning of the line, fx would get you there faster). Type x to delete the cursor character, then type p to add it after the e. Thus, to reverse two characters in text, type xp while in command mode.

Changing Uppercase/Lowercase

Now press the space bar or type l to move the cursor to the last letter in texT. Type ~ (tilde) to change the uppercase T to lowercase. Notice that the cursor advances to the period after the reversal is completed. Press (BACKSPACE) ~. What happens? Why? Press (BACKSPACE) ~ again to restore lowercase.

The sentence now reads as follows:

```
For example, Consider the following line of text.
```

Searching Within a Line: f and F Versus t and T

The cursor is now located at the end of the sentence underneath the period. We know from experience that FC would move the cursor to the uppercase C at the beginning of the third word in the current line. Type TC instead. What happened? Why? Press $, then type FC. Type ~ to drop C to lowercase. Now, type tx. Where did the cursor go? How is this different from fx?

The preceding pages have covered many concepts, but you now have the foundation for many skills that can be used with vi. Take some time to practice them on a few sentences of your own. The time will be amply rewarded as you move toward editing usable text.

Using Semicolon and Comma to Repeat a Search Within a Line

As you become more familiar with using f and F to search for characters in a line, you will discover that you frequently execute a search for a character (such as 5fl) only to find that you miscounted and got the wrong occurrence. Rather than typing another search command, it is usually easier to press semicolon (;) as a command to find the next occurrence of the character, possibly pressing it twice or more to get the correct one.

If you overshoot the character you want in a forward search, you can easily back up to the previous occurrence by using the comma (,) command. Thus 5fw , is equivalent to 4fw.

Both the comma and semicolon can be preceded by a number (such as 3; or 2,) to repeat the search more than once. Thus, 7fw 3, is equivalent to 4fw, and 3fw 3; is equivalent to 6fw.

The semicolon or comma repeat search command always works in any form with f and F. However, if used with t or T, the semicolon must be preceded by a number larger than 1 to obtain meaningful movement. If only the next occurrence of the search character is specified by the absence of a number greater than 1, the cursor does not move after the semicolon command because the search looks for the next occurrence of the character specified in the search, then moves to the previous or following character (depending on whether the search is forward or backward).

When the search is repeated by using ;, the character found in the previous search is again encountered, but when the cursor placement is determined, the result places the cursor in its location prior to the ; command, resulting in no movement. On the other hand, if the repeat command is preceded by a number larger than 1, the search is made for the nth occurrence of the search character, then the cursor returns to its correct position next to the specified character.

Examples of Replacing Text in a Line

We continue our discussion of editing within a line by using another example sentence with several errors:

```
Dis is a vewy junquey excyuse for a sentense, but wi'll uze it anyweigh.
```

Replacing a Single Character with Multiple Characters

This time, let's make the corrections in order, left to right. The first error is in the first word, so position the cursor at the first character in the line. We could use x to delete the first character, then insert two more characters to make the correction, but it is easier to use the s command. With the cursor positioned at the the D in Dis, type s. vi places a dollar sign ($) at the cursor location, indicating that this character will be replaced with zero or more characters (until you press (ESC) to restore command mode).

If you press (ESC) without entering any characters, the character space is deleted (the same as with the x command earlier). To correct the error, type Th and press (ESC). Notice how the remainder of the line was pushed to the right to accommodate new characters after the first was replaced.

Replacing Multiple Characters with Zero or More New Characters

The s command can be preceded by a numeric value to specify the number of characters that are to be changed. Thus, 10s replaces 10 characters beginning at the current cursor location with new text until (ESC) is pressed. If there are fewer than 10 characters between the cursor location and the end of the line, only the remaining characters in the line are replaced. The end-of-line position is extended, if necessary, to accommodate new characters being typed and can continue into multiple lines if enough characters are typed. This technique is demonstrated later in this example exercise.

Replacing a Single Character with Another

Now type 3w to move to the next incorrect word, then press the space bar twice to move to the incorrect character and type rr. The first r tells vi to replace the current cursor character with the next character typed. The second r is the replacement character. Since only one character is being replaced, vi does not require an (ESC) to return to command mode. However, if you type r, then decide not to make the change, you can use (ESC) to abort the change (unlike s, the character is not deleted when you press (ESC)).

Our sentence now looks like this:

```
This is a very junquey excyuse for a sentense, but wi'll uze it anyweigh.
```

Replacing Multiple Characters with a Single Character

Now press f (for "find character") q. This tells vi to move the cursor to the next occurrence of the character q in the line (if the character is not present in the current line, vi beeps). Now type 3s. Note that the cursor remains in its current position, but the dollar sign is located in the second column to the right. This means that new characters will be placed in the three character positions indicated until (ESC) is pressed. Type k and press (ESC). Now, type 2fy, then type x and press (ESC). What happened and why?

Note the present cursor position in the word excuse. Now type slowly and watch what happens when you type 3fsrc. What happened and why? What happens when you press (ESC)? Why? If you want to try it again, type u to undo the change, then move the cursor back to where it was. Our example sentence now looks like this:

```
This is a very junky excuse for a sentence, but wi'll uze it anyweigh.
```

Type 4w (BACKSPACE) se (ESC). Now type / (look at the bottom line of the screen) z (Return). This operation is explained in Chapter 4, but you just performed a forward search in the file for the next occurrence of the string expression z. Notice how much faster and easier it would have been simply to use fz to accomplish the same thing. Now type rs to make the change.

The sentence now looks like this:

```
This is a very junky excuse for a sentence, but we'll use it anyweigh.
```

Now type 10, then press the space bar. The cursor should be located at the e in eigh. Count the number of character positions from the previous cursor position to its present position (10 total). We need to change eigh to ay. There are several ways to accomplish this, and here are a few. Try and retry all of them until you understand the principles behind each technique.

First, type 4say (ESC). What happened? Four characters were replaced by two. Now type u to undo the change and put the cursor back where it was.

Next, type cfhay (ESC). What happened this time? c means change all characters from the current cursor position through the character position identified by the next command sequence, which must follow immediately. fh means find the the next occurrence of the character h and use ay as replacement characters as before. (ESC) again terminates the substitution and returns vi to command mode. Type u again to undo the change.

Here is another way to do the same thing: Type cway (ESC). As in the preceding method, c means change all characters from the current cursor position through the end of the "word" (as defined by our previous discussion of w versus W). Why did we use w instead of W? What happens if W is used instead?

The example sentence now looks like this:

```
This is a very junky excuse for a sentence, but we'll use it anyway.
```

There are many other ways to do the same thing, but these provide a useful sampling. The next section discusses the change (c) command in more detail.

Changing Words Within a Line

It is sometimes necessary to reword part of a line by changing one or more words in succession. It can be tedious to use the *n* s command because of the need to count characters before you know what *n* should be. vi provides an easy solution: the change (c) and delete (d) commands, which come in many varieties that were listed earlier in this chapter. Table 5-19 shows the delete and swap word commands.

More power comes to your fingertips when you use certain commands in convenient combinations. It is much easier to swap two characters, words, or lines with two to four keystrokes than to laboriously retype them.

Table 5-19. Delete or Swap Word Commands

Command	Action Taken
dw	Delete the current word consisting of all characters from the current cursor position up to, but not including, the next non-alphanumeric character unless it is a blank or tab character (if the first non-alphanumeric character is blank or tab, it and any additional contiguous whitespace excluding end of line is also removed).
d *n* w	Delete *n* words starting with the current word as defined by the dw command description. Count each non-alphanumeric character except blank (space), tab, and end of line as a separate word. Wrap to next line if necessary to match *n* word count. If the *n*th word is followed by a blank or tab, the blank or tab is also deleted, as are multiple contiguous blank/tab characters if present.
dW	Delete the word consisting of all characters from the current cursor position up to and including any following whitespace characters (one or more blanks or tabs but not end of line).
d *n* W	Delete *n* words consisting of all characters from the current cursor position up to and including the *n*th whitespace character or group of characters (blank, tab, or end of line or any contiguous multiple-character combination of the three). Wrap to next line if necessary to match *n* word count.
dwwP	Swap word beginning at cursor with word that follows (see dw). Treat non-alphanumeric characters as separate words.
dWWP	Swap word beginning at cursor with word that follows (see dW). Treat non-alphanumeric characters as part of the word(s) being swapped.

Let's modify our previous example sentence using some of these commands. Here is the sentence after our last changes:

```
This is a very junky excuse for a sentence, but we'll use it anyway.
```

Place the cursor at the beginning of the sentence, then type fa to move it to the third word, a. (You could also use 2w if the cursor was at the beginning of first word or 3w if the cursor was in the left column of the display screen but the sentence was indented one or more spaces — try it yourself and see.)

Now, let us reword part of the sentence. Type the command c6w, then type

    not a written well (ESC)

to produce a reworded sentence, as follows:

    This is not a written well sentence, but we'll use it anyway.
                          ^

Type the command 2b to back up two words. Now type the command dwwP to reverse the two words written and well. The sentence now reads:

    This is not a well written sentence, but we'll use it anyway.
                       ^

Now type (slowly) the command b (BACKSPACE) r-. What happened and why? (The b command is the opposite of w in that it moves backward. In like manner, B is the counterpart of W.) The result is now as follows:

    This is not a well-written sentence, but we'll use it anyway.
                      ^

While our sentence does not reflect the literary genius of a Milton or Shakespeare, you now have a good sampling of several simple commands that are quite useful when mastered.

Changing Multiple Lines of Text

The change and delete commands can also be used with line-oriented cursor movement commands. For example, c10 (Return) replaces the complete current cursor line and the 10 following lines with new text until you press (ESC). In like manner, c- replaces the current cursor line and the preceding line with new text until you press (ESC). In the first case, c10 (Return), c10+, and 11cc are equivalent and can be used interchangeably.

Likewise, d10 (Return) deletes the current cursor line and the 10 following lines while d- deletes the current cursor line and the preceding line. As when changing lines, d10 (Return) and 11dd are equivalent and can be used interchangeably.

Remember that when you use c or d and a line-oriented cursor control command such as +, -, G, j, k, H, L, or (Return), the current cursor line is replaced or deleted. On the other hand, when text-oriented cursor control commands such as w or W, b or B, and such, or text search commands (/ or ?) are used, the change or deletion begins at the present cursor character location and affects text from the current character to the new cursor location.

When using c or d with / or ?,[1] text is changed as follows:

- **Forward search** (/): Text is changed starting with the current cursor character up to, but not including, the first character in the text string that matches the search expression.

- **Backward search** (?): Text is changed starting with the first character in the text string that matches the search expression up to, but not including, the original cursor character.

Table 5-20 and Table 5-21 show several commands for changing, deleting, and swapping lines of text in a file. They are defined earlier in this chapter, but they are shown together here to illustrate various approaches to a given task.

Table 5-20. Line Change Commands

Command	Action Taken
c (Return), c+, or 2cc	Replace current cursor line and the line that follows with new text until (ESC) is pressed.
c n (Return) or cn+	Replace current cursor line and the n lines that follow with new text until (ESC) is pressed.
ncc	Replace n lines starting with the current cursor line with new text until (ESC) is pressed.
c-	Replace current cursor line and the line that precedes it with new text until (ESC) is pressed.
cn-	Replace current cursor line and the n lines that precede it with new text until (ESC) is pressed.

---

[1] The / and ? commands are discussed in greater detail later under "Pattern Searches".

Table 5-21. Delete or Swap Lines Commands

Command	Action Taken
dd	Delete current cursor line.
*n*dd	Delete *n* lines beginning at cursor line.
ddp	Swap cursor line and the line that follows it.

Pattern Searches

You will frequently want to search through a file for a certain (often a misspelled) word or expression during normal edits. vi provides a forward/backward pattern search capability that is very useful for locating a certain phrase or word in a file, finding a misspelled word, or locating a line in a program. You provide the phrase or word or an excerpt from the line, and vi does the work. If a word is misspelled, provide the word as misspelled, let vi find it, then make the needed correction.

You can also do repetitive searches for the same pattern so that you can make a change based on the location of the pattern, then repeat the change for all or some of the other occurrences of the same pattern in the file. Here is how it is done.

Forward Searches

To search forward in a file for a certain text pattern, use the forward search command

> /*pattern*

where *pattern* is a series of characters that matches a text word or phrase that occurs in the file. When you press (Return), vi searches the file beginning at the current cursor location and moving in the forward (toward end-of-file) direction until it finds the pattern or encounters end-of-file. If end-of-file occurs before the pattern is found, the search wraps to beginning-of-file and continues until the pattern is found or the current cursor line is reached. If the pattern cannot be found, the message

```
Pattern not found
```

is displayed and the cursor is returned to its original position prior to the search command.

If the pattern exists in the file, the cursor stops at the first character in the first detected occurrence of the pattern. You can then make text changes or choose not to.

Searching Backward in a File

You can search backward in a file from the current cursor position by using the ? command instead of /. Thus

   ?*pattern*

searches backward for the first occurrence of *pattern*. If beginning-of-file is encountered before *pattern* is found, the search wraps to end-of-file and continues until it returns full-circle to the current cursor line if the pattern is not found. As before, vi displays a `Pattern not found` message if the pattern is not present in the file or stops the cursor at the first character in the specified pattern if it is found.

Repeating the Search

Sometimes you may need to search for every occurrence of the pattern in the file. Obviously, it makes little sense to have to retype the pattern each time you want to continue to the next occurrence. You can use the n command to find the next occurrence without using (Return). When you type n, vi immediately resumes the forward search from the *current cursor position* (not from the previous pattern location).

You can reverse the direction of the search for the next occurrence of the pattern by using the N command instead of n. Thus, if your last search for *pattern* was in the forward direction, n searches forward from the current cursor position for the next occurrence of *pattern* while N searches backward. Conversely, if your last search was in the backward direction, n searches backward while N searches forward for the next occurrence of the same pattern.

Defining the Pattern

The pattern associated with a forward or backward search initiated by the / or ? command is most commonly a simple string of characters exactly matching the text or word of interest. However, it is not limited to only simple strings. Any valid regular expression recognized by vi and ex can be used for *pattern*. Using regular expressions in this manner harnesses some of the massive processing power implemented on UNIX, thus providing a great deal of flexibility. This means that regular expressions can become quite complex, depending on their use.

Refer to Appendix A on regular expressions for a detailed discussion about how to use them. If you are a beginner, you can easily use alphanumeric characters to form search patterns for finding text. If you use non-alphanumerics, remember that some of them are used to represent other characters or combinations of characters and their use requires special care.

Shifting Lines Horizontally Left or Right

vi has a shift left/right command that moves the entire current line (or specified number of lines starting with the current line) right (>> command) or left (<< command) shiftwidth columns. The default value for shiftwidth is 8, but it can be altered by using the :set shiftwidth=n command, where n is the number of columns to shift.

The shift right (>>) and shift left (<<) commands are useful on those occasions where you may need to move the left margin of a text block or paragraph right or left from the left margin or its current position. One method commonly employed by casual users is to insert or delete tabs or spaces at the beginning of each line. However, this can be cumbersome when a large number of lines are being shifted.

Consider the following lines of text:

```
These lines are about fifty characters in length.
They don't take a lot of space but they leave a
wide margin at the right-hand side.  If the lines
are shifted over, they move closer to the center.
```

By placing the cursor on the first line and typing 4>> (shift four lines, one shiftwidth to the right), they move one shiftwidth (eight columns) to the right:

```
These lines are about fifty characters in length.
They don't take a lot of space but they leave a
wide margin at the right-hand side.  If the lines
are shifted over, they move closer to the center.
```

Note that the cursor remains on the same line so you can easily press . (dot) to repeat the operation if you want to shift right again. To cancel the most recent shift, type u (undo). To shift four lines one shiftwidth to the left, type 4<<. Shiftwidth is discussed in Chapter 11.

Using Markers to Shift Lines

You can also mark a line at one end of the block of text (ma marks the line with a marker), then move to the other end and type >'a or <'a to shift every line from the cursor line through the marked line.

Automatic Indenting

When using structured programming languages such as C or Pascal, it is desirable to change indentation for each level in hierarchical source code structures. The vi/ex editor provides an autoindent option that supports this feature. It is described in detail in Chapter 11.

vi and ex are normally configured with autoindent disabled (default) unless a user configuration file named .exrc exists in a given user's home directory and contains the :set ai command explained below (see Chapter 11 for information about configuration files). To enable autoindent without disturbing other aspects of your editing session, simply type

    :set ai (Return)

To disable autoindent at any time during the session, type

    :set noai (Return)

Using Automatic Indentation

When autoindent is enabled, vi identifies the position of the first visible character on the current cursor line and sets that column number as the current indent value. Whenever a new line is created while in insert mode (o or O [open] creates a new line immediately; insert, append, change, and substitute create a new line whenever (Return) is pressed or whenever wrapmargin forces a new line if it is set), the new line automatically begins at the current indent.

Changing Current Indent

The current indent is easy to change. To increase the indent on a new line, use spaces or tabs to obtain the appropriate indent. To decrease the indent, use the special command (CTRL)-(D) (end-of-file character), which moves the current indent left by shiftwidth characters or to the left margin, whichever occurs first.

Good program structure also includes comment lines and other features to promote readability and ease of interpretation. It is often desirable to provide a single line (such as a comment) at the left margin, then resume normal indent for succeeding lines of program code. This is easily accomplished with a slightly different technique for moving the current margin to the left. Assuming that you just finished a line starting at the current indent and pressed (Return) to start the next line (or perhaps twice to obtain a blank line):

- Press the circumflex key (^) as the first character on the new line. The character is printed on the screen by vi.

- Press (CTRL)-(D) to select the extreme left margin for one line only.

- The circumflex character disappears from the screen, and the cursor is moved to the extreme left column on that line.

- Type the new line as desired, starting at the left column and inserting desired whitespace, if any, on the left before visible text.

- When the line is finished, press (Return). The cursor appears below the left margin of the previous line, not the left margin of the line that was just typed.

- Use the same procedure to type another line at the left margin, continue with the current margin, or change it right or left, as desired.

In Summary

- Use space or tab characters to move autoindent margin right.

- Use (CTRL)-(D) (must be first character typed on new line) to move margin left by one shiftwidth.

- Use (^) followed by (CTRL)-(D) to type a single line at left margin without changing current indent value.

Use of Tabs

Autoindent uses tab characters where possible to conserve the total character count in the file being edited. Some applications may require that all leading whitespace be only spaces. In such instances, you must either edit the file with autoindent disabled or process the file using the **expand** command, which converts tabs into spaces. This should be done after you write and quit editing; **expand** is not an editor command.

To expand tabs in a file, use a command similar to

> **expand** *filename* >*new_filename*

which replaces tabs with spaces such that text is lined up at intervals of eight characters starting at the left. Other forms of the command can be used to specify tab column positions other than every eight. Another technique in specifying options provides the ability to specify that tabs be assigned to stop on certain column numbers in each line. Refer to the **expand**(1) manual entry in the on-line UNIX reference (using the **man** command) for more information.

Chapter Summary

The following highlights were covered in this chapter:

Recovering from mistakes	ESC and u (for undo)
Inserting text into a file	i for insert a for append o for open line below
Typing control characters	CTRL-V e.g., CTRL-V ESC
Deleting text	x to delete character dw to delete word dd to delete line d) to delete sentence d} to delete paragraph d/*search_pattern* Return
Recovering deleted text from buffer	p put "in back of" P put "in front of"
Replacing text	r replace single character with single character R replace multiple characters s replace character with new text
Changing text	cw change word cc change line c/*search_pattern* Return change block of text
Swapping text	xp swap characters dwwp swap words ddp swap lines
Shifting lines horizontally	>> shift right << shift left

6

Copying and Moving Text
Using Buffers and Text Objects

What This Chapter Covers

- Overview of buffers

- Using buffers to copy and move text

- Using files to copy or move text

- Executing a buffer as an ex editor command

- Using text objects: words, lines, sentences, paragraphs, sections, and user-defined text objects

- Creating and accessing text markers

Using Buffers

vi makes 36 buffers available for copying or moving blocks of text. They are:

- The default, unnamed buffer

- 35 named buffers (a through z and 1 through 9)

The most commonly used buffer is the default buffer, which is sometimes referred to as the unnamed buffer. Whenever a delete or yank operation is performed, the deleted or yanked text is copied into the default buffer (unless another buffer name is specified). It can then be placed elsewhere or replaced in its original position by using the put (p or P) command. (Table 6-1 shows examples of copying text into named buffers.) However, the contents of the default buffer are maintained only until the next text modification command is executed.

Thus, if you delete a block of text (causing it to be placed in the default buffer), move elsewhere and execute another text modification command, then move again and try to place the buffer contents in your new location in the file, you will discover that the buffer text was destroyed by the command executed since the deletion. The buffer is destroyed even if the change is not a deletion or yank (for example, an insert or append).

Buffer names are accessed by using a double quote before the buffer name, which is specified prior to the delete or yank command in the command line. For example, "ayy yanks a line of text into buffer a and "ap puts the contents of buffer a on the following line.

The contents of the named buffers remain intact for the entire time that vi is running except when a new delete or yank to that named buffer overwrites the buffer contents. All buffer contents, both named and unnamed, are lost when vi terminates, not at the end of editing the current file. This means that information can be copied into named buffers when editing multiple files, then the contents of those buffers can be placed in other files being edited as part of the same session.

Named buffers a through z and markers (also named a through z) are completely unrelated and independent of each other.

Note	The default (unnamed) buffer contents are destroyed at the end of a file edit, even if several files are being edited in a single session. If you need to copy data between files using buffers, use named buffers instead to preserve contents until the appropriate file is open.

Table 6-1. Examples of Copying Text into a Named Buffer

Command	Buffer	Action
"a6dd	a	Delete six lines starting with current line.
"r3yy	r	Yank three lines starting with current line.
"xd4)	x	Delete four sentences starting at current location.
"cd'r	c	Delete current line through line at marker **r**.
"hdG	h	Delete all text from current line through end of file.
"b3x	b	Delete three characters starting at current position.
"gy/*text* [Return]	g	Yank from current position to (but not including) *text*.

Appending Text to Buffers

Text can be appended to an existing buffer instead of replacing any current buffer contents. Simply use the uppercase buffer names A through Z instead of the corresponding lowercase buffer names a through z.

Retrieving Text from Buffers

Anytime prior to the end of a session, data can be retrieved from a named buffer and placed in text relative to the current cursor position. To place the buffer contents after the current character or line use

   "*buffer_name*p

To place the buffer contents before the current character or line use

   "*buffer_name*P

If a yank or delete operation is performed on full lines (such as dd or 4yy), the put command places text before (P) or after (p) the current line.

When a yank or delete operation is performed on a character, word, sentence, section, and so on, the buffer text will be put before (P) or after (p) the cursor within the line as shown in the examples in Table 6-2.

Table 6-2. Examples of Using the Put Command

Command	Buffer	Text Placement
"ap	a	Six lines previously deleted are inserted after current line.
"rP	r	Three lines previously yanked are inserted before current line.
"xp	x	Four sentences are inserted starting after current character.
"cP	c	All lines deleted through line at marker r are inserted before the current line.
"hP	h	Lines to former end of file are inserted before current line.
"bP	b	Three characters are inserted before the current character.

Executing a Buffer as an ex Editor Command

Many commands, especially search-and-replace commands, can involve repetition and tedious typing with risk of mistakes. vi has a little-known but very useful feature that can be used in conjunction with the yank command to save much retyping for doing complex or repetitive ex operations. The procedure is simple:

1. Type in a valid ex command, including the colon at the beginning.

2. Use a yank line (Y) command to yank the entire current cursor line into a named buffer. For example, to use buffer h, the command is

```
"hY
```

3. Use the `vi` @ command, followed by the buffer name, to execute the buffer contents. For example, to execute the contents of buffer **h**, type

    @h

No [Return] is necessary in either case because both commands are processed by the `vi` command mode interpreter.

The editor places the command from the buffer on the bottom line of the display, just as it would appear if you had typed it in `ex` command mode, then executes the command. You will note that if the command was a substitute command, the substitution is made on the regular expression part of the command as well as anywhere else in the text file unless the address range was restricted to only part of the file. The substitute command is discussed in greater detail in the Chapter 7.

When using this technique, it is usually best to place lines being yanked at the beginning or end of the file for easy deletion before writing the file back to permanent storage at the end of the session.

Example of Executing a Buffer

In the following example, the > symbol along with a space before and after it will be attached to the beginning of every line in the file except the last line, which is the `ex` command.

```
This is an example of executing
an "ex" command stored in a
buffer. It places the ">" symbol
at the beginning of every line
in the file except the last.

:1,$-1s/^/ > /g
^
```

With the cursor at the bottom line (indicated by the ^), type

    "aY [Return]

Then type

@Y `Return`

The result should appear as shown below.

```
    > This is an example of executing
    > an "ex" command stored in a
    > buffer. It places the ">" symbol
    > at the beginning of every line
    > in the file except the last.
    >
 :1,$-1s/^/ > /g
```

Using ex Commands to Copy or Move Text

The ex commands, copy, move, yank, and put can also be used to copy or move text directly or through named buffers. Procedures are similar to using vi methods with some variations. Use of these commands is discussed in Chapter 9.

Using Files to Copy or Move Text

External mass storage files can also be used to copy all or part of a file to another location in the file or to other files. To move text, the lines of interest are written to a file, then the lines are deleted from the current workfile. To copy text, the lines are written to a file but not deleted. The external file can then be read back into the file being edited or into another file.

For more information about using the read and write commands, :r and :w, refer to Chapter 8.

Text Objects

One of the great strengths of `vi` is its ability to handle a variety of text objects, such as words, lines, sentences, paragraphs, and sections, and to allow each user to independently define certain objects such as sections by using `vi` configuration commands. Learning about and understanding these text objects and how they are used is a critical key to accessing and using the true power that is available from `vi` for the experienced user. Text objects were introduced in Chapter 4 and Chapter 5; this section explains them in greater depth so that more experienced users can make better use of them.

Word Objects: w or W

Word objects are treated in two ways: Words and words. When the uppercase W is used, word boundaries are delimited *only* by whitespace, which is defined by any one or more or a combination of blank, tab, or newline (end-of-line sequence) characters. When the lowercase w is used, word boundaries are delimited by whitespace or detection of any other non-alphanumeric character (except underscore). A sequence of one or more contiguous non-alphanumeric characters (other than whitespace and underscore) is treated as a single word. Thus the expression

    This, at least, is a sentence.

is treated as nine words or six Words (the lowercase w version treats each comma and period as a separate word). On the other hand, the expression

    $%one_word#&(@

is treated as one Word or three words: `$%`, `one_word`, and `#&(@`.

Line Objects: ˆ or $

The current line and the current position within the current line form the basic foundation from which `vi` operations are referenced. Two characters are used in `vi` and `ex` commands to represent the beginning and end of the current line:

   ˆ   When used in a regular expression, this character represents the position that would be occupied by a character if it were inserted in front of the first character in the line (left screen margin).

When used as a cursor control command, the cursor moves to the first visible (non-blank) character in the line.

$ When used in a regular expression, this character represents the position that would be occupied by a character if it were appended after the last character in the line.

When used as a command, the cursor moves to the last character (visible or invisible) at the end of the line.

Note   End-of-line refers to the end of the line as it exists in the buffer file, not as it is displayed on the terminal screen. If the line is longer than the width of the display screen, beginning- and end-of-line occur on separate lines of the display.

Sentence Objects: (or)

vi accommodates two types of sentences:

- A group of words terminated by ., !, or ?, followed by at least two spaces (blanks) or end-of-line. This defines a sentence as commonly used in normal spoken language and is consistent with standard typing practice. If the ., !, or ? is followed by fewer than two spaces (unless at end-of-line), it is not treated as an end-of-sentence condition.

- For the Lisp programming language, a sentence is a valid Lisp s-expression, provided the -l (Lisp) option was specified as part of the UNIX vi command at the beginning of the session (as discussed in Chapter 3) or the :set lisp command is included in the *.exrc* file or executed as a command from the editor (see Chapter 11).

Paragraph Objects: { or }

A paragraph is a group of one or more sentences that is bounded before and after by:

- One or more blank lines

- Either of the following:

  1. The default paragraph and section macros defined by vi.

2. An alternate set of macros defined by a :set paragraphs and/or a :set sections command.

but not both.

New paragraphs begin at a blank line, defined paragraph macro, or defined section macro.

Unless redefined by a :set paragraphs and/or :set sections command, the following default paragraph macros from various nroff/troff macro packages are recognized by vi:

    .IP   .LP   .PP   .QP   .P   .LI   .bp

To add new macros or change the current list of recognized paragraph macros, the entire string must be redefined. Refer to Chapter 11 for procedures to redefine macros.

Section Objects: [[or]]

A section is a block of text bounded by a section macro or end-of-file, where the section macro marks the beginning of a new section. Recognized section macros are defined by the :set sections command.

vi recognizes the following default section macros that originate from various nroff/troff macro packages:

    .NH   .SH   .H   .HU

To add new macros or change the current recognized section macros, the entire string must be redefined (see Chapter 11).

User-Defined Text Objects

In addition to the preceding text objects recognized by vi, you can define any other text object by specifying the text lying between the current cursor position and any standard cursor movement command, including text markers. User-defined text objects fall into two general categories:

- Line-oriented objects identified by beginning and ending line.
- Exact-position-oriented objects such as all characters between two markers.

Text Markers Within a File

A text marker is a locating device used by vi and other editors to accurately pinpoint a specific location in a file. vi text markers can be used to locate a specific character in the file or the beginning of the line containing the marked character, depending on the type of command used with the marker. vi text markers are not stored as part of the file, so they are lost at the end of the editing session.

Up to 26 text markers can be specified in any given file during the editing session. Each marker is given a lowercase single-character name in the range a through z.

Creating Markers

To mark a location in the file, use any normal combination of screen and cursor control commands to move the cursor to the desired location in the file. Once the cursor is in the correct location, type the command

m*marker_name*

where m is the "mark text location" command and *marker_name* is a single lowercase character in the range a through z. If an illegal character is specified for *marker_name,* the command is ignored and the editor sends a beep sequence to the terminal to signal the error.

Up to 26 simultaneous locations can be marked in the file during any given editing session. If a new marker command is given and the marker name is the same as an existing marker, the previous marker is canceled and redefined for the new location.

Using Markers for Cursor Control

One common use for markers is as a convenient means for moving quickly between arbitrary locations in a large file. For such uses, marked text locations can be reached by two methods. The first command form:

' *marker_name*

in which *marker_name* is preceded by an accent grave (also called a backquote) moves the cursor to the exact character in the file that is identified by the *marker_name* provided as part of the command.

On the other hand, using a single quote (apostrophe) as follows:

> ' *marker_name*

moves the cursor to the beginning (first visible non-blank character) of the line containing the marked character.

This subtle but important difference between forms is very useful in certain situations when you are editing text objects defined by marker-specified boundaries.

Using Markers for Text Object Operations

Markers can be used to define text objects being manipulated by a delete, change, or yank command. In general, the text object is bounded by the cursor position at the time the command is given and the location of the marker specified in the command sequence or by the lines containing each, depending on the cursor movement command associated with the marker name.

Note   If a line or character associated with a text marker is deleted, the marker definition is also canceled at the same time.

As indicated in earlier chapters on basic editing, the text characters contained within the text object depend on whether the cursor position before the move operation is at the beginning or end of the object in the file. Here is the general structure of the editing commands as they are used in conjunction with text markers:

1. Move cursor to beginning or end of text object being manipulated:

2. Specify operation type:

   - d to delete entire text object

   - d preceded by buffer name to delete text object into named buffer (buffers are described in "Using Buffers")

   - c to change text object to replacement text

   - y to yank text object into default buffer

   - y preceded by buffer name to yank text object into named buffer

3. Specify other boundary of text object being manipulated:

   - ` marker_name sets boundaries on marked character and current cursor position. Text object includes first boundary character in file and all text up to second boundary character, but does not include the second boundary character.

   - ' marker_name sets boundaries to include entire line containing marker and entire line containing cursor character, regardless of their relative positions in the file.

Examples of Editing Using Markers

The flexibility of text objects, especially when dealing with sentences, paragraphs, sections, and markers, makes it difficult to provide any quick useful examples involving large text blocks. However, Table 6-3 shows a few examples of commands that reference text objects so that you can become proficient in their use.

In Table 6-3, marker a is assumed to precede marker b in the file.

Table 6-3. Examples of Using Markers

Command	Action Taken
`ad`b	Remove all characters starting with the character marked by marker a up to but not including the character marked by marker b.
'ad'b	Remove all lines starting with the line containing marker a and continuing through the line containing marker b.
'adG	Remove all lines starting with the line containing marker a and continuing through the last line in the file.
'ad`b	Remove all lines starting with the line containing marker a and continuing through the character preceding marker b.
`ad'b	Remove all text starting at marker a and continuing through the entire line containing marker b.

Chapter Summary

The following topics were covered in this chapter:

Put text into unnamed buffer.	dw put deleted word into unnamed buffer yy put yanked line into unnamed buffer
Buffer names.	a through z (A through Z to append) 1 through 9
Put text into named buffer.	"adw put deleted word into buffer a "Cyy append yanked line into buffer c "hdG put text deleted from current line to end of file into buffer h
Retrieve text from buffer.	"ap retrieve text from buffer a "hP retrieve text from buffer h
Word objects.	w word delimited by non-alphabetic character W word delimited by whitespace only
Line objects.	^ first character in line $ last character in line
Sentence objects.	(beginning of sentence) end of sentence
Paragraph objects.	{ beginning of paragraph } end of paragraph
Section objects.	[[beginning of section]] end of section
Marker names.	a through z
Create a marker.	m*marker_name* ma marker a mm marker m
Access a marker.	'*marker_name* 'm accesses marker m

7

Search-and-Replace Operations

Search-and-replace capabilities are an important feature in any useful editor program. The search-and-replace features in this editor are accessible both from vi and ex as ex mode commands.

What's in This Chapter

- Several techniques for using search-and-replace.

- The substitute command.

- Line addressing to limit the scope of search-and-replace commands.

- Other useful techniques such as splitting lines that the substitute command provides.

The simplest form of search-and-replace is conducting a pattern search as described earlier in Chapter 2, then performing a character, word, or line replacement. The replacement can be done on other occurrences of the same pattern in the file by typing n to find the next occurrence, then typing . (dot) to repeat the previous change.

Obviously, this process becomes dull and tedious rather rapidly if a large number of changes are needed in the file. The ex capabilities addressed in this chapter can be used to automate this process greatly and save considerable time and effort. However, be wary because if you do not exercise adequate care in defining the string to be changed, you may get more changes than you really wanted. For example, changing every occurrence of the to xyz in a file also changes Athena to Axyzna—probably not what you would want.

Search-and-replace operations are most commonly performed using the substitute command in the `ex` command set with a global suffix on the command if the operation is to be performed more than once on any given line. The `ex` command set is accessed from `vi` command mode by typing a colon, which switches `vi` to `ex` mode operation for the duration of `ex` command execution.

Colon Commands

`ex` mode (or external mode) commands always begin with a colon when accessed from `vi` and are therefore often referred to as colon commands. When forming a colon command, the first character, the colon, is followed by a command sequence that can be any legitimate `ex` command (except for certain cases when program bugs or other considerations require a change to `ex` by using the `Q` command). `ex` commands are discussed in detail in Chapter 9. To execute a completed command, press (Return) or (ESC) after typing it. ((Return) is most commonly used and preferred, but (ESC) also works.)

Fixing Mistakes

If you make an error while typing a colon command, use (BACKSPACE) to move the cursor left to the appropriate position, then retype the rest of the command. As with normal `vi` operation, characters are not erased from the screen as you move the cursor left, but they are removed from the `vi/ex` command buffer. Hence, any extra characters that are not obliterated by retyping are ignored (you will notice that they disappear from the bottom line of the display as soon as you press (Return) or (ESC)).

If you make a mistake early in the line and prefer to retype the complete line, press the KILL (line-erase character, usually (CTRL)-(U)), which immediately moves the cursor to the first character following the colon so you can type a new line.

Aborting the Command

If you type part of a colon command, then decide you want to do something else instead, you can abort the command by pressing (BACKSPACE) several times (or press (CTRL)-(U) followed by (BACKSPACE)) to back the cursor up to the left margin past the colon. When the cursor passes the colon, the editor abandons the command and returns the cursor to where it was prior to the aborted colon command. This same method can be used to abort a partially typed vi search command (/ or ?).

An easier method is simply to press the (BREAK) key. This method has the side effect of setting the UNIX vi command return status flag to FALSE when vi terminates, but unless you are operating in an unusual environment, using the (BREAK) key should present no discernible disadvantage.

Aborting After Execution Begins

You may discover, particularly when performing global operations on a very large file, that you gave an incorrect command (such as inadvertently typing / or ? instead of :) or an inappropriate command and need to abort it. Press (BREAK). Command execution stops, and an error message is displayed as follows:

```
Interrupt
```

If you accidentally type a search command (/ or ?) and interrupt the search with (BREAK), the cursor usually returns to its original position prior to the command, and the file remains unmodified by the command. If you interrupt a substitution partway through the file or if the incorrect command runs to completion before being interrupted, you can use the u (undo) command to repair the damage and return to the pre-command state.

Should the screen be left in an unusable state (not likely but it can happen on occasion), simply press (CTRL)-(L) to redraw it.

Undoing Colon Commands

Like normal vi commands, the external mode commands are also subject to the u command. If you discover that the change you made did not produce the desired effect, type u immediately before executing any other command. As usual, if any command is executed after the colon command, the undo option for that command is forever lost, and you must either use another command or set of commands to fix the error or abort the session (:q! command) and start over.

File Safety

Because certain complex ex commands can have a disastrous effect on a file if they are incorrectly formed and you forget to execute an undo before you execute the next command, it is a good idea to write your buffer file to permanent storage before performing a complex instruction. That way, if the command happens to demolish your file beyond use, you can easily abort by using :q! without overwriting the backup, then use the vi command again to reopen the file. Use of write and quit commands is discussed in greater detail in Chapter 3.

Command Structure

The search-and-replace command consists of the following parts in the following sequence:

- A colon to identify the command as an ex mode command.

- A starting line number or address.

- An ending line number or address.

- A substitute command.

- A regular expression that defines the search string to be identified.

- A substitute string to replace the search string when found.

- A global suffix if the operation is to be performed more than once on any lines containing two or more strings that match the search string expression.

Line Addresses

Colon search-and-replace commands start with a colon, which tells vi to execute the ex mode command (ex can also execute the same command except that the ex personality provides a colon prompt so it is not necessary to type a new colon, although if you do type a colon while in ex it is not treated as an error). The colon is then followed by zero, one, or two line addresses where:

- If no address is present, it implies that the operation is to be performed on the current line only.

- One address tells the editor to perform the operation on the addressed line only.

- When two line addresses are provided, the operation is performed on all lines starting with the first line addressed and continuing through the second addressed line. The first line address must precede the second address in the file. A comma separates the first and second line addresses.

Whitespace (space or tab character) is optional but rarely used before, between, and after line addresses.

All colon commands include a line address for a single line, a double line address for a group of contiguous lines, or an implied address when no specific address is included in the command. Table 7-1 lists the line address forms recognized by ex.

Table 7-1. Recognized Colon Command Line Address Forms

Address	Corresponding Line
none	Current line only (implied address).
$	Last line in file.
.	Current line.
n	nth line in file.
.-n	nth line before current line.
.+n	nth line after current line.
%	Abbreviation for 1,$, which means every line in the file.

When two addresses are present to define starting and ending line numbers for the command, they must be separated with a comma (,) as shown in the examples in Table 7-2.

Table 7-2. Examples of Colon Command Line Address Forms

Address	Corresponding Line
1	First line in file.
3	Third line in file.
.	Current line in file.
.-4	Fourth line before current line in file.
.+8	Eighth line after current line in file.
$	Last line in file.
g	All lines in file.
1,.	All lines from beginning of file to current line.
.,$	All lines from current line to end of file.
.,.+5	Current line through fifth following line.
1,.+5	First line in file through fifth line after current line.
.-10,.+5	Tenth preceding line through fifth following line.

Global searches (described next) can also be used to identify certain lines in the file in lieu of the address forms in the preceding list, as can file markers.

Global Searches

Suppose you are working on a large file such as a large computer program or text file and need to look at every line in the file that contains a certain word, program label reference, or operand name. Rather than using a cumbersome series of / or ? followed by n or N search sequences, you can print all occurrences of the desired text pattern with a simple command of the form

: g/ *text_pattern*/p (Return)

where *text_pattern* is any regular expression of the form described in Appendix A on regular expressions that is compatible with vi and ex. The g command specifies that the search is to be made globally (on every line) throughout the file, and the p command specifies that the results are to be printed on the display screen. Experienced users will recognize that this command is very similar to the UNIX grep command.

After the lines are printed to the screen, the message

```
[Hit return to continue]
```

appears at the bottom of the screen. Press any typing key to restore the normal editor display.

Limited Searches

You can easily limit the search for a given expression to a certain part of the file by specifying the starting and ending line numbers. Here is the command form:

: *start_line*, *end_line* g/ *text_pattern*/p (Return)

where *start_line* is any valid line number identifier that specifies the starting line and *end_line* specifies the last line in the search space. Valid line specifiers can be the actual line number (1 is the first line in the file, $ specifies the last line, and 25 specifies line 25, etc.), line locations relative to current line, or any other form recognized by ex.

Displaying Tabs and Other Non-Printing Control Characters

Suppose you need to find any non-printing control characters hidden in a file. This can be particularly important when examining a computer program file as well as in many other circumstances.

The l (lowercase L) command accomplishes this task in this form:

: *start_line*, *end_line*l (Return)

Any control characters contained within the specified file segment are displayed in **hat** format, hat being a common vernacular name among UNIX users for the circumflex character (^). Tabs are displayed as ^I, and end-of-line is displayed as $. For example, consider the following rather innocent looking line of text:

```
If this looks like a simple sentence, look between the words
```

Placing the cursor anywhere on the line and executing the command

: .l (Return)

reveals more than meets the eye:

```
If this looks like a^Isimple sentence, look between the words   ^I  $
```

showing two hidden tabs plus several spaces at the end of the line. Likewise, a command of the form

: ., .+10l (Return)

displays all control characters in the current plus the 10 following lines.

After listing the lines, press any key to restore the normal editor display.

Displaying Tabs and Ends of Lines

Tabs and ends of lines can be viewed by using the ex command :set list. The tab character is indicated by ^I, and the end-of-line character is indicated by $. This can be useful when tabs are embedded in the text or when spaces follow the last character of text in a line. To toggle back to normal mode, use :set nolist.

For example, suppose the following information is displayed:

```
      This is a table of some ASCII
      characters that appears to
      contain white space.

            Octal    Character        Octal    Character
            000      nul              010      bs
            001      soh              011      ht
            002      stx              012      nl
            003      etx              013      vt
            004      eot              014      np
            005      enq              015      cr
            006      ack              016      so
            007      bel              017      si
```

Now type

    :set list

The display should appear as:

```
      This is a table of some ASCII $
      characters that appears to              $
      contain white space.$
$
^IOctal^ICharacter^IOctal^ICharacter$
^I000^Inul^I^I010^Ibs$
^I001^Isoh^I^I011^Iht$
^I002^Istx^I^I012^Inl$
^I003^Ietx^I^I013^Ivt$
^I004^Ieot^I^I014^Inp$
^I005^Ienq^I^I015^Icr$
^I006^Iack^I^I016^Iso$
^I007^Ibel^I^I017^Isi$
```

The embedded tab and end-of-line characters now show up clearly. Notice the extra spaces at the end of the second line after the word to.

Splitting Lines

One very perplexing problem for many vi users lies in how to split lines during a pattern search-and-replacement operation. In other words, when a certain pattern is found, how can an end-of-line be placed near that location so that multiple lines are formed? Likewise, how can a pair of lines be combined in a global search-and-replace sequence?

Unfortunately, regular expressions cannot have newlines escaped into them, so it is not possible to join lines using global search-and-replace operations. (However, the UNIX sed editor can join lines in the pattern space. While holding one line in the pattern space, read the next line, then convert the newline to a space character. Use the on-line man command for an explanation of the sed editor.)

Switch to ex

Since the vi command interpreter cannot handle multiple-line command input, we must use ex. To switch from vi to ex, type Q (press (SHIFT)-(Q)). ex then responds with the usual colon prompt.

Forming the Command

Like any normal search-and-replace command, the colon prompt is followed by typing an address or pair of addresses followed by the s (substitute) command. A regular expression followed by replacement text forms the substitution part of the command, and any flags or options are added at the end of the command.

For illustration, let us use the following paragraph as original text:

```
This paragraph is only one of the many possible demonstrations
of the substitute command for splitting lines.  However, the
result may make you writhe in pain or laughter as your friends
watch the scene.
```

With the cursor on the first line of the paragraph, type Q to get the colon prompt, then type the following command:

```
:.,.+3s/the /the\(Return)
/g(Return)
```

Now for the explanation. The colon prompt was provided by ex. The `.,.+3` specifies the current and three following lines. s says substitute the replacement text for the text pattern defined by the first expression. The first expression is identified by the slash characters before and after. The second expression consists of the followed by a backslash (\\), which is in turn followed by (Return) and another slash, meaning that the replacement ends with an end-of-line (the \\ at the end of the first line in the command escapes the newline character from interpretation by the editor as end-of-command). The g option tells ex to make the substitution for every occurrence of the first expression throughout the specified body of text, even when it occurs more than once on any given line.

Executing the command yields the following displayed line:

```
scene.
```

Now, change back to vi by typing vi (Return). The previous line appears at the top of the screen. Scroll the text down to reveal the following:

```
This paragraph is only one of the
many possible demonstrations
of the
substitute command for splitting lines.   However, the
result may make you writhe
in pain or laughter as your friends
watch the
scene.
```

As expected, every occurrence of `the` followed by a space was replaced with `the` and a newline sequence. Even `writhe` was subjected to the same treatment, as you would expect since no restrictions were placed on the text preceding `the`.

Another Example

Using the first sentence from the previous example, let us change a few of the ASCII space characters to tab characters as follows:

```
This paragraph is only one of the many possible
demonstrations of the substitute command for
splitting lines.
```

Now, using the previous procedure, place the cursor on the first line of the three, type `Q` to switch to `ex`, then execute the following command:

> `:.,.+2s/`[*space tab*]`/\`⃞Return⃞
> `/g`⃞Return⃞

where the regular expression [*space tab*] contains a space and tab character—that is, [*space tab*]. This tells the editor to search for any space or tab character and replace it with the replacement expression, which is an end-of-line preceded by an escape character to protect it from being devoured by the editor's command interpreter. The `g` option at the end tells the editor to perform the substitution for all matches throughout each line in the body of text being searched. After executing the `vi` command to restore the `vi` personality, the sentence looks like this:

```
This
paragraph
is
only
one
of
the
many
possible
demonstrations
of
the
substitute
command
for
splitting
lines.
```

There is a defect in this example in that if two or more spaces and/or tabs appear in succession, each is converted to a newline, which results in blank lines in the output. This is easily solved by the following command:

> : . , . +2s/ [*space tab*] [*space tab*] ∗/\ ⌈Return⌋
> /g⌈Return⌋

which tells the editor to replace any space or tab followed by *zero* or more spaces and/or tabs with a newline (treating the series of one or more characters as a single entity) and perform the substitution globally across the line. The asterisk after the second closing square bracket tells the regular expression evaluator to look for zero or more of the previous character, which can be either a space or a tab as specified by the enclosing square brackets.

If no tabs exist in the file, the search expression can be simply two spaces followed by an asterisk. The technique of searching for spaces and/or tabs is used because UNIX and other similar operating systems use the term **blank** to mean either a space character or a tab character.

Double-Spacing Text

To double-space text by placing a double newline at the end of each line, use the command

:%s/$/\ [Return]
/g [Return]

Strip Unneeded Blanks

It is often desirable to remove unneeded blanks (space and/or tab characters) at the end of every line in a text file in order to conserve disk or tape storage space. This is easily accomplished by using the following command:

:%s/[*space tab*]*$// [Return]

where *space tab* is a single space and a single tab character (or vice versa) placed between square brackets. The asterisk after the closing bracket and the dollar currency symbol after the asterisk tell the editor to search for zero or more blanks and/or tabs at the end of every line in the file and replace them with nothing. Even blank lines that may contain invisible blanks are trimmed to empty strings by this command.

Save Time by Executing a Buffer

Having to retype a complex substitution command can be frustrating. You can easily alter, fix, or modify a command and execute it over and over without retyping the entire command by using buffers.

For example, suppose you made a minor mistake when typing a substitute command, which created an unwanted result. You can easily use the undo command to fix the damage and restore the original to its state before the command was executed, but you are now faced with retyping the whole command, and you don't have the previously typed line to use as a reference.

An easier way is to execute a buffer (an example is in Chapter 6). If the results of the command are not what you wanted, type u to undo the changes, then type G to return to the line containing the command (assuming it is the last line in the file), edit as needed, then repeat the procedure. When you have finished, delete the line from the end of your file.

Forming Multiple Substitute Commands

In complex edits, you will likely use many substitute commands. You can easily take a previous command on the last line of the file, modify it as needed, yank it to a buffer for execution, then repeat the process as required. Again, as before, delete the command line from the file before you terminate the edit.

Chapter Summary

The following topics were covered in this chapter:

Perform global search	:**g/**_text_pattern_**/p** :**g/world/p**
Perform limited search	:_start_line_,_end_line_ **g/**_text_pattern_**/p** :**12,25g/chapter/p**
Display tabs and other non-printing control characters	:_start_line_,_end_line_**l** :**l**
Display tabs and ends of lines (entire file)	:**set list**
Switch to ex	Type **Q** (press SHIFT - Q). **ex** responds with the colon prompt.
Replace characters with newline	:**.,.+3s/the /the** Return **/g**
Replace spaces and tabs with newline	:**.,.+2s/[**_space tab_**]/** Return **/g**
Double-space text	:**%s/$/** Return **/g**
Strip unneeded spaces and tabs	:**s/[**_space tab_**]*$//**

8

Working with Files

As you gain experience, you will likely encounter times when you need to edit several files at a time or insert the contents of a text file into the file you are editing. These types of file manipulation activities and others described below are covered in this chapter.

- Arbitrarily switch back and forth between the two files while performing similar operations on each file.

- Move text back and forth between two or more files without terminating the edit.

- Change the list of files to be edited without leaving the editor.

- Edit two files simultaneously and use shared buffers to move text between the two files.

- Insert the contents of an existing text file into the file being edited.

- Copy part of the file being edited into another file.

- Copy all or part of the file being edited into one or more other files.

- Split the current file being edited into several smaller files.

- Edit two files simultaneously and use shared buffers to easily move text between the two files.

This list is not complete. There are many reasons and combinations of user needs that require writing all or part of the buffer file to other locations in the UNIX file system.

In addition, you may need to access the UNIX operating system to perform some necessary task without terminating the editing session. Perhaps you need to list a directory before selecting a filename to be used with a write command to store the current workfile. Or you may need to mail a file to someone or perform some other task. The vi editor provides a "shellescape" capability so that you can exit to a user shell to perform the task, then return to vi.

Editing Multiple Files in Succession

The most common type of multiple-file editing usually involves normal editing on two or more files in succession. The procedure is simple and very straightforward.

Opening the Session

As in any editing session, start by executing the vi command. The only difference between this session and a single-file edit is that you specify more than one file to be edited. There are several ways to do this. For example, to edit files *one, two,* and *three* in the current directory, execute the following command:

    vi one two three (Return)

vi opens file *one* and, if it exists, displays the beginning part of the file on the display screen. If the file does not exist, the new file message explained in an earlier chapter is displayed.

Edit the first file as if it were the only file being edited. You can close the edit on that file by using a write (:w) or terminate (ZZ) command. If you use the :w command, a message at the bottom of the screen shows the filename and number of lines and bytes in the file as follows:

    "one" 179 lines, 6511 characters

If you use ZZ, the filename and size message is displayed briefly while the file is being written, then it is replaced by a new message indicating that you still have two files to edit:

```
  2 more files to edit
```

In either case, to proceed to the next file, use the "next file" command

   :n (Return)

vi terminates the edit on the first file and opens the second file specified in the original UNIX command that started the session. Edit and close the second file in the same way as you did the first file.

When the third file is opened, proceed as usual, and terminate as usual. Upon termination of the last file in the series, a :wq or ZZ command closes the file, ends the session, and returns to the shell process from which the session started. The shell then displays a new shell prompt on the terminal display screen.

Using Buffers in Multi-File Edits

When using this method to edit multiple files, *named* buffers are preserved between files. Thus you can yank or delete text into a named buffer as described in Chapter 6 while editing one file, then copy (using p or P) the named buffer contents into a later file in the series. The contents of the unnamed buffer cannot be transported between files, but the last command is remembered so you can use the dot (.) command from file to file without losing the last operation.

Going Back to the First File

Sometimes, especially on long, complex edits, you may want to make additional changes on files already edited. First set autowrite on (described in Chapter 11) as follows:

   :set autowrite

Next, reset the file pointer to the first file while editing any other file (but before you close the last file) by executing the command

   :rewind (Return)

This closes the current file, then reopens the first file for editing.

An alternate form of the `rewind` command can be used to abort the current file and immediately reopen the first file:

    `:rewind!` (Return)

Using Shell Characters in Filenames

When specifying filenames in the `vi` command line, all normal shell special characters (sometimes called metacharacters or wild-card characters) such as * can be used. For example, suppose you have several files, each containing a chapter in a book project, and you need to make some minor corrections in each chapter. If each file was named *chap1, chap2, chap3*, etc. the easiest way to specify the files being edited would be

    `vi chap*` (Return)

or even

    `vi c*` (Return)

if no other files in the directory started with c. You can use any legitimate expression that the shell can correctly interpret when specifying filenames. The use of shell special characters and their expansion is discussed in Appendix A. This topic is also discussed in any good textbook on the UNIX system and in texts that address the use of the Bourne, C, or Korn shells.

Editing Two Files Simultaneously

Situations occasionally arise in computer programming and technical composition when it is useful to be able to open two files simultaneously and perform editing operations on both files with the ability to switch between files without losing the contents of buffers or memory of the last editing operation. Such a capability enables you to conveniently:

■ Delete or yank text from one file and insert it in the other or vice versa.

■ Perform identical changes, one pair at a time, on both files.

- Search for an expression through one file using / and ? followed by **n** or **N**, then switch files and continue in the other file.

vi does not have the ability to handle multiple files simultaneously, but it does allow you to switch between two files being edited without losing memory of the last operation, including yanked or deleted text using named buffers. Thus you can switch to the other file and repeat the last change (using the . command) or put yanked or deleted text in the chosen location in the other file. This capability works best when the **autowrite** option is set as discussed in Chapter 9.

Opening the Files

To start editing the two files *file1* and *file2,* open *file1* with the command

> vi file1 (Return)

This command opens *file1* and loads it if it exists. The buffer must be written to permanent storage if any editing operations were performed before the second file can be opened. If the **autowrite** option is set, this is done automatically; if not, the :w command must be used before opening the second file.

To open the second file, use the external mode command, :e, as follows:

> :e file2 (Return)

The **vi** editor then writes the current file to permanent storage if **autowrite** is set (or clears the buffer if it has been written already or has not been altered since it was opened), then copies *file2* into the buffer area if *file2* exists or opens a new file if it does not.

Switching Files

You can easily switch back and forth between files by using the (SHIFT)-(CTRL)-(^) command (press (^) while holding down the (SHIFT) and (CTRL) keys simultaneously). Using this method preserves the contents of all named buffers (but not the default buffer), search strings (used by **n** and **N** commands), and so on, and the last operation (.) is also remembered. Thus if you add text to one file in a single operation, then switch files and move the cursor to a desired location in the other file and press the period (.) key, the same operation is repeated in the new current file.

The ex command `:e #` reopens the previous file. Use the `:w!` command to save the contents before switching files, even when the `autowrite` option is set.

Merging Another File into Text

Probably the most common file manipulation task is merging all of an existing file into the current text file. The vi editor cannot copy only part of a file. If you don't want the entire file, you must edit it first or copy it to a different file and edit the copy if the original must be preserved intact. The procedure for merging a file into the file being edited is simple. Place the cursor at the location you want the other file inserted. Then simply give vi the following command:

> `:r` *filename* `Return`

The vi editor then uses UNIX to locate the file and copy it into the file being edited beginning *after* the current cursor line. Subsequent lines in the file being edited are pushed down to make room for the file being inserted. For example, consider the following excerpt from a sample file:

```
This line represents the early part of the file.

This line is the current cursor line.
        ^
This line represents the remainder of the file.
```

The cursor could be located anywhere on the second text line when the read file command is given. After the file has been read and inserted, the cursor is moved to the first line of the inserted file (the line following the cursor line before the insertion began). Thus, the result looks like this:

```
This line represents the early part of the file.

This line is the current cursor line.
This line represents the inserted file.
^

This line represents the remainder of the file.
```

The cursor is relocated to the first visible character in the third test line.

Merging a File After a Text Pattern

You may occasionally need to merge a file into the file being edited starting after the line that contains a certain text pattern, although you may not know the location of the pattern in the file. Of course, you could search for the pattern, then use the :r command to read the file being merged, but you can also combine an ex global search command with the read command to perform the same operation. Assuming you are already familiar with ex commands (described in Chapter 9), the command form is as follows:

   :g/*text_pattern*/r *filename*

to read a file or

   :g/*text_pattern*/r ! *UNIX_command*

to read standard output from a UNIX command or command sequence into the file. Also note that any standard ex line address form described in Chapter 9 can be used instead of the g address form shown. For example, consider the following text segment:

```
However, be wary because if you do not exercise adequate care
in defining the string to be changed, you may get more changes
than you really wanted.  For example, changing every occurrence
of the to xyz in a file also changes Athena to
Axyzna; probably not what you would want.
:g/xyz/r junk
            ^
```

The bottom (command line) on the display shows an ex command that is interpreted as follows:

g/xyz/   Tells ex to search every line in the file for the text pattern xyz.

r   Opens a new line after any line containing the pattern xyz and fills it with the text contained in file *junk*. In this example, the file *junk* consists of a single line containing the text junk file.

^ (caret)   Represents the cursor. When (Return) is pressed, the following change occurs in the displayed text:

```
However, be wary because if you do not exercise adequate care
in defining the string to be changed, you may get more changes
than you really wanted.  For example, changing every occurrence
of the to xyz in a file also changes Athena to
junk file
Axyzna; probably not what you would want.
junk file
2 lines added
```

Note that since the pattern xyz appears on more than one line, the file is merged after each line where the text appears.

This technique can be used for various purposes such as form letters or other applications. The example shown should be sufficient for you to develop other more useful ideas.

Note	The example shown reads a file into the file being edited. However, changing r (read file) to w (write file) does not write the line containing *text_pattern* to a file but rather writes the entire file being edited to the specified file each time *text_pattern* is encountered and is therefore not useful.

The Write Command:
Saving All or Part of the Current Workfile

The ZZ command is most commonly used to save the current workfile at the end of an editing session and was discussed in an earlier chapter. However, there are times when you may want to save all or part of the current file in its present form elsewhere, then edit it further. One obvious method for doing so is to copy the file before invoking vi by using the UNIX cp command. However, it is not uncommon to take an existing file and edit it before creating the copy. You can avoid having to terminate the edit before copying the file by using the :w command. As discussed in Chapter 3, the command

> :w *filename* (Return)

is used to save the current workfile in its present form in a specified file. You can also specify that only certain lines are to be copied into the file by specifying a starting and ending line. There are several ways to do this. For example:

> :10,88w junk (Return)

tells vi to copy lines 10 through 88 into a file named *junk*. If *junk* already exists, you must use the forced form of the command:

> :10,88w! junk (Return)

which overwrites (and destroys the previous contents of) the file *junk* if it already exists (if the file does not exist, a new file is created without complaint).

Other methods can also be used to identify the beginning and last line to be saved. For example:

> :.,.+2w junk (Return)

copies the current line and the two following lines into file *junk*. Note that the ex notation for line numbering (.+2) is used, rather than the vi cursor command sequence 2+.

> :.,$w junk (Return)

copies the current line through end-of-file into file *junk*.

When using this command, you can use any combination of addressing methods that is recognized by ex, as described in Chapter 9. Several methods are illustrated in the remainder of this chapter.

Using File Markers

File markers can also be used to specify start and finish lines. Markers can be accessed by using the accent grave (') or apostrophe (') in normal editor operation. The accent grave is used to move the cursor to the exact location where the marker was placed, while the apostrophe moves the cursor to the first visible character of the line where the marker was placed. When using file markers to locate the beginning and ending lines in a file write command, only the apostrophe form can be used. Thus, to write all of the current file from marker a through marker c, use the command

    : 'a, 'cw junk (Return)

If both markers reside on the same line of the file, only one line is written to the output file. If you attempt to write part of a line by placing both markers on the same line, then use the accent grave form to identify cursor location, an error message results and no write operation is performed.

Using Text Patterns

As with any ex command that uses line addresses, a text pattern can be used instead of a line number to define the beginning or ending line in the file being written. For example:

    : . , /*pattern*/w! junk (Return)

writes all lines starting with the current line through the line containing the text pattern *pattern* to the file *junk*. The exclamation point (!) forces the file to be overwritten if it already exists. Likewise

    :/*pattern_a*/,/*pattern_b*/w! junk (Return)

writes all lines starting with the line containing *pattern_a* through the line containing *pattern_b* to file *junk* with overwrite if the file exists.

Other combinations are also possible using addressing forms discussed in the chapters dealing with **ex** commands.

Appending to a File

You can also append to an existing file instead of writing to a file by using the "double redirection" symbol. For example, to write lines 1 through 25 to a file named *junk,* then append lines 150 through 200 to the same file, use the sequences

    `:1,25w junk` `Return`

then

    `:150,200w >>junk` `Return`

To append the entire workfile to an existing file named *existingfile,* use

    `:w >>existingfile` `Return`

If the named file does not exist, the specified text is written to a new file having the specified name. This is a useful way to write the file and ensure that any existing text is not overwritten as well as a convenient means of merging text from various sources.

Changing Filenames

In the course of normal editing, you will commonly encounter the need to change the name of the file being edited before writing or closing a session or to store various versions of a file under multiple names that are similar, yet unique.

Amending Current Filename During Write

Another version of the write command can be used to amend the name of the file slightly. For example, suppose you are currently editing file *filename* and execute the following command:

> :w %1 (Return)

The vi editor remembers the filename used when it was invoked, in this case *filename*. The percent sign (%) is used to represent the name of the file currently associated with the buffer file. Thus, when the example command is executed by vi, the 1 is appended to *filename,* and the buffer is stored in file *filename1*. Note that if a directory pathname is associated with %, the new file will be stored in same directory as *filename*.

Other variations on these basic themes can be used. Possibilities should be self-evident as you gain experience.

Changing the Name of the Current File

Sometimes, as when creating various versions of a file, it is helpful to be able to write the current file, change the current filename to something else, edit the file again and store it under the new name, and possibly continue. To change the name of the current file, execute the :file command as follows:

> :file *new_filename* (Return)

Piping the Workfile to a Command

All or part of the current workfile can be piped to the shell (actually a new shell is spawned) for filtering or other processing. A shell can also be spawned and results from the process inserted or appended to the current buffer file. The techniques used for performing such tasks are described in detail along with several examples in Chapter 10.

Escaping to a UNIX Shell

The vi editor provides an escape mechanism for escaping to an external UNIX shell where you can run programs, manipulate files, or perform other tasks. This is accomplished by entering external mode (as discussed in Chapter 2), then using the shell escape character (!) as follows:

> : ! *command* (Return)

Where *command* can be any valid UNIX command. If you need to perform several UNIX operations before returning, you may prefer to spawn a new user shell. Then you can execute the commands and later use a logout command or keypress sequence ((CTRL)-(D)) to return to the undisturbed editing session. You have several options.

You can use the ex command : sh to spawn a new Bourne shell directly from the editor as follows:

> : sh (Return)

This command can be used only to access the Bourne shell. It cannot be used to access other shells such as the C shell or Korn shell.

A second method involves typing only one more character but creates a different sequence of events to obtain an equivalent result. It also provides access to any available shell on your system. Here are three examples:

> : !sh (Return)   *to access the Bourne shell*
> : !csh (Return)   *to access the C shell*
> : !ksh (Return)   *to access the Korn shell*

This command form behaves as follows:

- The : ! sequence spawns a new user process (Bourne shell) to execute a UNIX command.

- The remainder of the command is the name of a shell program name such as sh, csh, or ksh. The shell spawned by the : ! sequence then spawns a new process to execute the shell you specified on the remainder of the line.

The efficient method for spawning a Bourne shell is to use the : sh command. However, both methods are equally effective and do not measurably affect system performance. For other shells, the : ! form must be used.

When you are ready to return to the editor, type the normal logout sequence for the shell you are using or use the exit command if it is supported by the shell. This terminates the processes that were spawned during the detour from the editing session and resumes the editing session. You will probably have to press another key such as [Return] or the space bar to redraw the screen if the : ! command form was used. Also remember that you must eventually return to vi to prevent possible loss of the buffer file unless you have written it to permanent storage immediately before executing the shell escape command.

Dealing with Special Characters

The command interpreter in vi/ex is similar in some respects to the C shell interpreter in csh. Thus the special characters used by csh are also significant to vi when using shell escapes. This can be a problem if you are sending mail by using a vi shell escape. For example, suppose you used a command similar to the following to originate a mail message:

    :!mailx ihxp5!netsys_a!corpsys_b!john[Return]

This tells vi to spawn a new shell to handle mail, run the mail program, and originate a message to john who resides on corpsys_b, which can be accessed by our system by making two hops through backbone systems ihxp5 and netsys_a. Or does it? csh uses the exclamation point (!) to represent the previous command. Other characters such as % are also significant to the command interpreter (% represents the current filename). To successfully mail a note, use a backslash (\) to escape the special character. Thus the previous command should be:

    :!mailx ihxp5\!netsys_a\!corpsys_b\!john[Return]

If the address includes a path to an external mail handler where % is used, the % should also be preceded by a backslash.

csh special characters include the following:

    ! & | % + - * ? / ^ < > ( ) && || << >> # ; and $

Which of these characters is interpreted as a special character depends on the context in which it is used. In any case, preceding the character with a backslash cancels its interpretation as a special character.

Using Tag Files to Edit Large or Multiple Programs

vi and ex include a tag file capability that, when used in conjunction with the ctags command (use the on-line man command for information about the ctags command), greatly simplifies editing random code segments in a large program or group of programs. This section uses a simple example to illustrate the general technique. Expanding the technique to extremely large multiple-file code structures, however, is not difficult.

An Example Multi-File Program

Here are three C files that make up a counting program that is about 50 lines long. For this example, the program is stored in the files *count.h, count.c,* and *countsubs.c* in the current directory.

File *count.h:*

```
#include        <stdio.h>
#include        <ctype.h>
#define NUM_OK          1
#define NUM_NOT_OK      0
#define TRUE    0
#define FALSE   1
```

File *count.c:*

```
#include "count.h"
/*
 * This program outputs a string of numbers.
 * Its syntax is:
 *      count <start> <end> [<increment>]
 *
 * If no <increment> is specified, it defaults to 1 or -1, depending on
 *      the values of <start> and <end>: if <start> is less than <end>,
 *      it defaults to 1; if <start> is greater than <end>, it defaults
 *      to -1.  To override the default increments, you must supply an
```

```
 *          <increment> on the command line.
 */
main (argc, argv)
int     argc;
char    *argv[];
{
void    syntax_error();
int     s_to_n();
int     not_done();
int     start, end, inc;
int     idx;

        if (argc < 3 || argc > 4) {
                syntax_error();
                exit(9);
        }
/*
 * Convert each argument to the appropriate parameter:
 */
        if (s_to_n(argv[1], &start) == NUM_NOT_OK) {
                syntax_error();
                exit(1);
        }
        if (s_to_n(argv[2], &end) == NUM_NOT_OK) {
                syntax_error();
                exit(2);
        }
        if (argc < 4) /* <increment> not provided on command line */
                if (start < end)
                        inc = 1;
                else
                        inc = -1;
        else if (s_to_n(argv[3], &inc) == NUM_NOT_OK) {
                        syntax_error();
                        exit(3);
                }
/*
 * Output a string of numbers:
 */
        for (idx=start; not_done(idx, end, inc); idx += inc)
                printf("%d ", idx);
        printf("\n");
        exit(0);
}
```

File *countsubs.c:*

```
int      not_done(idx, end, inc)
int      idx, end, inc;
{
        if (inc >= 1)
                if (idx > end)
                        return(TRUE);
                else
                        return(FALSE);
        else
                if (idx < end)
                        return(TRUE);
                else
                        return(FALSE);
}
void     syntax_error()
{
static char *emsg="\
\n\t'count' doesn't understand the command you've given.\n\
\tThe format of 'count' is:\n\
\n\
\t    count <start> <end> [<increment>]\n\
\n\
\twhere <start> and <end> are the starting and ending numbers\n\
\tof the string of numbers generated.  The optional <increment>\n\
\tcan be used to specify a default other than +1 or -1.\n\
\n";
        fprintf(stderr, emsg);
}
/*
 * Convert 'str' to 'num'.  If an error occurs, return 'NUM_NOT_OK'.
 * If no error occurs, return 'NUM_OK'.
 */
int      s_to_n(str, num)
char     *str;
int      *num;
{
int      neg;

        if (strlen(str) == 0)
                return(NUM_NOT_OK);

        if (*str == '-') {
                neg = -1;
```

```
            str++;
            if (strlen(str) == 0)
                    return(NUM_NOT_OK);
    }
    else
            neg = 1;

    *num = 0;
    while (*str != '\0')
            if (isdigit(*str)) {
                    *num = *num * 10 + (*str - '0');
                    str++;
            }
            else
                    return(NUM_NOT_OK);
    *num = *num * neg;
    return(NUM_OK);
}
```

Creating a Tags File

Before the tags option can be used with **vi**, the tags file must be created by the **ctags** command. To create a tags file on the example files, execute the **ctags** command on them as follows:

    ctags count* [Return]

This command produces a new file named *tags* in the current directory. The *tags* file contains the following information:

```
Mcount    count.c /^main (argc, argv)$/
not_done          countsubs.c      /^return(FALSE);$/
s_to_n    countsubs.c     /^int   s_to_n(str, num)$/
syntax_error      countsubs.c      /^void  syntax_error()$/
```

Using the Tags File

Suppose you want to edit the code segment **syntax_error** in the file *countsubs.c*. Suppose further that the file *countsubs.c* is only one of a complex collection of programs and program segments and you don't have time to sift through 500 pages of source code listings to find which file contains the code segment. Fortunately for you, someone has run **ctags** on the entire set of files and the previous tags listing is only a small segment of the total tags file. You have three options:

- Use the -t option on the vi or ex command.

- Use the :ta command from vi or ex while editing a program source file.

- While editing a program source file, place the cursor on the first character of the name of a program tag (such as on the line that calls a tagged subroutine) and press CTRL-].

Note	When using tags files, the current directory must be the directory containing the tags file. However, since the path to the file to be edited is specified on each line in the tags file, it is not necessary that the file being edited be in the same directory.

If starting a new session, execute the command

    vi -tsyntax_error [Return]

or

    ex -tsyntax_error [Return]

where the —t option tells vi (or ex) to use the specified tag from the tags file to determine which file to edit. vi searches the tags file for the identifier syntax_error in the first column. The second column on the same line contains the name of the file where the code segment resides. vi opens the file, then uses the third column on the tag line as a search string to find the requested code segment.

A few moments after the command is given, vi produces the following image on the screen with the cursor in the first column of line with the tag syntax_error in the middle of the screen:

```
                    if (idx > end)
                            return(TRUE);
                    else
                            return(FALSE);
            else
                    if (idx < end)
                            return(TRUE);
                    else
                            return(FALSE);
}
void    syntax_error()
{
static char *emsg="\
\n\t'count' doesn't understand the command you've given.\n\
\tThe format of 'count' is:\n\
\n\
\t    count <start> <end> [<increment>]\n\
\n\
\twhere <start> and <end> are the starting and ending numbers\n\
\tof the string of numbers generated.  The optional <increment>\n\
\tcan be used to specify a default other than +1 or -1.\n\
\n";
        fprintf(stderr, emsg);
"countsubs.c" 61 lines, 1098 characters
```

Mixed-Language Programs

The ctags command is also useful when you have a collection of mixed C and FORTRAN (and possibly Pascal) source files. For example, suppose you have a collection of program files located under various directories that are, in turn, all collected under a single parent directory. For this example, suppose all C source files end with .c, FORTRAN source files end with .f, and Pascal source files end with .p. To create a single tags file, change to the parent directory of the directories containing the source files (use the cd command), then execute the command

    ctags */*.[cfp] (Return)

The result is a new tags file in the current directory. You can also specify other pathnames to the files of interest if they reside in other directory trees or subtrees.

When using this or an equivalent method, ctags complains if it creates a tag from a given file, then finds another tag having the same name in another file. When such duplicate names are encountered, the first tag is retained and subsequent tags are not included. This is usually not a big problem, but care should be taken to avoid duplicate names. This condition can also occur when a program line looks like a procedure declaration but isn't.

Editing Other Program Segments

Programmers often change several program segments during an editing session. This can become especially cumbersome as programs become large or involve a large number of files. Using tags to move around greatly simplifies the problem, and you can move from file to file without terminating vi (or ex) by using the :ta command.

Again using the previous example tags file, suppose you have modified the routine named syntax_error and want to look at Mcount in the main program. Simply execute the ex command

        :ta Mcount (Return)

The editor examines the tags file, then immediately moves back in the current file and displays the main program with the cursor at the beginning of the line. Since the new tag is in the file currently being edited, no file change is needed so the editor does not write the buffer back into permanent storage before moving to the new tag.

When the New Tag Opens Another File

Suppose you decide to edit the file containing tag new_tag. Using the command

        :ta new_tag (Return)

(or (CTRL)-(])) causes one of two results. If the autowrite option has not been set (options are discussed in Chapter 11) and the file has not been preserved by using the :w command, the editor ignores the new tag command and displays the following error message at the bottom of the display screen:

```
No write since last change (:tag! overrides)
```

To recover, save the buffer by executing

    :w (Return)

or

    :set autowrite

then repeat the :ta new_tag command.

If the autowrite option is set and the :ta command needs to open a new file, the current buffer is written back to permanent storage before the new file is opened.

Overriding Autowrite When Changing Files

You may occasionally need to change to another file after changing the current file, but for some reason you do not want to overwrite the original file (in other words, abort the edit and continue on another file). You can use the tag command to abort the current file without writing it back and open a new file by using the command form

    :ta! new_tag (Return)

The exclamation point after :ta tells vi to abort (same as :q!) and open a new tagged file. If you need to write the current file to a file whose name is the same as the current file plus added *text,* use a write command:

    :w %*text* (Return)

where *text* is the character or characters used to alter the original filename, as discussed earlier in this chapter under "Changing Filenames."

Important   The tag command writes the current buffer *only* when changing files with the `autowrite` option set. The tag command followed by an exclamation point unconditionally aborts the current edited file and opens a new file. Any changes made to the current file are *always* lost when `:ta!` is used.

Chapter Summary

The following topics were covered in this chapter:

Edit multiple files in succession.	`vi one two three` end edit with `ZZ` or `:w` edit next file using `:n`
Copy between files in multi-file edit.	Yanked or deleted text in a named buffer from one file can be copied (using `p` or `P`) from the named buffer into a later file.
Go back to the first file in a multi-file edit.	first, `:set autowrite` next, `:rewind`
Merge a file into text.	`:r` *filename*
Merge a file after a text pattern.	`:g/`*text_pattern*`/r` *filename*
Merge a output from a UNIX command after a text pattern.	`:g/`*text_pattern*`/r !` *UNIX_command*
Save the current workfile.	`:w` *filename* `:w!` *filename* (overwrite *filename*) `:w junk`
Save part of the current workfile (lines 10 through 88).	`:10,88w junk` `:10,88w! junk` (overwrite `junk`)
Copy the current line through end-of-file into file *junk*.	`:.,$w junk`
Copy the text between two markers (a and c) into file *junk*.	`:'a,'cw junk`
Append text to a file.	`:w >>junk`
Change the name of the current file.	`:file` *new_filename*

Escape to a UNIX Shell.	`:!`*command* `:!sh` (Bourne shell) `:!csh` (C shell) `:!ksh` (Korn shell)
Create a tags file.	`ctags count*`
Use a tags file.	`vi -tsyntax_error`

9

Using ex Commands

This chapter discusses how to use ex commands from the ex editor and from vi as ex mode commands (colon commands). Most commands are used identically from either editor. Any exceptions are explained in the command description.

Access to these commands is obtained from vi by typing a colon while in command mode. Startup and use of vi is discussed in previous chapters.

These commands can also be directly accessed when using ex instead of vi. Few UNIX users use ex directly because most of them prefer to access ex features directly from vi. However, if you need to use ex directly, this chapter describes the necessary procedures.

Editing Modes

The ex editor has five editing modes, as shown in (Table 9-1).

Table 9-1. ex Editing Modes

Mode	Description
Command	Commands are entered after a colon (:) prompt and executed each time a complete line is sent.
Text input	ex places lines of text in the file. append, insert, and change commands use text input mode to alter existing text.
	No prompt is printed when you are in text input mode. To exit this mode, type period (.) (Return), and command mode resumes.
Open	Enables you to edit text in the file. This mode is accessed using the open command, which displays text one line at a time on any terminal.
Visual	Enables you to edit text in the file. This mode is accessed using the visual command, which switches to vi.
Text insertion	Enables you to insert text within open and visual modes.

Colon Commands

The user prompt displayed by ex when it is ready for a new command is the colon. If you are in vi command mode, typing a colon switches vi to ex (external) mode so that you can use any appropriate ex command without leaving vi except while executing the command. For this reason, ex commands are often referred to as colon commands when used from vi. To form a colon command, the colon character, whether an ex prompt or a vi command, is followed by a command sequence that can be any legitimate ex command. To execute the command, press (Return) or (ESC) after typing it.

Command Format

In general, ex commands follow one of two formats.

Standard form

> : *line_address command parameters count flags*

Variant form

> : *line_address command*! *parameters count flags*

where all items except the colon are optional and can be included or omitted as the situation dictates. The function of each item when present in a command line is presented in Table 9-2.

Table 9-2. Elements in a Command Line and Their Purpose

Element	Description
:	Starts command (vi) or prompt (ex). To avoid confusion over whether a colon was typed from vi or automatically provided by ex and whether another colon needs to be typed, the editor ignores the second colon if one is present (three colons, however, produce an error message).
line_address	Defines which line or lines are to be processed by the command. For commands that accept an address, zero, one, or two addresses may be present. If more addresses are provided than the command can use, extra addresses are ignored beginning with the first. If no address is present but one is needed by the command, the current line is assumed.

Table 9-2.
Elements in a Command Line and Their Purpose (continued)

Element	Description
command	Defines the type of operation to be performed. If no command is provided, the last previous command is repeated.
command!	Variants of commands, if available, can be invoked by using the ! with the command. The ! also toggles the default for variants controlled by options.
parameters	Arguments or options to a command, such as option names in a :set command, filename in an :edit command, regular expression in a :substitute command, or a target address for a :copy command.
count	Usually specifies the number of lines affected by *command*. Optional or required, depending on the command. Value is rounded down if rounding is necessary.
flags	Identifies action to be taken upon completion of *command*. Flag characters include **p** (print line), **c** (confirm each change before making it), and **g** (repeat *command* globally across the line). Any number of + or − characters can be used immediately before a flag to introduce an offset from the current line before executing the action specified by the flag. With the exception of the confirm and global flags associated with substitutions, flags are of little interest to **vi** users, although they can be important when using **ex** on an electro-mechanical printer/terminal.

The topics that follow describe the components of a command line in greater detail.

Line Address Forms

The first item after the colon is usually a line address of some form (if absent, the current line is assumed) unless the command does not require or does not accept an address. A missing address or a single address identifies a single line. Two line addresses separated by a comma specify the starting and ending lines for a group of contiguous lines. Table 9-3 shows the forms of line address (also sometimes referred to as **addressing primitives**) that the ex editor recognizes

Table 9-3. Line Address Forms

Address	Corresponding Line in the File Being Edited
1	First line in file.
$	Last line in file.
.	Current line.
n	*n*th line in file.
.-*n*	*n*th line before current line.
.+*n*	*n*th line after current line.
%	Abbreviation for 1,$, which means every line in the file.
/*pattern*/ or ?*pattern*?	Searches forward (/) or backward (?), respectively, for a line containing text that matches *pattern* where *pattern* is any regular expression, usually a string of text characters. The number of that line is then used as an address. Searches normally wrap around the end of the buffer file. If you want to print only the next line containing *pattern*, the trailing / or ? can be omitted. If *pattern* is omitted or explicitly empty, the last previous pattern is used.
'' or ' *marker_name*	Locates previously marked lines. Before each non-relative motion of the current line (.), the previous current line is marked with a tag, subsequently referred to by a double single quote (acute accent) character pair (''). Thus, you can easily refer or return to this previous location. A line can also be marked by using the **mark** command followed by a *marker_name* consisting of any single lowercase letter in the range **a** through **z**. Marked lines can then be referred to in addresses by using *marker_name* preceded by a single quote (').

Combining Line Addresses

Addresses can be combined using a comma (,) or semicolon (;) to separate the beginning address (on left) from the ending address (right). If no beginning address is given, the current cursor line (.) is used. For example, ,5 is the same as .,5, and ,+5 is the same as .,.+5. Line addresses are combined to specify a range of lines that the command can act upon.

■ When a comma separator is used, the beginning address (or the current line address if no beginning address is given) becomes the current line address for that command. For example

    `:1,10 p`

instructs the editor to print lines 1 through 10, beginning with line 1.

■ When a semicolon separator is used, the address preceding the semicolon becomes the current line address (.) for the next address reference. The semicolon is most useful when the location of the current line address is important for the command to function properly. For example, assume you have the following text in a file

```
1 squares and triangles
2 triangles and cubes
3 pyramids and rectangles
4 cubes and squares
```

and you want to print all lines between and including the lines containing the word cubes. The command

    `:/cubes/;/cubes/p`

would find the first occurrence of cubes on line 2 and set the current address to line 2. The editor would then search for the next occurrence of cubes after line 2 and would find it on line 4. Thus, the editor would print lines 2, 3, and 4 as a result of this command.

However, if the command had been typed

    `:/cubes/,/cubes/p`

the editor would have found and printed only line 2. Since the comma does not reset the current line address, both address searches would begin at the current line address (line 1) and would find the same occurrence of cubes in line 2.

Address ranges are evaluated from left to right. If the command line contains more addresses than the command requires, all but the last one or two addresses are ignored. If two addresses are required by the command, the line of the first address must precede the line of the second address. Providing a prefix address for a command that expects none produces an error diagnostic.

Several examples of commonly used address forms, including single-line addresses and combined addressing primitives for multiple-line operations, are given in Table 9-4. Note that space characters after the colon and on either side of the comma are optional but not normally used.

Table 9-4. Common Address Forms

Address	Affected Lines(s)
1	First line in file.
n	Line n in file.
.	Current line in file.
.-4	Fourth line before current line in file.
.+8	Eighth line after current line in file.
$	Last line in file.
g	All lines in file.
1,.	All lines from beginning of file to current line.
.,$	All lines from current line to end of file.
.,.+5	Current line through fifth following line.
1,.+5	First line in file through fifth line after current line.
.-10,.+5	Tenth preceding line through fifth following line.

Pattern searches and markers can also be used to specify lines in the buffer file that are to be subjected to *command*. Some examples of how they are used follow in Table 9-5. Note that space characters after the colon and on either side of the comma are optional but not normally used.

Table 9-5. Pattern Searches and Markers

Address	Affected Line(s)
/reg_exp1/	First line in forward search direction containing text pattern that matches the valid regular expression reg_exp1.
?reg_exp1?	First line in backward search direction containing text pattern that matches the valid regular expression reg_exp1.
/reg_exp1/,/reg_exp2/	First line in forward search direction containing a text pattern that matches the valid regular expression reg_exp1 through first following line in forward search direction containing a text pattern that matches the valid regular expression reg_exp2. Second line must not precede first line in file due to end of file wraparound.
?reg_exp2?,?reg_exp1?	First line in backward search direction containing a text pattern that matches the valid regular expression reg_exp1 through first encountered line in same search direction containing a text pattern that matches the valid regular expression reg_exp2. Line containing reg_exp1 must not precede line containing reg_exp2 in file due to beginning of file wraparound.
'',.	All lines starting with previous current line through current line (previous line must precede current line in file).
'marker_1,'marker_2	All lines starting at line containing marker_1 through the line containing marker_2. marker_2 must not precede marker_1 in file. The name of each marker is any distinct lowercase letter in the range a through z.

Building the Command

Once you have defined and structured the address, you are ready to form the command part of the line. Most command names are English words, and the first letter in the word or a prefix form of the word is acceptable as an abbreviation. However, similarity between two commands can result in ambiguous or conflicting abbreviations. All ambiguous or conflicting abbreviations are resolved in favor of the more commonly used commands. Thus, for example, the abbreviated form of the substitute command is s, while the shortest available abbreviation for set is se because substitute is used more often by more people than set.

Command Parameters

The number and type of parameters associated with each command varies, depending on the command. This section describes those parameters, their purposes and their uses.

Address Parameter

Many commands require one or two addresses where each address can have any of the valid forms previously described. Some commands can use either one or two addresses. If only one address is present, operations are performed relative to that line. If two addresses are present, they identify the starting and ending lines in the text block that is to be processed by the command. If no address is provided on the command line but one is required by the command, the current line is assumed.

Command Name

The command name or its abbreviation comes after the address (if any). A complete list of command names and corresponding abbreviations follows this section along with a full description of each command and its use. Some commands require other information or parameters that are always appended following the command name; for example, option names in a set command, a filename in an edit command, a regular expression in a substitute command, or a target address for a copy command as in 1,5 copy 25 or .,.+5 copy 12.

Flags and Options After Commands

Various flags and options can be used after many commands to specify additional action to be taken upon completion of the command (Table 9-6).

Table 9-6. Command Flags and Options

Flag	Option	Description
	c	The confirm option is used mainly with the `substitute` command. Confirm each change before continuing to next. Editor displays the line being changed with a circumflex (^) underneath each character that will be affected if the change is made. To accept the change, type **y**, then press [Return]. To reject it, type **n** (or any other character except **y**), then press [Return], or simply press [Return]. (This option may not work on some implementations.)
	g	Global option. If proper conditions exist, executes *command* across entire line. This option is most commonly used with the `substitute` command where a text pattern to be changed may exist more than once in a given line. If the **g** option is not present, only the first matching pattern in the line is changed. With the **g** option, the text pattern is processed every time it appears in the line.
p		Print flag. Prints the current line after *command* has been processed. If this colon command is initiated directly from **vi**, the editor will print the current line and prompt you to [Hit return to continue].
l		List flag. Prints the current line after *command* has been processed, but also show the position of tab characters and end of line position. If this colon command is initiated directly from **vi**, the editor will list the current line and prompt you to [Hit return to continue].
#		Print-line-number flag. Prints the current line after *command* > has been processed, but precede the printed line with its corresponding line number in the current buffer file.

You can give any number of + or - characters with these flags if you are using **ex** to move the current line in the specified direction. If any + or -

flag is present in the command, the specified offset is applied to the current line value *before* the command is executed. For example, the command `:s/new/old/p+++` would print (display) the third line following the modified line.

`vi` users have no need to use the `p` flag since the display shows the current file contents at all times. If you are running `ex` directly (or after a `Q` command from `vi`), `ex` normally prints the new current line after each change, so `p` is still rarely necessary.

Named Buffers

The `ex` editor can use named buffers to save blocks of text during editing. These named buffers can be especially useful when editing multiple files. You can name the buffers `a` or `A` to `z` or `Z`. Commands *append to* uppercase named buffers and *replace* lowercase-named buffers. While named buffers are similar to normal buffers, only a limited number of operations can be used with them.

Comments

This feature is used where comments are needed to explain complex editor scripts. The editor takes no action with comment commands. Comments can be placed at the ends of commands unless they would be interpreted as part of the command text (for example, in shell escape sequences or `substitute` or `map` commands). Begin the comment line with a double quotation mark (`"`). For example,

```
"Change CLEAR LINE key to vi delete-to-end-of-line command (D):
map ^[K D
```

The first line in this example is the comment; the second is the actual command.

Multiple Commands on One Line

To combine multiple commands on one line, use the | character to separate adjacent commands. For example:

```
set wrapmargin=10|set nolist
```

demonstrates the structure of a multiple command. Note that global commands, comments, and the shell escape (!) cannot be terminated by a | and must appear last on a line of multiple commands.

Reporting Large Changes

To help you detect large changes in the editor buffer file, you can set a threshold of change using the `report` option. Most commands that change the contents in the buffer file will notify you if this threshold is exceeded. If the change is undesirable, you can reverse it using `undo`. For example, if a global substitution command changed a greater number of lines (17, for example) in the buffer than allowed for in the threshold (12, for example), you would receive a message similar to this:

```
15 substitutions on 17 lines
```

Regular Expressions

A regular expression specifies a set of strings of characters. A member of this set of strings is said to be matched by the regular expression. `ex` remembers two previous regular expressions: the previous regular expression used in a `substitute` command and the previous regular expression used elsewhere (referred to as a previous scanning regular expression). The previous regular expression can always be referred to by a null regular expression; for example, '//' or '??'. For a more detailed discussion of regular expressions, see Appendix A.

Magic and Nomagic

The regular expressions allowed by `ex` are constructed in one of two ways, depending on the setting of the `magic` option. The `ex` and `vi` default settings of `magic` give quick access to a powerful set of regular expression metacharacters. The disadvantage of `magic` is that you must remember that these metacharacters are "magic" and precede them with the character \ to use them as ordinary characters. With `nomagic`, the default for `edit`, regular expressions are much simpler, there being only two metacharacters. The power of the other metacharacters is still available by preceding the (now) ordinary character with a \. Note that \ is thus always a metacharacter. For more information on the `magic` setting, see Chapter 11.

Using ex Commands

Editing the Command

If you make an error while typing a colon command, use (BACKSPACE) to move the cursor left to the appropriate position, then retype the rest of the command. As with normal vi operation, characters are not erased from the screen as you move the cursor left, but they are removed from the vi/ex command buffer. Hence, any extra characters that are not obliterated by retyping are ignored (you will notice that they disappear from the bottom line of the display as soon as you press (Return) or (ESC)).

An alternate and sometimes easier method for correcting a command is pressing the terminal "kill" character (usually (CTRL)-(U)), which immediately moves the cursor to the first character following the colon so you can retype the entire line as a different command.

If the command is complicated and you want to be able to change or fix errors in it easily, type the command as a line in the file, yank the line to a buffer, and execute the buffer. Procedures for doing so are described in Chapter 6.

Aborting or Changing the Command

If you type part of a colon command and then decide you want to do something else instead, you can abort the command by using (BACKSPACE) or (CTRL)-(U) followed by (BACKSPACE) to back the cursor up to the left margin past the colon. When the cursor passes the colon, the editor abandons the command and returns the cursor to the position it occupied prior to the aborted colon command.

An easier method is simply to press the (BREAK) key (on some computers, the (DEL) key can be set to produce the same result). This method has the side effect of setting the UNIX vi command return status flag to FALSE when vi terminates, but unless you are operating in an unusual environment, using the (BREAK) key should present no discernible disadvantage.

Aborting After Execution Begins

You may discover, particularly when performing global operations on a very large file, that you gave an incorrect command (such as inadvertently typing / or ? instead of :) or an inappropriate command, and need to abort it. Press (BREAK). Command execution stops, and an error message is displayed:

```
    Interrupt
```

The cursor may or may not return to its original position prior to the command, and the file may or may not be untouched by the command, depending on what was happening at the time of interrupt. If you made changes before the command was interrupted, you can use the u (undo) command to repair the damage and return to the pre-command state. After the undo, the cursor may move to a different location in the file, depending on the situation.

Undoing Colon Commands

Like normal vi commands, the external mode commands are also subject to the u command. If you discover that the change you made did not produce the desired effect, type u immediately before executing any other command. As usual, if any command is executed after the colon command, the undo option for the previous command is lost forever and you must either use another command or set of commands to fix the error or abort the session (:q! command) and start over.

ex Command Descriptions

As we said before, all `ex` commands are constructed around a variation on

address command '' ! '' parameters count flags

where all parts are optional (or not allowed in some cases as described later). The simplest case in `ex` is the empty command, which prints the next line in the file (if part of a `vi` colon command, it does nothing). To preserve the user's sanity when operating from `vi` or visual mode from `ex`, `ex` ignores a : preceding any command.

In each of the following command descriptions, summary tables present the command, its standard abbreviation, its default value (if any), and a brief description.

Abbreviations as Typing Aids (vi/ex)

`vi/ex` maintains a table of abbreviations that can be used as typing aids. When a text pattern is typed that matches the abbreviation *word* and it is preceded and followed by a whitespace character, (space, tab, end-of-line, or beginning-of-line), the pattern is replaced by *text* in the buffer file and on the display screen. The table of abbreviations is lost at the end of each session. To construct a permanent set of abbreviations, use an *.exrc* file in your home directory as described in Chapter 11.

To abbreviate the term `cathode ray tube`, for example as `crt` for ease in typing, use the command:

    :abbreviate crt cathode ray tube (Return)

or

    :ab crt cathode ray tube (Return)

Whenever you type the abbreviation, the editor will automatically expand it to the full form if it is preceded and followed by whitespace (space, tab, end-of-line, or beginning-of-line).

Canceling an Abbreviation (vi/ex)

It is possible to cancel a defined abbreviation. For example, to cancel the previous abbreviation `crt`, type the command

```
        unabbreviate crt (Return)
```

or

```
        una crt (Return)
```

Table 9-7 summarizes the abbreviations commands.

Table 9-7. Abbreviations

Command Format	Command Description
:abbreviate *word text* or :ab *word text*	Adds the specified abbreviation to the current list of abbreviations. *word* is the abbreviated form of *text* that is being defined by the command. When vi is in insert/append mode, if *word* is typed as a complete word (whitespace before and after), the editor expands the abbreviation, replacing it with *text*. Defined abbreviations are discarded at the end of the editing session. No address is allowed with this command.
:unabbreviate *word* or :una *word*	Deletes *word* from the list of abbreviations.

Appending Text After Specified or Current Line (ex Only)

The append command is used to enter new text after the specified or current address. Press (Return) after the :a or :append, type the text being added, and then press (Return) after the last (or Only) line being added followed by . and (Return) to terminate your input.

For example, to add three lines after the 12th line following the current line, type the following:

```
:.+12a (Return)
This is added line 1. (Return)
This is added line 2. (Return)
This is added line 3. (Return)
. (Return)
```

Appending Text but Toggle Autoindent Option (ex Only)

The `append!` command is the same as `append`, but the `!` toggles the `autoindent` option to its opposite state for the duration of text input. Table 9-8 summarizes the forms of the `append` command. For more information about autoindenting, refer to the discussion near the end of Chapter 5, and to the section on the `:set autoindent` command in Chapter 11.

Table 9-8. Append Text

Command Format	Command Description

`:append`
text
or
`:a`
text
Default addr: current line
Uses one address
	Inputs one or more lines of new text, starting after the specified line. If the address preceding the `append` command is the current-line address (.) or absent, new *text* is placed after the current line. If address zero (0) is given, *text* is placed at the beginning of the buffer file. To terminate the append, type . at the beginning of a new line and then press (Return), with no further text on that line. This command is not recognized by `vi` in `ex` mode.

`:append!`
text
or
`:a!`
text
Default addr: current line
Uses one address
	Same as `append` except `!` toggles the setting of the `autoindent` option to its opposite state for the duration of text input. Upon termination of `append`, `autoindent` reverts to its normal state. This command is not recognized by `vi` in `ex` mode.

Print Current Command Argument List (vi/ex)

This command is sometimes useful when you are editing several files in succession and need to know which file in the list of files is currently being edited or what other files are in the list.

This command can be used only in the following form, exactly as shown, with no other arguments:

`:args` (Return)

An example response to the `:args` command is

```
    file1 [file2] file3
```

where `file2` is the current working file. Table 9-9 summarizes the `args` command.

Table 9-9. Print Argument List

Command Format	Command Description

`:args`
or
`:ar`
	Prints the files of the argument list that was provided as part of the UNIX command line when the editor was started. The current argument is identified by left and right brackets in a form resembling: *arg arg [arg] arg arg*. No address or other argument is allowed with this command.

Change One or More Lines to New Text (ex Only)

This command can be a bit confusing because it can take several line addressing forms, including:

■ First and last address specified

   : *start_addr, end_addr* c (Return)

■ Starting line and number of changed lines specified

   : *start_addr* c *line_count* (Return)

■ Start at current line with number of changed lines specified

   :c *line_count* (Return)

Replacement text is then typed on subsequent lines following the form described for the `append` command.

The templates above show the general form of the command. You can use any accepted address, whether line number, marker, or regular expression, provided it can correctly identify the line or lines being affected by the command.

Here is an example in which 13 lines are replaced by three lines, starting at the second line after the current line:

```
:.+2c13 (Return)
This is changed line 1. (Return)
This is changed line 2. (Return)
This is changed line 3. (Return)
.  (Return)
```

A period (.) terminates the command.

Change One or More Lines to New Text but Toggle Autoindent (ex Only)

The change! command is the same as change, but the ! toggles the autoindent option to its opposite state for the duration of text input. Table 9-10 summarizes the change commands.

Table 9-10. Change Text

Command Format	Command Description
:change *count* *text* or :c *count* *text* Default addr: current line Uses one or two addresses	Replaces lines specified by *count* with the input *text*. Upon completion, the current line becomes the last line in *text*. If no text is provided, the command is treated as a delete. Uses one address if count is specified or implied or two addresses if changing multiple lines without using count. This command is not recognized by vi in ex mode.
:change! *count* *text* or :c! *count* *text* Addressing: same as above	Same as :change except ! toggles the setting of the autoindent option to its opposite state for the duration of text input. This command is not recognized by vi in ex mode.

Change Current Directory (vi/ex)

The current buffer file is written to permanent storage (if `autowrite` is set) or discarded as appropriate, and the new file is opened from the new directory specified by the `:cd` command. If `autowrite` is not set, the current buffer must be written before the directory can be changed, unless you override with a `:cd!` command. This lockout feature prevents you from changing directories and then writing the current buffer into the wrong directory after making the change.

You can use this feature to move from directory to directory and edit various files without terminating and restarting `vi` or `ex` between each file. When you terminate the editor program with ZZ or the `quit` command, the current directory changes back to what it was before editing started. Thus, this command has no visible effect if the `:edit` *file* or `:n`*file* command is not used. This command does not affect the location of the directory where the buffer file is stored (the buffer directory is determined by the `:set directory` command, which is described in Chapter 11).

Any legitimate directory and pathname descriptors can be used when specifying *directory_name,* including (..) and (.). If the `:cd!` form of the command is used, the buffer file is not lost. If this command is used during an editing session, commands such as `:w` and ZZ write the buffer to a file whose name matches the current filename being edited. Thus, if you are editing a file named *file_a* in directory *directory_X* and then change to *directory_Y,* `:w` or ZZ writes the buffer to a file named *file_a* in *directory_Y,* creating a new file if necessary. If *directory_Y* already contains a file of that name, the existing file is overwritten by the new buffer file contents. Table 9-11 summarizes the `cd` command.

Table 9-11. Change Directory

Command Format	Command Description
:cd *directory_name*	Changes the current working directory to the directory specified by *directory_name*. If autowrite is set and the file has been modified, the buffer file is written to permanent storage before the change is made. If autowrite is not set, the file must be written to permanent storage before the command can be executed. To change directories without writing the current buffer file to permanent storage, use the command form :cd! *directory_name*.

Copy One or More Lines to New Location (vi/ex)

The copy command lets you copy specified lines to a specified location. The addressing parameters preceding the copy command are similar to the addresses preceding the change command. A single address (or implied single address) copies one line to the specified target address *address*. Two addresses, when present or implied, specify the starting and ending lines when multiple lines are to be copied.

Commands can have any of the following general formats:

- First and last address specified

    :*start_addr*,*end_addr* co *destination_address* (Return)

- Starting line and number of copied lines specified

    :*start_addr* co *line_count destination_address* (Return)

- Start at current line with number of copied lines specified

    :co *line_count destination_address* (Return)

Below are some examples of copying lines to a new location:

- Copy the second line after the current line, placing it after line 13 in the current file:

    :.+2co13 (Return)

- Copy the current line through the second line after the current line (three lines total), placing them after line 22 in the current file:

  :.,.+2co22 ⌈Return⌉

- Copy the entire buffer file, placing it after the last line. This produces the equivalent of two files concatenated head-to-tail in a new single file and is equivalent to the UNIX command `cat buffer_file >>buffer_file`:

  :%co$ ⌈Return⌉

Flags

The `copy` command accepts the following flags:

Print current line preceded by line number after copy.

p   Print current line without line number after copy.

Table 9-12 summarizes the copy commands.

Table 9-12. Copy Lines to New Location

Command Format	Command Description
:copy *address flags* :co *address flags* or :t *address flags* Default addr: current line	Places a copy of the lines specified by the address primitives that precede the `copy` command after the line identified by *address*, which can be zero. Upon completion, the current line (.) addresses the last line of the copy. The :t command is a synonym for :copy. Addressing rules are the same as for the `change` command with or without *count*. *flags* is pertinent only when using `ex`.

Encrypt Files (vi/ex)

The encrypt option allows you to edit encrypted files (Table 9-13).

Table 9-13. Encrypt Files

Command Format	Command Description
:cr or :X	If your system is properly licensed and has file encryption software installed, this command provides editing for encrypted files.

Delete One or More Lines (vi/ex)

The delete command removes specified lines from the buffer. If a named buffer is specified in the command by a single letter, the deleted lines are saved in that buffer.

Again, the addressing parameters are similar to those of the copy and change commands. A single address deletes a single line unless the delete command is followed by a *count* parameter. A pair of addresses identifies a block of lines to be deleted, provided no *count* parameter is present. If *count* is present in the command line, the second address is used and *count* lines are deleted starting at that address (the first address is ignored). To store the deleted lines in a named buffer, specify the buffer name between the delete command and the *count* parameter as indicated above.

If a p, l, or # flag is included in the command and ex is being used instead of vi, the new current line after the deletion is completed is printed as specified by the flag that is present.

- First and last address specified

    : *start_addr , end_addr* d (Return)

- Starting line and number of deleted lines specified

    : *start_addr* d *line_count* (Return)

- Current line and number of deleted lines specified

    :d *line_count* (Return)

■ Current line, number of deleted lines, and overwrite buffer **u** specified

    `:d u` *line_count* `Return`

■ Current line, number of deleted lines, and append to buffer **u** specified

    `:d U` *line_count* `Return`

Here are more examples that are similar to those given for `change` and `copy` but that show some variations on the use of *pattern* addressing:

■ Delete three lines starting at the second line after the first encountered line containing *text* and append to buffer **r**:

    `:/text/+2,dR3` `Return`

■ Delete the current line and the next two lines after the current line:

    `:.,.+2d` `Return`

■ Delete all lines starting at the 5th line after the line that contains marker **a** and continuing through the 4th line before the last line in the file:

    `:'a+5,$-4d` `Return`

Table 9-14 summarizes the `delete` command.

Table 9-14. Delete Lines

Command Format	Command Description
`:delete` *buffer count flags* or `:d` *buffer count flags* Default addr: current line	Removes the lines specified by *count* and *flags* from the text buffer file, and the line following the last line deleted becomes the new current line. If the deleted lines were originally at the end of the text buffer file, the new last line in the file would become the current line.

Edit a Different File (vi/ex)

The `edit` command ends the current editing session and starts a new one with a specified file. That the three names and abbreviations for this command are identical to three UNIX commands used to access various personalities of the `ex` editor is purely coincidental. When used as commands within the editor, `edit`, `e`, and `ex` are synonymous. They are also synonymous with the UNIX commands `e` (if it exists in the system in the form of a link to the `vi/ex` editor program file) and `ex`.

When this command is given, the editor checks the current file to see whether it has been modified. If the file has been modified, the editor checks the `autowrite` option to see whether it is set. If `autowrite` is not set, an error message is sent to the terminal and the command is aborted. If `autowrite` is set, the buffer file is written to permanent storage and the buffer is destroyed.

When the current buffer is cleared (current file not modified or modified file copied to permanent storage), the editor then examines the specified new file to make sure that it is a valid text file. If so, it is copied to the buffer area for editing and a new session begins in the usual manner.

After ensuring that this file looks reasonable, the editor reads the source file into its buffer. If the transfer is completed without error, the number of lines and characters in the file is displayed. For versions of the `vi` editor that support international language capabilities, any 8-bit characters in the file are handled as 8-bit values. This capability provides the editor with international language support.

Under certain conditions, the new file is sometimes treated as a modified file. If the last line in the new file is missing its trailing newline character, one will be supplied and a complaint message will be displayed. The current line (`.`) is the last line in the new buffer file.

The `:e` command and its variants cannot be used with a multiple filename list, unlike the `:n` (next) command.

Edit a Different File; Forced Command Version (vi/ex)

The `edit!` option ends the current editing session, destroys the current buffer file, and copies the new file into the editing buffer. Any error or complaint message that would normally result when switching to a new file without saving the current file is suppressed. Even if the `autowrite` option is set, the buffer is not written to permanent storage before it is destroyed.

Edit New File Starting at Specified Address (vi/ex)

It is possible to edit a new file beginning at a pre-determined line using the `edit` command. For example, `:e+1 myfile` will let you edit *myfile* beginning on line 1; `e+/standard myfile` would open *myfile* with the current address being the first occurrence of the word `standard`. Table 9-15 summarizes the edit commands.

Table 9-15. Edit a Different File

Command Format	Command Description
`:edit` *file* `:e` *file* or `:ex` *file*	Terminates the current editing session and starts a new session on the specified *file*. If the `autowrite` option is not set (see Chapter 11) and the current file has been modified but not written, the command is aborted and an error message is displayed. If `autowrite` is set and the file has been modified, the current buffer is written to permanent storage before the new file is loaded into the buffer for editing. This command is commonly used from `vi` as well as `ex`.
`:edit!` *file* `:e!` *file* or `:ex!` *file*	Terminates the current editing session, destroys the current buffer file whether it has been modified or not, and then copies the specified new *file* to the editor buffer for editing.
`:e!`	With no *file* specified, the editor reloads the current file.
`:edit+`*n* *file* `:e+`*n* *file* `:edit+/`*pattern* `:e+/`*pattern*	Same as the `edit` command, but causes the editor to begin at line *n* rather than at the last line or to start with the first line containing *pattern*. *Important: pattern* must contain no spaces or tabs.

Print Current Filename and Description (vi/ex)

To obtain a description of the current file, type `:f`. The editor will respond with information similar to the following:

```
myfile line 500 of 1140 --43%--
```

Table 9-16 summarizes this use of the `file` command.

Table 9-16. Print Filename and Description

Command Format	Command Description
:file or :f	Prints the current filename and provides the following information: whether the file has been modified since the last `write` command; whether it is read-only; current line number; number of lines in the buffer; and the relative location of the current line in the buffer (expressed as a percentage). This command is equivalent to the `vi` command (CTRL)-(G).

Change Name of Current File (vi/ex)

To change the filename without modifying the file, type `:f` *file* (see Table 9-17). For example, to change *myfile* to *oldfile,* type `:f oldfile`.

Table 9-17. Change File Name

Command Format	Command Description
:file *file*	Changes the current filename to *file,* which is considered *not modified.*

Global Searches

Suppose you are working on a large file, such as a large computer program or text file, and need to look at every line in the file that contains a certain word, program label reference, or operand name. Rather than using a cumbersome series of / or ? followed by n or N search sequences, you can print all occurrences of the desired text pattern with a simple command of the form

   `:g/` *text_pattern*`/p` (Return)

where *text_pattern* is any regular expression (see Appendix A for more information on regular expressions) compatible with `vi` and `ex`. The `g` command specifies that the search is to be made globally (on every line) throughout the file, and the `p` command specifies that the results are to be printed on the display screen. Experienced users will recognize that this command is very similar to the UNIX `grep` command.

After the lines are printed to the screen, the message

```
[Hit return to continue]
```

appears at the bottom of the screen. Press any key to restore the normal editor display.

Limited Searches

You can easily limit the search for a given expression to a certain part of the file by specifying the starting and ending line numbers. The command form is

> : *start_line* , *end_line* **g**/ *text_pattern*/**p** ⌊Return⌋

where *start_line* is any valid line number identifier that specifies the starting line and *end_line* specifies the last line in the search space. Valid line specifiers can be the actual line number (**1** is the first line in the file, **$** specifies the last line), line locations relative to the current line, or any other form recognized by **ex**.

Process All Lines Containing a Pattern (vi/ex)

The *commands* parameter represents all of the remaining commands on the current input line. The current input line can consist of multiple lines, provided that each line except the last line in the multiple-line command ends with a backslash (\), which is interpreted as a line-continuation flag. If *commands* (and possibly the trailing (/) delimiter after *pattern*) is omitted, each line matching *pattern* is printed. This means that the following two commands are equivalent:

> : **g**/ *pattern* /**p**

> : **g**/ *pattern*

When using the : **global** command from **ex**, note that **append**, **insert**, and **change** and their associated text can be included in the *commands*. You can omit the terminator (.) for these commands if the last line of the associated text coincides with the end of the `global` command line or lines. You can also use `:open` and `:visual` in the command list, although you will need to enter any input text from the terminal keyboard since these commands do not take text arguments. When using the `global` command from `vi`, do not use commands that `vi` does not accept (like `append`).

Do not use the `:global` command itself or the `:undo` command in *commands*. Using `:undo` could reverse a `global` command. The `:global` command inhibits `autoprint` and `autoindent`, and sometimes the `/` delimiter, and temporarily sets the value of the report option to infinite so that the editor can report the entire operation. Before the `global` command begins, the context mark (`"`) is set to the current line (`.`). The context mark does not change during the command unless an `:open` or `:visual` command is embedded in the `:global` command.

Below are some examples:

■ Delete all lines containing *pattern*

    `:g/dog/d`

■ Yank all lines containing *pattern* and append to buffer `a`

    `:g/dog/y A`

Table 9-18 summarizes the `global` command.

Table 9-18. Process Lines Containing Pattern

Command Format	Command Description
`:global`/*pattern*/*commands* or `:g`/*pattern*/*commands* Default: All lines in file	Scans each line among those specified and marks those lines that match the regular expression in *pattern*. Current line is then set to each marked line in sequence, and *commands* are then executed from each successive new current line before advancing to the next marked line.

Process All Lines Not Containing a Pattern (vi/ex)

The global! command runs the specified commands on all lines that do not contain the specified pattern (Table 9-19).

Table 9-19. Process Lines Not Containing a Pattern

Command Format	Command Description
:global!/*pattern*/*commands* :g!/*pattern*/*commands* or :v/*pattern*/*commands*	Runs *commands* on each line that does not contain text that matches *pattern*. Note that the v command is synonymous with g! but that there is no v! variant.

Insert New Text Before Specified or Current Line (ex Only)

To insert text from ex, type

    :i [Return]
    text

    .

For example, to insert two lines of text above line 100, you could type:

```
:100 i
This is inserted line 1.
This is inserted line 2.
         .
```

The period (.) terminates the command.

Insert New Text but Toggle Autoindent (ex Only)

The insert! command sets autoindent to its opposite state for the duration of the command. For more information about insert!, refer to the earlier text related to the append! command. Table 9-20 summarizes the forms of the insert command.

Table 9-20. Insert Text

Command Format	Command Description

`:insert`
text
`:i`
text
Default addr: current line
Uses one address
	Places *text* before the specified line. Upon completion, the new current line becomes the last line in *text*. If no *text* is given, it is set to the line before the addressed line. This command is equivalent to `append` except that the new text is inserted in the file before the current line instead of after it. As with `append`, *text* must be terminated by a line that contains a period in the first column position, with no other characters on the line (except for certain situations in `:global`). `vi` does not recognize this command in `ex` mode.

`:insert!`
text
`:i!`
text
Default addr: current line
Uses one address
	Same as `:insert` except the variant flag on `insert` toggles the setting of the `autoindent` option to its opposite state for the duration of text input. Upon termination of `insert`, `autoindent` reverts to its normal state. `vi` does not recognize this command in `ex` mode.

Join (Combine) Lines on Single Line and Trim Whitespace (vi/ex)

The `join` command places a specified number of lines on one line.

Addressing

If *address* and *count* are absent, the current and next lines are combined. If two addresses are present without a *count,* the lines starting with the first address and ending with the last address are joined to form a single line. If *count* is specified, only one address is used (if two addresses are present, the first is ignored) and *count* lines are joined. If *count* is specified but no address is given, *count* lines are joined, starting with the current line.

For example, to join the following lines

```
This line is broken
and

needs to be joined.
```

type :j 4, assuming that the current address is the line beginning with
This. Table 9-21 summarizes the join command.

Table 9-21. Join Lines and Trim Whitespace

Command Format	Command Description
:join *count flags* :j *count flags* Default addr: current and next line Uses one or two addresses	Places the text from a specified range of lines together on one line. Whitespace is adjusted at each junction to provide at least one blank character, two if there was a period, question mark, or exclamation point at the end of the line, or none if the first following character is a right-hand parenthesis. If there is already whitespace at the end of the line, the whitespace at the start of the next line is discarded.

Combine Multiple Lines on Single Line with Retained Whitespace (vi/ex)

The join! command combines multiple lines on a single line, but does not
eliminate whitespace.

Table 9-22 summarizes the join! command.

Table 9-22. Join Lines and Retain Whitespace

Command Format	Command Description
:join! *count flags* :j! *count flags*	Causes a simpler join with no change in whitespace. Adjacent lines are simply concatenated, and no whitespace is eliminated. Addressing is same as with the join command.

Finding Tabs and Other Control Characters

Suppose you need to determine whether and where any control characters might be hidden in a file. This can be particularly important when you are examining a computer program file, as well as in many other circumstances.

The l command accomplishes this task quite handily with the following form:

    : *start_line* , *end_line* l (Return)

Any control characters contained within the specified file segment are displayed in "hat" format, "hat" being a common vernacular name among UNIX users for the circumflex character (^). Tabs are displayed as ^I, and the end of the line is displayed as $. For example, consider the following innocent looking line of text:

```
If this looks like a simple sentence, look between the words.
```

Placing the cursor anywhere on the line and executing the command

    : .l (Return)

reveals more than what meets the eye:

```
If this looks like a^Isimple sentence, look between the words  ^I.  $
```

Two hidden tabs plus several spaces are at the end of the line. Likewise, a command of the form

    : . , .+10l (Return)

displays all control characters in the current line plus the 10 following lines. After listing the lines, press any key to restore the normal editor display.

Table 9-23 summarizes the list command.

Table 9-23. List Lines Showing Control Characters

Command Format	Command Description
:list *count flags* or :l *count flags* Default addr: current line Uses one or two addresses	Prints the specified lines so that tab characters and end of line are recognizable. Tabs are printed as (CTRL)-uppercase I (^I), and the end of each line is marked with a trailing $. The last line printed becomes the new current line.

Map Text Pattern or Macro to a Function Key (vi Only)

The map command defines macros and associates them with specific keyboard key codes. This command can be executed from vi or ex, but the macro or text pattern produced by the definition can be used only when in vi mode.

An example of the map command is the following:

    :map (A) /Example

This command would map key (A) with the instruction to search for the word Example. Further examples of how this command is used are shown in the example *.exrc* file in Chapter 11.

To cancel the meaning attached to a mapped key use the command :unmap *key*.

Mapping Keys in Insert/Append Modes

The variant map! has the same effect as map except that it works in both command and insert/append modes. Use unmap! to cancel the meaning of these keys.

Using the | Command Separator Character in Map Commands

The vertical bar character (|), since it is used as a command separator, must be escaped when using it in a :map command in order to protect it from interpretation as a separator between two commands on the same line. To escape the character, it must be preceded by a ^V. However, the ^V character is also interpreted as a special character, so it must, in turn, be preceded by another ^V. Thus, to place a vertical bar command separator character in an argument to the :map command, you must press (CTRL)-(V) twice, followed by the | character.

Table 9-24 summarizes the forms of the map command.

Table 9-24. Map Meaning to Key

Command Format	Command Description
:map *key replacement*	Defines macros that are associated with specific keyboard key codes. This form of the command has an effect only when vi is in command mode.
	key should be a single character or the sequence #*n* where *n* is a digit referring to function key *n*. When the character or key specified by *key* is typed from vi, the corresponding *replacement* expression is substituted (and displayed if appropriate). On terminals that do not have function keys, you can type #*n* to represent the missing key.
:unmap *key* or :unm *key*	The macro expansion defined by a previous :map command for *key* is canceled.
:map! *key replacement*	Same as :map command but variant form has effect in both command and insert/append modes.
:unmap! *key* or :unm! *key*	The macro expansion defined by a previous :map! command for *key* is canceled.

Mark Current or Specified Line (vi/ex)

The mark command assigns a specified marker name to the specified line(s). The marker name can then be used as an address in subsequent commands to specify this line (Table 9-25).

Table 9-25. Mark Lines

Command Format	Command Description
:mark *x* :ma *x* or :k *x* Default addr: current line Uses only one address	Assigns the specified marker name *x* to the current line. *x* is a single lowercase letter that must be preceded by a blank or a tab. The current line does not change. :mark, :ma, and :k are synonymous. A blank or tab between :k and the marker name is optional.

Move One or More Lines to a New Location (vi/ex)

To move one or more lines to a new location, type :m *address* (see Table 9-26). For example, the command : .,+5 m 10 moves the current line plus the following five lines to the line immediately following line 10.

Table 9-26. Move Lines

Command Format	Command Description
:move *address* or :m *address* Default: current line only Uses one or two addresses	Deletes the specified lines and copies them to a new location immediately after the line identified by *address*. The first of the moved lines becomes the new current line. This command is functionally equivalent to a copy followed by a delete or a delete followed by a put. Refer to the copy command for information about line addressing for the lines being moved.

Edit Next File in Argument List (vi/ex)

The next command lets you edit the next file in a list of multiple filename arguments. If the file currently being edited has been saved or has not been modified since the session began, the new file is opened. If the current file has been modified but has not been saved, it is written to permanent storage if autowrite is set and the new file is opened. If autowrite is not set and the file has been modified, an error message is produced and the command to open the next file is aborted. The previous file in the argument list must be written unless the autowrite option is set.

Force Edit Next File in Argument List (vi/ex)

The next! command lets you exit the current edit file without writing to storage. Any warning or error message that would normally result from terminating the session and starting a new file is suppressed. Any change that may have been made to the current file is irretrievably discarded.

Table 9-27 summarizes the forms of the next command.

Table 9-27. Edit Next File in Argument List

Command Format	Command Description
:next or :n	Starts editing next *file* in list containing multiple filename arguments.
:next! or :n!	This variant of the next command forces the termination of the current edit file without rewriting to permanent storage whether the file has been modified or not.

Print Line(s) Preceded by Corresponding Buffer Line Number (vi/ex)

The number command prints the specified line preceded by its line number.

Addressing

Addressing is the same as for the print command. If *address* and *count* are absent, the current line is printed. If two addresses are present without a *count,* all lines starting with the first address and ending with the last address are printed. If *count* is specified, only one address is used (if two addresses are present, the first is ignored) and *count* lines are printed. If *count* is specified but no address is given, *count* lines are printed, starting with the current line.

Below are some example command structures. Addresses can take any form previously described in the section titled "Line Address Forms." *count* can be any numerical value that does not exceed the boundaries of the buffer file. Each command line that follows shows a different form of the number command.

- First and last address specified

    : *start_addr , end_addr* number (Return)

- Starting line and number of changed lines specified

    : *start_addr* nu *line_count* (Return)

- Start at current line with number of changed lines specified

    :# *line_count* (Return)

Table 9-28 summarizes the forms of the number command.

Table 9-28. Print Lines with Buffer Line Numbers

Command Format	Command Description
:number *count flags* :nu *count flags* :# *count flags* Default: current line	Prints one or more lines, with each line preceded by its line number in the buffer file. Can be used with one address (specified or implied) and optional *count* or two addresses with no *count* specified, as described below. The last line printed becomes the new current line.

Enter Open Mode (ex Only)

The open command enables open mode editing. The open command is of little interest to most users who have ready access to display terminals, but it can be useful for bringing many vi features to printing terminals for more interactive operation than can be obtained from ex in normal line mode or if you are using ex to circumvent vi on an unknown type of terminal that is not supported by the *terminfo* database.

Open mode operation essentially amounts to changing to vi instead of ex, except that only the current line is printed as with normal ex operation instead a full-screen file window being displayed as with normal vi. Thus you can use all of the normal vi commands—i, I, a, A, o, O, cw, cW, dw, dW, cfx, and so forth. If a *pattern* is used to define the line address, the cursor is initially placed at the beginning of the string matched by the pattern. (ESC) is used at the end of each change just as in vi. Cursor control keys, such as h, j, k, and l, as well as the nG and other commands, can be used to move from one line to another.

To exit open mode, use Q. The Q command that is used to exit the open mode is related to, but is not the same command as, the Q command used to switch from vi to ex.

Table 9-29 summarizes the open command. For more information about vi editor commands and operations, consult earlier chapters of this book.

Table 9-29. Enter Open Mode

Command Format	Command Description
:open *flags* or :open/*pattern*/*flags* Default: current line Uses only one address	Enables open mode editing on the current or addressed line. To exit open mode, type Q.

Emergency File Preservation (vi/ex)

You may, on rare occasion, encounter an error during a write operation, placing the contents of the buffer file in jeopardy if you follow the error with a quit command. Use the preserve command to save the buffer just as it would be saved in a system crash (see Table 9-30). This command is for emergency use when a write command has resulted in an error and you don't know how to save your work. Refer to "Recover File After Hangup, Power Fail, or System Crash (vi/ex)" to recover a preserved file.

Table 9-30. Emergency File Preservation

Command Format	Command Description
:preserve or :pre	Saves the buffer just as it would be saved in a system crash. This command is for emergency use.

Print One or More Lines (vi/ex)

The print command is used to print one or more specified lines.

Addressing

Addressing is the same as for the number command. If *address* and *count* are absent, the current line is printed. If two addresses are present without a *count,* all lines starting with the first address and ending with the last address are printed. If *count* is specified, only one address is used (if two addresses are present, the first is ignored) and *count* lines are printed. If *count* is specified but no address is given, *count* lines are printed, starting with the current line.

Below are some example command structures. Addresses can take any form previously described in the section titled "Line Address Forms." *count* can be any numerical value that does not exceed the boundaries of the buffer file. Each command line that follows shows a different form of the print command

- First and last address specified

    : *start_addr, end_addr* print (Return)

- Starting line and number of lines specified

    : *start_addr* p *line_count* (Return)

- Start at current line with number of lines specified

    :P *line_count* (Return)

Table 9-31 summarizes the print command.

Table 9-31. Print Lines

Command Format	Command Description
:print *count* :p *count* :P *count* Default: print only current line	Prints one or more lines with non-printing characters displayed as control characters in the format ^x (the DEL character is printed as ^?). Can be used with one address (specified or implied) and optional *count* or two addresses with no *count* specified, as described below. The last line printed becomes the new current line.

Put Yanked or Deleted Text Back in File (vi/ex)

The put command restores previously deleted or yanked lines after the line specified in the put command. Normally, put is used with delete to move lines or with yank to duplicate lines. If no buffer is specified, the last deleted or yanked text is restored. By using a named buffer, you can restore text that was saved there at any previous time in the current session. Table 9-32 summarizes the put command.

An example of putting yanked text back in a file follows.

1. Type :.,+5 y b. This command copies the current line plus the following five lines and places them in a buffer called b.

2. Type :50 pu b to place the six yanked lines of the b buffer after line 50.

Table 9-32. Put Text Back in File

Command Format	Command Description
:put *buffer* or :pu *buffer* Default: current line	Restores previously deleted or yanked lines after the line specified in the put command.

Quitting an Editing Session (vi/ex)

The `quit` command terminates the editing session if the current buffer is not modified or has been saved if modified. If the buffer file has not been modified, termination is immediate. If the buffer file has been modified and the `autowrite` option is set (see Chapter 11 for information about setting options), the buffer is written to permanent storage before the session is terminated.

If `autowrite` is not set, an error message is displayed indicating that the file has been modified but not written and the command is aborted. To save the changes, use a `write` command and then a `quit` or combine both commands using the form `:wq`.

Quit Editing Session and Discard Buffer File (vi/ex)

The `quit!` command terminates the editing session without saving the buffer file regardless of whether or not the `autowrite` option is set. This command is commonly used to force termination of the editor when a buffer file has been badly damaged by inappropriate edits or when a list of files was specified for editing but the user does not want to edit the remaining files in the list.

Table 9-33 summarizes the forms of the `quit` command.

Table 9-33. Quit an Editing Session

Command Format	Command Description
:quit or :q	Terminates the editing session if the current buffer is not modified or has been saved if modified. If the buffer file has not been modified, termination is immediate. If the buffer file has been modified and `autowrite` is not set, an error message is displayed indicating that the file has been modified but not written and the command is aborted. To save the changes, use a `write` command and then a `quit` or combine both commands using the form :`wq`.
:quit! or :q!	Terminates the editing session without saving the buffer file regardless of whether or not the `autowrite` option is set. :`q!` unconditionally discards any changes to the current buffer.

Merge File from File System into Buffer File (vi/ex)

In most situations, this command is very simple and does exactly what is expected: It reads a specified file into the current file after the current or specified line. However, under certain circumstances the result may be different:

■ If no filename argument is provided when the editing session is started, the editor opens a buffer file but does not assign a filename to it for permanent storage. If this condition exists when the `read` command is executed, the filename specified with the `read` command is assigned to the buffer. This means that when you execute a `write` command to save the buffer in permanent storage, the file you read when the `read` command was executed will be overwritten by the `write` command. This result may not be what you want (play it safe—specify a working filename when you start the session or be very careful about specifying a filename every time you use `write` during the session).

■ If you use the `read` command but do not specify a filename, the current file being edited is used instead. This means that the file as it existed at the start of the session (or after the last `write` in the current session, if any) is inserted into the buffer file, which again may not be what you want.

- If the current buffer is empty (you are editing a new file or you deleted all lines from the existing file) and the `read` command has no filename specified, an error message is displayed.

Table 9-34 summarizes the `read` command.

Table 9-34. Read File into Buffer

Command Format	Command Description
`:read` *file* or `:r` Default addr: current line Uses only one address	Copies the entire contents of text file *file* into the editing buffer beginning after the current line if no address is specified or after the specified line if an address primitive is provided before the `read` command. Specifying address zero inserts the file before the first line in the buffer. Upon completion of the `read`, the number of lines and bytes read are displayed as when starting a new session.

Merge Standard Output into Buffer File (vi/ex)

The `read !` command merges standard output from UNIX commands into the editor buffer (Table 9-35). This is not a variant form of `read`, but rather it is a `read` command that inputs standard output from a UNIX command sequence directly into the buffer instead of sending it to the terminal display.

Table 9-35. Read Output into Buffer

Command Format	Command Description
`:read !` *unix_command* or `:r !` *unix_command* Default addr: current line	Reads standard output from any UNIX command *unix_command* in the editor buffer starting on the next line after the line specified by *address*. A blank or tab before the (!) is strongly recommended and may be mandatory in some earlier versions of vi/ex.

Recover File After Hangup, Power Fail, or System Crash (vi/ex)

The `recover` command retrieves a file from a system save area (Table 9-36). This command is used after an accidental hangup of the phone, a system crash, or a `preserve` command. You will be notified by mail when a file is saved (except after a `:preserve` or a modem hangup).

Table 9-36. Recover File Command

Command Format	Command Description
`:recover` *filename* or `:rec` *filename*	Recovers *filename* from the system save area. You can also recover the preserved file by using the `-r` option to the `vi` or `ex` command at the beginning of the session as described near the end of Chapter 3, which discusses recovery procedures.

Rewind Argument List to First Argument (vi/ex)

This command, which apparently got its name from its similarity to rewinding tapes, rewinds the argument list associated with the UNIX command that started the current editing session. The file corresponding to the first file in the list is then copied to the buffer and opened for editing. See the description of the `next` command earlier in this section for details.

Rewind Argument List to First Argument; Discard Current Buffer (vi/ex)

The `rewind!` command rewinds the argument list and discards any changes made to the current buffer (Table 9-37).

Table 9-37. Rewind Argument List

Command Format	Command Description
:rewind or :rew	Rewinds the argument list associated with the UNIX command that started the current editing session. The same restrictions apply with respect to the **autowrite** option and modified files as for any new file when changing from the current file to a new file.
:rewind! or :rew!	Rewinds the argument list, discarding any changes made to the current buffer.

Set or List Editor Options (vi/ex)

The `set` command sets or lists current editor configuration parameters (Table 9-38). Chapter 11 provides a detailed discussion of this command.

Table 9-38. Set or List Editor Options

Command Format	Command Description
:set *parameter* :set *parameter*? :set all :set No address allowed Abbreviated form: :se	Sets or lists current editor configuration parameters. If *parameter* is included after the command, that parameter is set to the value specified. If *parameter* is followed by a question mark (*parameter*?), the current setting of that parameter is printed or displayed. The **set all** command lists all available parameters with their current settings, while **set** lists only those options whose values have been changed from their defaults.

Create New Shell from Editor (vi/ex)

This command spawns a new shell as specified by the `:set shell` configuration command or your global environment variable $SHELL (the default is the Bourne shell). Table 9-39 summarizes the **shell** command. Chapter 10 also describes additional shell information. The following alternate forms can also be used.

- For the Bourne shell

    : ! sh (Return)

- For the C shell

    : ! csh (Return)

- For the Korn shell

    : ! ksh (Return)

However, when these forms are used, the exclamation point after the colon spawns a shell, which, in turn, spawns another shell. (A more efficient method is to use one of these commands: : ! exec sh, : ! exec csh, or : ! exec ksh.)

Returning to the Editor From a Shell Escape

To return to the editor, use a normal shell termination command. For example, to terminate a Bourne or C shell, press (CTRL)-(D) or type:

    exit (Return)

The spawned shell dies, the intermediate shell, if one was spawned, also dies, and control returns to the editor program.

Table 9-39. Create New Shell

Command Format	Command Description
:shell or :sh	Creates a new shell. When you terminate the shell with a (CTRL)-(D) or other termination command, the shell dies and editing resumes at the same location in the file. This is a convenient way to depart temporarily from the editor, change directories if you wish, perform other tasks or take care of any other spur-of-the-moment need and then return without terminating the edit or disturbing the editing environment (for example, the current directory). A typical use is when you are editing a program and need to use the man command to look at a manual page entry so you can verify an option or some other operating detail and then return.

Input ex Editor Commands from a File (vi/ex)

This command provides a means for collecting a series of ex commands into a file, then using that file to edit another file. If you were editing a large number of files, the stream editor sed would probably be a better choice, but this command provides a convenient means for collecting several global changes that need to be made on a file before you manually make other changes that are not suitable for execution from a command file. Table 9-40 summarizes the source command.

Note   This command does not work correctly on some versions of the editor when accessed from vi in ex command mode due to a bug in the vi program. From vi, :so executes the first command in the file, then returns without executing the remainder of the file. However, the command works correctly when using the ex editor. To work around the problem when using vi, use the Q command in vi command mode to change to ex, then type the so command after ex displays its colon prompt. When ex provides another prompt after completing the command file, type vi (Return) to resume editing with vi.

Table 9-40. Input ex Commands from a File

Command Format	Command Description
:source *file* or :so *file*	Causes the editor to read and execute ex commands from the specified commands file *file*. Commands in the file can be nested.

Substitute Text Within Line or Lines (vi/ex)

The substitute command lets you find text using a pattern search and then replaces that text with new text. If the global (**g**) option is present in the command line, all occurrences are substituted. If the confirm option (**c**) is specified, you are asked to confirm each substitution beforehand. The line to be substituted is displayed (with the string to be substituted marked with ^ characters underneath). To accept the substitution, type **y**. Any other input causes no change to take place. Note that by omitting the pattern and replacement text, you can repeat the most recent substitution. Table 9-41 shows options and flags used with the substitute command.

Table 9-41. Substitute Options and Flags

Option or Flag	Description of Action Taken
c	Confirms each substitution before making it.
g	Performs the substitution for every occurrence of *pattern* in each addressed line.
r	Reuse the previously specified search pattern or replacement text. The :*address* s r command reuses the search pattern and replacement text from the last substitute command, but on the lines specified by the current *address*. It is equivalent to the :*address* & command in the same situation (& is discussed later in this chapter).
p	Prints current line after replacement without line number.
#	Prints current line preceded by line number after replacement.
l	Prints current line after replacement and show tabs and end-of-line position.

Search and substitute command lines can be split (only when in ex, not from vi colon command) by substituting newline characters into the line. In Table 9-42, the newline in *repl* must be escaped by preceding it with a backslash (\). Other non-printing characters are available in *pattern* and *repl* also. Table 9-42 summarizes the forms of the substitute command.

Below are examples of the substitute command.

- Substitute the phrase date unknown with October 17, 1989 on lines 5 through 20, confirming each substitution:

    :5,20 s/date unknown/October 17, 1989/c

- Substitute 101 with 111 for all occurrences in the file:

    :% s/101/111/g

Table 9-42. Substitute Text

Command Format	Command Description
:substitute/*pattern*/*repl*/ *options count flags* or :s/*pattern*/*repl*/*options count flags* Default addr: current line Uses one or two addresses	On each line as defined by the one or two addresses preceding the substitute command or the combination of an address and count, substitutes the replacement text pattern defined by *repl* for the first text encountered that matches the regular expression *pattern*. After a substitute, the current line is the last line substituted.
:substitute *options count flags* or :s *options count flags* :& Addressing: same as above	If *pattern* and *repl* are omitted from the substitute command, repeats the last substitution.

Using Tags to Edit a New Location

A file named *tags* file is normally created by a program such as ctags and consists of a number of lines with three fields separated by blanks or tabs. The first field in each line contains the name of the tag, the second field is the name of the file where the tag resides, and the third field contains an addressing primitive that can be used by the editor to find the tag in the file specified in the second field. The address field is usually a contextual scan using /*pattern*/ to maintain immunity from minor changes in the file. Scans for /*pattern*/ are always performed with the nomagic option temporarily set for the duration of the scan, independent of its normal setting. (See the section "Regular Expressions" in this chapter for more information on the nomagic option.)

tag names in the *tags* file must be sorted alphabetically. Sorting is done automatically by the ctags command (use the man command to review the on-line reference to the ctags(1) command). Table 9-43 summarizes the tag command.

Table 9-43. Tags for Editing New Location

Command Format	Command Description
:tag *tag* or :tag *tag*	Changes the defined current line from its present location to a new location defined by *tag,* which may be in the current file or in a different file. If *tag* is located in a different file, the present file is saved in permanent storage and the file containing the new *tag* is copied to the buffer and opened for editing. Refer to Chapter 8 for more information about creating and using tag files.

Reverse (Undo) Changes Made Previously

The undo command restores all changes made in the buffer by the most recent buffer-editing command to their original forms prior to the command. If the command included global operations, all changes resulting from the global command would be treated as a single operation, whether the changes are made by vi, ex, or ex in open mode. However, commands that interact with the file system, such as write and edit, cannot be undone. If you use undo to reverse a change only to find that the result is not what you wanted, you can restore the changes by another undo before executing any other command that alters the buffer file. In other words, undo is its own inverse.

Undo always assigns the file mark ' to the current line prior to performing any undo changes so that you can readily return to that position by typing the backward single quote twice (' '). When the undo is completed, the new current line is usually the first line restored or the line before the first line deleted if no line was restored. However, for commands such as global that affect larger blocks of text, the current line position is not changed by the undo. Table 9-44 summarizes the undo command.

Table 9-44. Undo Changes

Command Format	Command Description
:undo or :u	Restores all changes made in the buffer by the most recent buffer-editing command to their original forms prior to the command. undo is its own inverse.

Print Editor Version Number and Last Change Date

While this command is rarely of interest to most users, it may be useful on occasion if you need to identify what version of the vi/ex editor you are using. The version command prints the current version number of the editor and the date the editor program was last changed (Table 9-45).

Table 9-45. Print Editor Version

Command Format	Command Description
:version or :ve	Prints the current version number of the editor and the date the editor program was last changed.

Change from ex to vi Editor or from vi to ex

The visual command changes the editor from ex to visual operation and vice versa (Table 9-47).

Window Size and Location

If no parameters are provided with the vi command, a full-screen window is created with the current line located at the top. (For terminals that communicate at a slow baud rate with the UNIX system the default window size will be smaller.) If *type* is specified, window size, text placement, and format are as shown in Table 9-46.

Table 9-46. Window Type

Type	Description
Not specified	A window *count* lines high and ending at the bottom of the display screen is displayed with the current or addressed line at the top of the window. If *count* is not specified or if it is greater than the available screen size, a full-screen display window is used.
-	Same as type not specified except that the current or addressed line is placed at the bottom of the window.
.	Same as type not specified except that the current or addressed line is placed at the center of the window.
#	Displays a full window starting at the current or addressed line, but each line is preceded by its corresponding line number in the editor buffer. *count* cannot be used with this type.

Returning to ex from vi

To return to ex from vi or to change from vi to ex at any time, press Q
([SHIFT]-[Q]) while in vi command mode. :Q cannot be used from vi and
causes an error message if attempted. Table 9-47 summarizes the forms of
the visual command.

Table 9-47. Entering Visual Mode

Command Format	Command Description
:visual *type count flags* or :vi *type count flags* Default addr: current line	Changes from ex to visual operation and displays a text window whose height and location in the file are defined by the parameters provided on the command line. Uses only one address (specified or implied), regardless of whether or not *count* is specified.
Q	While in vi command mode, switches the editor to its ex personality.
:visual *file* or :visual +*n file* Abbreviated forms: :vi *file* or :vi +*n file*	Equivalent to comparable forms of the ex edit command except that the visual editor is used instead of the line editor. See the section "Edit a Different File (vi/ex)" earlier in this chapter for more information about each form. *n* specifies the line number where editing starts in the new file.

Write All or Part of Buffer to a Permanent File

The most common form for this command is simply

> :w (Return)

which writes the current buffer back to the original file if it exists. If no file exists (new file edit), a file is created and written to. If no filename was specified at the beginning of the edit, a new file is created and the current filename is changed to *file* before the new file is written.

If *file* already exists, and the filename does not match the current file, an error message is displayed and the write operation is aborted. This protects files from being accidentally overwritten in a moment of carelessness or inattention. If the current filename matches the specified *file,* the file is overwritten even if you don't want it overwritten (unless the readonly flag is set).

The current line is not changed by this command. If an error occurs while the file is being written, the editor treats the buffer file as a modified file whether it has been modified or not since the beginning of the session.

Append All or Part of Buffer to a Permanent File

This command, which takes the form :`write` >> *file,* is equivalent to `write`, except that the buffer or specified lines are appended to *file,* which must already exist (an error message is displayed if it does not exist).

Force Write All or Part of Buffer to a Permanent File

The `write!` command overrides checking for an existing file and forces a `write` to the named file if the file system's permissions allow the `write` operation to proceed. If the file does not already exist, this command is equivalent to :`write`.

Write, Then Quit: Terminate a Session

To `write` to a file and then immediately end the session, type `wq`. Table 9-48 summarizes the forms of the `write` command.

Table 9-48. Write Buffer to File

Command Format	Command Description
:write *file* or :w *file* Default addr: entire file Uses one or two addresses	Writes the contents of the current buffer to the specified *file*. If *file* is not specified, the buffer is written to the original file currently being edited. If two addresses are specified, all lines starting at the first address through the line identified by the second address are written to the specified or default file. If only one address is provided, only one line is written. If no address is included in the command line, the entire file is written.
:write >>*file* or :w >>*file* Default: entire file	Equivalent to the previous write command description, except that the buffer or specified lines are appended to *file,* which must already exist (an error message is displayed if it does not exist).
:write! *name* or :w! *name* Default addr: entire file Uses one or two addresses	Overrides checking for an existing file and forces a write to the named file if the file system's permissions allow the write operation to proceed. Note that there is no space between the write command and the variant flag (!). If the file does not already exist, this command is equivalent to :write.
:wq *name*	Combines write file and quit session command on a single line. Similar in effect to the vi command ZZ. (For more information on the ZZ command, refer to Chapter 3.)
:wq! *name*	Does not protect an existing file from being overwritten (equivalent to :w!); terminates the session as soon as the write operation is complete.

Write All or Part of Buffer to a UNIX Command

The write ! command is not a variant form of the write command, but rather a shell escape form of the write command (Table 9-49). The w ! command writes the specified lines into *command.* Note the difference between :w!, which can overwrite a file, and :w ! (space before !), which writes to a command.

Table 9-49. Write Buffer to UNIX Command

Command Format	Command Description
:write ! *command* or :w ! *command* Default: entire file Uses one or two addresses	Writes the specified lines into *command*. Note the difference between :w!, which can overwrite a file and :w ! (space before !), which writes to a command.

Terminate Editing Session

The xit command lets you terminate a session (Table 9-50). If the buffer file has been modified but not yet written to permanent storage, the file is saved before the editor is terminated. If the file is not writable (readonly option is set or no write permission is on the file being edited), the exit command is aborted, and you can save the buffer in a different file before it is discarded.

Table 9-50. End Editing Session

Command Format	Command Description
:xit *name* or :x *name*	Equivalent to the vi command ZZ. Terminates the editing session.

Yank Text into a Buffer for Use in Copy Operations

The yank command copies specified lines into a buffer. The *buffer* can be named with any lowercase letter in the range a through z. If a buffer name in the range A through Z is specified, yanked text is appended to the named buffer instead of replacing it.

Note   If the ex commands yank and put are used directly from vi as colon commands to copy text from one location to another, undo may not work correctly. Instead use the vi commands for yank and put (which work correctly), as explained in earlier chapters of this book.

Addresses for Yank

yank can be used with one or two addresses specified. One address with no *count* specified copies the specified line into the named buffer. Two addresses with no *count* specified copies multiple lines starting and ending with the specified lines. Two addresses and a *count* value copies *count* lines starting at the second specified address (the first address is ignored). If no address is specified, the current line address is used by yank. Table 9-51 summarizes the yank command. Below are some examples:

■ First and Last Address Specified

    : *start_addr* , *end_addr* y ⌊Return⌋

■ Starting Line and Number of Yanked Lines Specified

    : *start_addr* y *line_count* ⌊Return⌋

■ Current Line and Number of Yanked Lines Specified

    : y *line_count* ⌊Return⌋

■ Current Line, Number of Yanked Lines, and Buffer **e** Specified

    : y e *line_count* ⌊Return⌋

Table 9-51. Yank Lines to Copy

Command Format	Command Description
: yank *buffer count flags* or : y *buffer count flags* Default addr: current line	Copies the lines specified by *count* and *flags* from the text buffer file into the specified *buffer* or into the default buffer if no buffer name is provided. The current line does not change.

Print Window Containing Line Count

With the **z** command it is possible to print a window containing a specified number of lines (*count*). Upon completion of the command, the current line is changed to the last line printed in the window. By specifying the type of window, it is possible to specify the placement of the addressed line in the window.

Text Positioning in the Window

The window *type* determines the position of the displayed text in the window, as shown in Table 9-52.

Table 9-52. Window Type

Type	Description
– (minus)	Places the addressed line (or current line if no address primitive is provided) at the bottom of the window.
(period)	Places the addressed (or current) line at the center of the window.
+	Displays window of lines following specified line. Successive **z+** commands scroll down through the buffer.
^	Displays window of lines that are two windows prior to the specified line. Successive **z^** commands scroll up through the buffer.
=	Displays specified line at center of window with a line of 40 dashes (–) above and below the specified line. The current line becomes the specified line (not the last line of the window as with the other *types*).

No other values for *type* are accepted. *count,* if present, specifies the window length in lines. If no window length is given, the current value of the `scroll` option to the `set` command (see Chapter 11) is doubled and used as a window length, provided the value does not exceed available screen display space. If any window size value exceeds screen capacity, the full screen is used. If a full-screen window is needed, the display screen is cleared before the new window is displayed. Table 9-53 summarizes the forms of the print window (`:z`) command.

Table 9-53. Print Window

Command Format	Command Description
:z *count* Default addr: next line	Prints *count* lines starting at next line after addressed line. If address is omitted, printing starts at next line after current line. If *count* is not specified, a default window is printed that contains the number of lines specified by the `scroll` option to the `set` command, provided it does not exceed display screen capacity.
:z *type count* Default addr: current line	Similar to the preceding :z command, except a *type* parameter specifies the placement of the addressed line in the printed text window. If *count* is not specified, the default window contains twice the number of lines specified by the `scroll` option to the `set` command, provided the number of lines does not exceed display screen capacity. Upon completion of the command, the current line is changed to the last line printed in the window.

Execute a Shell Command

The shell escape character (!) in this command is an editor command that spawns a new shell and sends the remainder of the command following the exclamation point to the shell for execution. When the command has been executed by the shell, the spawned shell dies and control returns to the editor.

If the buffer has been modified since the beginning of the session or since the last buffer `write` command to permanent storage, whichever occurred later, the warning message No `write since last change` is displayed. However, if the shell escape command is followed by another shell escape command before any other change is made in the file, no warning is given on the second escape.

If the characters % and # appear within the specified command, they are expanded as the current working filename and the alternate filename, respectively. An example of this occurrence is working with two files and switching between them. If the ! character occurs in *command*, it is replaced with the most recent command. Therefore, !! repeats the previous shell escape. Expanded lines are echoed to the terminal screen if they are performed. This command does not change the current line position in the buffer. (For more information on the use of special characters in regular expressions, see Appendix A.)

Table 9-54 summarizes the forms of the shell (!) command.

Table 9-54. Execute a Shell Command

Command Format	Command Description
: ! *command*	The shell escape character (!) in this command is an editor command that spawns a new shell and sends the remainder of the command following the exclamation point to the shell for execution. When the command has been executed by the shell, the spawned shell dies and control returns to the editor. When this command is executed from **ex**, a single ! is printed on a line by itself after the text currently displayed on the terminal screen. The prompt for the next command is printed on the following line. If this command is executed from **vi**, the message [Hit return to continue] is displayed instead (press any key to continue with **vi**).
: ! !	Repeats the most recent shell escape command. The existing shell command buffer is again sent as command input to a newly spawned shell.

Pipe Part or All of Buffer to a Command (vi/ex)

You can use the ! to pipe all or part of a buffer to a command (Table 9-55). Standard output from *unix_command* is then returned to the editor, where it replaces the original lines that were sent to standard input.

Table 9-55. Pipe Buffer to Command

Command Format	Command Description
: (*addr1* , *addr2*) ! *unix_command* Uses one or two addresses Default: none Address must be specified	Copies all text lines within the specified line address range to UNIX standard input for processing by *unix_command*. If no address is specified and the command requires input from standard input, *stdin* is switched to the keyboard and the command hangs, waiting for keyboard input.

Print Current or Addressed Line Number

Use = to print the current or addressed line number (Table 9-56).

Table 9-56. Print Line Number

Command Format	Command Description
: = Default addr: last line in file Uses only one address	Prints line number of current or addressed line. If an address primitive is provided before the = command, the line number of the addressed line in the buffer file is printed. If no address precedes the command, the line number of the last line in the file (address **$**) is printed instead. The location of the current line remains unchanged.

Shift Lines Left or Right

This command allows you to shift white space left (<) or right (>) in specified lines. The quantity of shift is determined by the shiftwidth option and the repetition of the specification character (Table 9-57).

Table 9-57. Shift Lines Left or Right

Command Format	Command Description
: (. , .)> *count flags* : (. , .)< *count flags*	Performs intelligent shifting on the specified lines; < shifts left and > shifts right. Only whitespace (blanks and tabs) is shifted; no non-whitespace characters are discarded in a left shift. The current line becomes the last line that changed due to the shifting. This command is related to the vi >> and << commands.

Execute a Buffer (vi/ex)

This command allows you to execute ex commands you have put into a buffer as though the buffer were a valid ex command (Table 9-58). The buffer must contain a valid ex command that does *not* begin with a colon. This feature is useful for yanking a complex editing command that has been placed in the file being edited, executing it, and being able to edit the command, then yank and execute it again to fix errors in the command or perform a similar but different operation.

Table 9-58. Execute a Buffer

Command Format	Command Description
: *buffer_name*	Executes the contents of buffer *buffer_name* as a valid ex command. If the command is accessed while in vi, a colon must precede the asterisk.
: @*buffer_name*	Executes a valid ex command stored in *buffer_name* directly from vi. The command residing in the buffer must begin with a colon. The @ command cannot be used from the ex editor (use the * command instead).

Miscellaneous Commands

The ~ command can be used, for example, to search for a pattern using a `global` command, review the lines that contain patterns matching the regular expression, construct a new substitute command with appropriate address or addresses, and then complete the command with the following form:

```
s/~/<new_text>
```

You can add any flag or option that may be appropriate. The & command can then be used to repeat the command on a new set of addresses, if desired.

A summary of a few miscellaneous commands follows in Table 9-59.

Table 9-59. Miscellaneous Commands

Command Format	Command Description
: ^D	An end of file from a terminal input scrolls through the file. The scroll option specifies the size of the scroll, which is normally a half-screen of text.
: *address_1* , *address_2* or : *address_1* , *address_2* |"	An address or pair of addresses without a command causes the addressed lines to be printed. A blank line created by pressing the carriage return (no address or command) prints the next line in the file.
: *address* & *options count flags* 0, 1, or 2 addresses	The ampersand (&) command repeats the previous `substitute` command.
: *address* ~ *options count flags* 0, 1, or 2 addresses	Equivalent to the & command if the most recent previous regular expression was the search pattern part of a `substitute` command. If the most recent regular expression was part of a `global` command (not a global flag on a `substitute` command), you can use a tilde between slash characters (\~\) as a regular expression and supply new replacement text to save retyping the previous expression.

Getting ex Started

Like vi, ex uses the environment variable TERM to determine the terminal type. When you invoke ex:

- If the TERM variable matches an entry in the *terminfo* database, that description is used.

- If variable EXINIT exists in the environment, ex executes the commands in this variable.

- If EXINIT does not exist in the environment, ex looks for an *.exrc* file in your home directory and configures the editor using those commands.

- ex also looks in the current directory for an *.exrc* file and executes it if it is there.

The ex editor sets options in EXINIT and *.exrc* before each editing session.

You can start ex with no options by executing the following:

    ex *file* (Return)

The ex prototype is as follows (options appear in brackets):

    ex [-] [-v] [-t*tag*] [-r][-l] [-w*n*] [-x] [-R] [+*command*] *file* ...

Table 9-60 briefly describes the ex command line options.

Table 9-60. Command-Line Options

Option	Description
-	Suppresses interactive-user feedback; use to process editor scripts.
-v	Invokes vi.
-r	Recovers file(s) after an editor or system crash. If no file is specified, prints a list of saved files.
-R	Sets read-only option to prevent overwriting file inadvertently.
+*command*	Indicates that the editor should execute the specified command first. If *command* is omitted, the argument defaults to the last line of the first file. Useful commands are patterns (*/pattern*) or line numbers, such as +50 (which starts at line 50).
-l	Sets the showmatch and lisp options for editing Lisp.
-t	Edits the file containing the tag and positions the editor at its definition.
-w	Sets the default window size to *n*.
-x	Causes ex to prompt for a key that is used to initiate creation or editing on an encrypted file.
file	Indicates file(s) to edit.

Manipulating Files

Current File

Usually, ex is used to edit one file at a time. The name of the file to be edited typically becomes the *current* filename. The contents of the original file are copied into a temporary buffer file. All editing is done on the buffer file, and the original file remains unchanged until it is replaced by the edited buffer (using a write command). If the buffer file is not edited, ex usually will not write over the original file (you will see the message `not edited` when you use the write command).

Alternate File

When you give the current filename a new value, the previous current filename is saved as the alternate filename. If a filename is given, but it does not become the current file, it is considered the alternate filename.

Filename Expansion

You can specify filenames within the editor using normal shell-expansion conventions. Also, the characters `%` and `#` are expanded into the current working filename and the alternate filename, respectively. For example, you could use filename expansion when working with two files alternately or to eliminate the need to retype filenames on an edit command after receiving a diagnostic message such as `No write since last change`.

Multiple Files

In the editing of multiple files, command-line arguments for the first and subsequent files are typed in an argument list (use the `args` command to display the current argument list). The first file listed is edited as explained previously. To edit the next file on the list, use the `next` command. You can also use the `next` command to destroy the original argument list and filenames by appending new arguments and filenames to the `next` command. UNIX expands the `next` command with the new arguments, and `ex` edits the first file on the new list.

Read-Only Mode

Use `ex` in read-only mode to look at files you do not intend to modify and do not want to alter accidentally. Read-only mode is active when:

- Using the `-R` command-line option.
- The `readonly` option is set.

You can clear the read-only setting by typing `:set noreadonly` (Return). You still can write to a file while in read-only mode by writing to a different filename. Or, if you have write permission on the file being overwritten, you can use :w! If a file is marked read-only, only the superuser[1] can overwrite it.

Errors and Interrupts

The ex editor prints an error diagnostic when an error occurs, and it can also, at your option, ring the terminal bell. If ex receives an interrupt signal, it prints Interrupt and returns to its command level. If the primary input is a file, ex will exit in response to both errors and interrupts.

Recovery

If ex receives a hangup signal and you have already modified the buffer, ex will try to preserve the buffer. If the system crashes, the system will try to preserve the modified buffer once it reboots. After a hangup or a crash, you should be able to recover the work you were doing by using the -r option. At most, you will lose only a few changes from the point you were at when the hangup or crash occurred. As an example, suppose you were editing the file *data1* and a hangup or crash occurred. You would change to the directory where you were when the problem happened and type:

    ex -r data1

Next you would check to see that the recovered file was intact, then write it over the original file.

After a crash, the system will usually send you a mail listing of the saved files. Type

    ex -r

to print a list of files that have been saved. This listing will not show files lost during a hangup.

---

[1] The superuser is the person who manages the UNIX system and has the ability to modify system files.

Chapter Summary

The following highlights were covered in this chapter:

Address a command.	: *start_addr* , *end_addr* : *start_addr* , +*n* : *start_addr* , -*n* /*pattern*/ or ?*pattern*?
Define abbreviations.	:abbreviate or :ab
Add text.	:append or :a
Print argument list.	:args or :ar
Replace text.	:change or :c
Change directory.	:cd *directory_name*
Copy text.	:copy or :co :t
Encrypt file.	:cr :x
Delete text.	:delete or :d
Edit a different file.	:edit or :e :ex
Print current filename/description.	:file or :f
Process all lines with *pattern*.	:global or :g
Insert text.	:insert or :i
Join lines.	:join or :j
Show tabs and ends-of-lines.	:list or :l
Map pattern/macro to function key.	:map
Mark lines.	:mark or :ma :k
Move lines.	:move or :m
Edit next file in list.	:next or :n

Enter open mode.	`:open`
Preserve file (emergency use).	`:preserve` or `:pre`
Print lines.	`:print` or `:p`
Put text back in file.	`:put` or `:pu`
Exit editor.	`:quit` or `:q`
Merge file into buffer file.	`:read` or `:r`
Recover file.	`:recover` or `:rec`
Rewind list to first argument.	`:rewind` or `:rew`
Set editor options.	`:set` or `:se`
Create new shell.	`:shell` or `:sh`
Input ex commands from file.	`:source` or `:so`
Substitute text.	`:substitute` or `:s`
Use tags to edit new location.	`:tag`
Undo previous change.	`:undo` or `:u`
Change to visual operation.	`:visual` or `vi`
Write buffer to file.	`:write` or `w:`
End a session.	`:wq`
	`:xit`
	`:x`
Yank text into a buffer.	`:yank` or `:y`
Print window.	`:z`
Execute a shell command.	`:!` *command*
Repeat previous shell command.	`:!!`
Repeat previous substitute command.	`&`

10

Advanced Editing: Shell Operations

As you gain experience, you will commonly encounter situations in which you need to access UNIX commands and capabilities directly from within the vi editor without terminating or disturbing the editing session. vi command mode supports several methods for accessing UNIX commands, opening a vast field of possibilities for the imaginative user.

When UNIX commands are accessed, all or part of the current vi buffer is used as the standard input source for those UNIX commands requiring standard input and as standard output when the command's standard output is to be placed in the text file. This ability to use the buffer as the source for standard input as well as the destination for standard output opens a wide realm of possibilities that fall into three general categories:

- All or part of the current buffer can be sent to a series of one or more UNIX commands whose final output is brought back to replace the original text that was sent to standard input.

- The tee command can also be used to send the output of any of the commands in the series to another file. This technique for accessing UNIX commands is commonly called piping the buffer to a command.

- All or part of the buffer can be sent as standard input to a UNIX command in a write operation where the command output is sent elsewhere and is not brought back to replace the original text. This is called writing the buffer to a command. A comparable read operation imports standard output from a UNIX command and is called reading from a command.

This chapter presents several typical examples of each of these types of operations, discusses some useful techniques, and is intended to serve as a source of ideas that you can use in your own text-editing applications.

For more information about the UNIX commands used in the examples in this chapter, refer to the corresponding on-line manual page entry using the UNIX `man` command[1].

Operation Types

As we mentioned earlier, shell operations fall into three general categories:

- Operations that modify (replace after processing) existing text in the file.

- Operations that insert new text from a UNIX command into the file after the current line.

- Operations that send existing text in the file to a UNIX command and produce output elsewhere without altering the existing buffer contents.

The remainder of this chapter addresses each category separately.

Text Replacement Shell Operations

When shell operations are used to modify text currently residing in the `vi` buffer, that portion of the buffer being modified by UNIX is sent by `vi` as standard input to the specified UNIX command or commands. Standard output from the command is then sent back to `vi`, which uses it to replace the original text. The text from `vi` that was sent to UNIX can also be used or stored elsewhere by using the `tee` command, in addition to being brought back for replacement in its modified form.

When you use this method for altering text, the command to `vi` that specifies the work to be done causes `vi` to spawn a new shell in response to the shell escape sequence. The spawned shell process then executes the shell command specified in the remainder of the shell escape command

---

[1] A feature of nearly all UNIX implementations is the on-line reference that provides quick access to information on the commands that come with the system. For example `man vi` would diplay on your screen the quick reference for the `vi` command.

line that spawned the process. The command can consist of a single shell program/command, or it can be a series of commands piped together. Upon completion of the specified shell command, standard output from the last command is returned to the editor and replaces the original text object. You can use the undo command to restore the original text if the result is not what you wanted.

Text Replacement: Command Format

Text replacing shell commands generally have the following form:

! *count text_object shell_command(s)* (Return)

Table 10-1 gives the format for text replacement commands.

Table 10-1. Command Format for Text Replacement

Element	Description
!	Exclamation point (!) is used to escape from vi to the shell interpreter.
count	Number of *text_objects* (such as sentences or paragraphs) to pass to the shell for processing.
text_object	Any valid vi text object definition; can be preceded by a *count* parameter (for example, 2} defines the text object as all text from the current position to the second following end of paragraph).
shell_command(s)	Any valid sequence of one or more UNIX commands, including pipe (|) and tee connections between commands. Standard input for commands is the text object defined by *text_object*. *text_object* is replaced by standard output from *shell_command(s)*.

Text Replacement: Adjusting Text Paragraphs

As any experienced user of text processors and editors knows, text consisting of choppy lines of varying length are common. Here is an example:

```
This paragraph
consists of several lines of varying length.
It
would look much better if
it were rearranged into a group of lines of more uniform length.
Do you
agree?
```

Shell operations provide a convenient means for easily justifying paragraphs or other text blocks while in `vi`. While several programs could be used to do this (as well as your own custom shell script), the UNIX `adjust` command is probably the most convenient. (The `adjust` command is not available on all UNIX implementations. However, the `fmt` command works similarly. See the manual page entry on `fmt` (`man fmt`) for more information on justifying text with this command.)

In its default form, `adjust` arranges contiguous lines of text (in this case taken from standard input provided by `vi`) into a paragraph of successive lines separated by word boundaries and containing the maximum possible number of characters per line up to the default limit of 72 characters per line. If the `adjust` command does not include any non-default options, no extra spaces are provided and the finished paragraph has an even left margin and a ragged right margin.

Below is what `adjust` does to the previous example paragraph following the command `!}adjust` with the cursor placed anywhere on the first line in the paragraph:

```
     This paragraph consists of several lines of varying length.  It would
     look much better if it were rearranged into a group of lines of more
     uniform length.  Do you agree?
```

To obtain even margins on both right and left boundaries, use the -j option.
Below is the result of the same paragraph using the !}adjust -j command:

```
     This   paragraph  consists  of several lines of varying  length.  It would
     look   much   better  if it were   rearranged   into a group of lines of more
     uniform length.  Do you agree?
```

The -m option is used to change line length. Below is the result of the
command !}adjust -j -m40 or !}adjust -jm40. Note the smooth right
margin and observe how the options can be separate or combined.

```
     This paragraph consists of several lines
     of varying  length.  It would  look much
     better  if it  were  rearranged  into   a
     group of lines of more  uniform  length.
     Do you agree?
```

Below is the result when the -j option is omitted:

```
     This paragraph consists of several lines
     of varying length.  It would look much
     better if it were rearranged into a
     group of lines of more uniform length.
     Do you agree?
```

Refer to the adjust(1) entry in the on-line UNIX reference (using man adjust) for more information about available options. The topics that follow show several other ways of using the adjust command.

Adjusting Multiple Paragraphs

Suppose you have four paragraphs of text that are separated by empty lines or lines consisting of paragraph macros. For the purpose of illustration, let's assume that each paragraph contains four sentences (16 sentences in four paragraphs) and that the cursor is located somewhere on the first line of the first paragraph.

Since vi passes any defined text object to the shell without knowing what you want to do with it, the following two commands are equivalent:

>   !4}adjust (Return)   *adjust next 4 paragraphs*

or

>   !16)adjust (Return)   *adjust next 16 sentences*

Either form adjusts all four paragraphs with a left-justified, ragged right margin, with up to 72 characters per line. The first command adjusts the next four paragraphs starting with the cursor line. The second adjusts the next 16 sentences starting with the line of the sentence that contains the cursor. When the operation is complete, the cursor is returned to the left margin of the line it was on when the operation started.

Note	When text objects are being piped to a command, the current cursor position represents the beginning or end of the object sent to the pipeline unless a move command precedes the text object definition sequence. Therefore, be careful when using text objects this way to ensure that the correct text is being sent.

Speeding It Up: Tradeoffs

Whenever you perform an adjust operation this way, `vi` must spawn a new process, load the `adjust` program, run it on the text object, return the result to `vi`, and terminate the process. This involves a lot of overhead. Thus, it is much faster to adjust 16 paragraphs at once than to adjust the same number of paragraphs one at a time. However, as the number of paragraphs adjusted in a single operation increases, so does the risk of encountering a text object within the defined text object (such as a table or heading) that you do not want to adjust.

Using Left/Right Shift with Adjust

The shift-right (`>>`) and shift-left (`<<`) commands are useful on those occasions when you may need to move the left margin of a text block or paragraph right or left from the left margin or its current position. One method commonly employed by casual users is to insert or delete tabs or spaces at the beginning of each line. However, this can be cumbersome, especially if `adjust` is used to justify the margins (`adjust` has no provision for altering the left margin indent to a given column position).

To solve the problem, consider the following paragraph that was formatted by using the `vi` command `!}adjust -j` Return :

```
Occasionally,  you may need to move the left  margin of a text  block or
paragraph  right or left from the left margin or its  current  position.
One method commonly employed by casual users is to insert or delete tabs
or  spaces  at  the  beginning  of  each  line.  However,  this  can  be
cumbersome,  especially if adjust is used to justify the margins (adjust
has no provision  for altering the left margin  indent to a given column
position).
```

Suppose we need to indent the left margin five columns while holding the same right-margin position. First, repeat the previous `adjust` command, but use a right margin of 67 instead of 72 to gain five columns:

```
!}adjust -j -m67
```

```
Occasionally,  you may need to move the left margin of a text block
or  paragraph  right or left from the left  margin  or  its  current
position.  One  method  commonly  employed  by  casual  users  is to
insert or  delete  tabs or spaces at the  beginning  of each  line.
However,  this can be  cumbersome,  especially if adjust is used to
justify the margins  (adjust has no provision for altering the left
margin indent to a given column position).
```

Note the narrower paragraph width. To change the default shiftwidth
(`shiftwidth` is discussed in Chapter 11), use the command

   `:set shiftwidth=5` `Return`

then type `7>>` (shift 7 lines right beginning with the current line). The entire
paragraph moves to the right with the following result:

```
        Occasionally,  you may need to move the left margin of a text block
        or  paragraph  right or left from the left  margin  or  its  current
        position.  One  method  commonly  employed  by  casual  users  is to
        insert or  delete  tabs or spaces at the  beginning  of each  line.
        However,  this can be  cumbersome,  especially if adjust is used to
        justify the margins  (adjust has no provision for altering the left
        margin indent to a given column position).
```

Reversing the Adjust Command

If you are not satisfied with the effect of `adjust`, or if you get an error
message because `adjust` does not exist on your system, remember that the
`undo` command can reverse the effect of typing the `adjust` command. The
`undo` command will return the text to its previous state.

Text Replacement: Sorting Lists

A common problem in text processing involves taking a random list of items and sorting them in some pre-determined fashion — sometimes one word or item per line, sometimes multiple-column lines sorted according to a certain column, sometimes simply long lines that need to be sorted — and getting the job done with a minimum of effort or difficulty. Normally, this could be a very tedious task. With `vi` it becomes surprisingly simple.

The techniques shown here for sorting are simple. However, they can be readily expanded to fit more sophisticated needs. The examples that follow can serve as a seed bed for more ideas. Refer to the information on the `sort` command (using `man sort`) for more information.

Sorting the List

Suppose you have the following list of colors somewhere in the middle of a large text file, arranged as indicated, one color per line with one or more empty lines before and after the list (thus forming one paragraph):

```
red
blue
green
orange
yellow
maroon
brown
cyan
purple
chartreuse
violet
crimson
```

First, let's sort the list into alphabetical order, still one color per line, without disturbing surrounding text. Place the cursor on the word `red` in the first line, then execute the `vi` command:

!}sort (Return)

The ! command tells vi that this command is to be sent to the shell for interpretation. The } command is a vi directive identifying the text object to be processed. It tells vi to send the text from the current cursor line through the end of the current paragraph to the shell as standard input for the command that follows. sort is the UNIX command that is to be executed by the shell. Upon completion, the shell returns its standard output from the sort to vi, which, in turn, uses the processed text to replace the original text that was previously sent to the shell for processing.

As you type the command, notice that when you type !, nothing visible happens (vi is holding the character in a buffer and is waiting for your next command character). The } character represents the text object (the object can be preceded by a count). As soon as vi recognizes a valid text object, the ! character is displayed at the bottom of the screen on the command line, but the object is never displayed—just as in normal vi editing operations. Once the text object has been defined, the remaining characters in the command are treated as a valid shell command and are sent directly to the shell for interpretation. After processing by vi, only the following characters from the command sequence are visible on the command line at the bottom of the terminal screen:

```
!sort
```

The result that replaces the original text is the following:

```
blue
brown
chartreuse
crimson
cyan
green
maroon
orange
purple
red
violet
yellow
```

Working with Multi-Column Lines

Occasionally, you may have a similar series of lines except that each line contains several columns of text separated by tabs or other whitespace or delimiter characters. You may want to sort the lines based on the contents of the first column of each line. However, you may also need to sort the lines based on the contents of column 3 or 4, for example, or based on contents from any position in the line to any other position in the same line. For more information, refer to the sort(1) manual page (using `man sort`) and to discussions of the `sort` command earlier in this chapter.

For example, to sort a paragraph containing several lines, each of which contains five columns, in alphabetical order according to the contents of column 2, and ignoring uppercase/lowercase differences, you would use the following:

```
!}sort -f +1 -2
```

Text Replacement: Rearranging Lists into Tables

Another common text processing problem entails rearranging a single column of text or data, one item per line, into a multiple-column table. The UNIX `pr` command provides an easy way to do this. For example, using the unsorted list of colors from the previous section, execute the following `vi` command

    !}pr -4t (Return)

while the cursor is on the first color (`red`). The following single-column list

```
red
blue
green
orange
yellow
maroon
brown
cyan
purple
chartreuse
violet
crimson
```

is replaced by this four-column layout:

```
red             orange          brown           chartreuse
blue            yellow          cyan            violet
green           maroon          purple          crimson
```

However, the list is not sorted into alphabetical order. To sort and format the list in a single operation, execute both commands in a single pipeline as follows:

    !}sort | pr -4t

The resulting table is now in alphabetical order:

```
    blue            crimson         maroon          red
    brown           cyan            orange          violet
    chartreuse      green           purple          yellow
```

As discussed previously, the **sort** part of the command sequence sorts the paragraph into alphabetical order in a single-column format. The **pr** command option **-4** specifies four-column output (columns are separated by an appropriate combination of tab and space characters); the **t** option suppresses page headers, footers, and any empty lines that would normally be created before or after the processed text when formatting printed pages. The processed output text from **pr** is returned to **vi** by the shell so it can be used to replace the original text object.

However, the embedded tab characters in the formatted multi-column output may not be acceptable for some situations. To see the tabs in the text file set the list option:

```
    :set list
```

The text will appear as:

```
    blue^I^I    crimson^I      maroon^I        red$
    brown^I^I   cyan^I^I       orange^I        violet$
    chartreuse^I  green^I^I      purple^I         yellow$
```

The ^I represents the space on the terminal screen that is consumed by the corresponding tab character in the sorted output.

Expanding Tabs to Spaces in Columnar Output

If the table must not contain tab characters, they are easily eliminated by using another UNIX command, expand, in the pipeline:

```
!}sort | pr -4t | expand (Return)
```

As before, the sort part of the command sequence sorts the specified text object into alphabetical order in a single-column format; pr formats the sorted output into four-column output with columns separated by tab characters, and expand converts each tab character into a string of blanks to create the correct appearance on the terminal screen (pr and expand use the same default column numbers for tab stop positions). The shell returns the processed result to vi without any embedded tab characters:

```
blue            crimson         maroon          red
brown           cyan            orange          violet
chartreuse      green           purple          yellow
```

Adding tbl Macros

The table preprocessor tbl converts table source text in a special form into a series of command sequences that can be used in conjunction with an nroff or troff text formatting program or mm (memorandum macro) processing program. The output from the sort | pr command shown previously would not be suitable for use with tbl (table formatter) preprocessor macros because tbl expects a single tab character as a field separator between items on each line.

In both examples shown earlier, the table contains either multiple adjacent tab characters and spaces or multiple spaces between items. Therefore, both are incompatible with tbl unless some changes are made. To convert a combination of multiple tabs and spaces to the single tab separator expected by tbl, use a global substitution technique similar to the following (the cursor is anywhere on the first of the three lines in the table) on the unexpanded table

```
:.,.+2s/<tab> <tab>*<space>*/<tab>/g
```

where *<tab>* is a single tab character and *<space>* is a single space character.

To convert each occurrence of a series of one or more spaces (as in the second example where tabs were expanded to spaces) to a single tab, use a construction like this:

:.,.+2s/*<space space>**/*<space>*/g

Either method applied to the appropriate text produces the following (source text contains no leading blanks or tabs):

```
blue<tab>crimson<tab>maroon<tab>red
brown<tab>cyan<tab>orange<tab>violet
chartreuse<tab>green<tab>purple<tab>yellow
```

where *<tab>* represents a single tab character. This format is now compatible with **tbl** formatting requirements. To arrange the three lines into a boxed table with each pair of adjacent columns separated by a single vertical line, add three lines before and one line after, as follows:

```
.TS
center box;
1 | 1 | 1 | 1 .
blue<tab>crimson<tab>maroon<tab>red
brown<tab>cyan<tab>orange<tab>violet
chartreuse<tab>green<tab>purple<tab>yellow
.TE
```

As always, the table definition sequence on the second and third lines could be changed to add more information, such as column headings.

Sorting by Field Before Formatting in Columns

Occasionally you may need to sort a list consisting of two or more words (such as first and last names in a name list) based on the second (or later) column. For example, the following list of notable names:

```
George Washington
Henry Clay
John Adams
Napoleon Bonaparte
Abraham Lincoln
John Calvin
Martin Luther
```

is easily sorted into three columns by placing the cursor anywhere on the first line in the list, then using the command:

```
!}sort -t\  +1b |pr -3t
```

```
John Adams<tab><tab>Henry Clay<tab><tab>Martin Luther
Napoleon Bonaparte<tab>Abraham Lincoln<tab><tab>George Washington
John Calvin
```

The -t*space* option defines the ASCII space character between first and last names as the field separator. A backslash precedes the space to protect it from interpretation by the shell. A second space separates the -t option from the +1b option that tells **sort** to arrange entries according to the contents of the first field following the left or first field on the line, thus sorting by surname. (A bug in **pr** may place an unwanted tab character between first and last name on some names in the list.)

Text Insertion: Reading Shell Output

Suppose you are writing a procedure for how to use a new program you have written and need to include an example of expected program output. Obviously, you want the result to be accurate. What better way than to let the program provide the result and place it directly into the file you are editing instead of sending it to the standard output, which usually shows up on the terminal display screen?

In Chapter 9 we talked about merging a file into text using the :r command, which reads a file into the buffer file starting on a new line following the current cursor line. Suppose we replace the filename (following the space after the r command) with the shell escape character (!) and a UNIX command sequence as follows:

> :r ! *unix_command* (Return)

Voila! Standard output appears in the file right where the text normally goes when a filename is read in. An example follows.

Suppose you have three files, each containing 10 items, one item per line. *file1* contains the letters a through j, *file2* contains the numbers 0 through 9, and *file3* contains the words zero through ten (note that *file3* contains 11 lines instead of 10 like the other two files). With the cursor in the current line of visible text followed by another visible text line, the command

> :r !paste file1 file2 file3 (Return)

produces the following result:

```
a    0    zero
b    1    one
c    2    two
d    3    three
e    4    four
f    5    five
g    6    six
h    7    seven
i    8    eight
j    9    nine
          ten
```

There is an important difference between

    :w! *filename*

and

    :w ! *unix_command*

To reinforce the difference, the command form

    :r ! *unix_command*

is emphasized instead of the equivalent :r! *unix_command,* which produces identical results for read operations only.

Check Your Spelling the Easy Way

One perplexing problem for typists, terminal users, and humans in general is having an easy way to check for spelling and typing errors. This becomes very easy when using vi in the UNIX environment, and as usual, there are several ways of doing it. The method shown here is simple, effective, available on most systems, and not significantly more cumbersome than using specialized programs to accomplish the same thing.

To check spelling on the entire file, type the command:

`:w !spell >spell.errors` (Return)

When the prompt to continue is displayed upon completion, press any key to restore the display screen and continue. Misspelled words are now stored in the file named *spell.errors*. However, it is a bit of a nuisance to have them in an external file, so let's import the errors file to the working file being edited. Type G to move the cursor to the last line in the file, then type

`:r spell.errors` (Return)

to read the errors file in at the end of the file. If you prefer to have the errors at the beginning of the file, place the cursor on the first line of the error file text, type the command dG, type 1G to move the cursor to the beginning of the file, and then type P to insert the deleted text before the first line.

Now it is a simple matter to scan through the merged errors file and delete those lines that may be correctly spelled but that were not included in the UNIX spelling dictionary database. After eliminating the correctly spelled words that showed up as misspelled, you can search for the others, make the needed corrections, delete each entry from the errors list after it has been corrected, and then continue with the next error.

Writing to a Shell Command Instead of a File

The previous spelling example shows a typical situation in which a block of text needs to be written as standard input to a shell command without bringing the standard output back to replace the original text object. The command used is deceptively similar to the standard forced write command (`:w!`) except for the placement or absence of a blank (space or tab) before the exclamation point. The command format to force the buffer to be written to *filename,* even if the file already exists (provided you have write permission), is

`:w!` *filename* (Return)

To send the entire file as standard input to a *unix_command,* use

```
:w ! unix_command  Return
```

The type of output produced by the command (or shell script or other program) and its destination are determined by the command and what options, if any, are used with it.

As discussed in the section on using the **write** command in Chapter 8, text blocks (instead of the entire file) defined by file markers, text object specifications, and so on can be sent to the command by preceding the w with marker names, line numbers, **ex** addresses, or any other compatible construction that can be used with the w command.

Custom Processing

The :w ! construction can also be used to process the file through a shell script, **awk** script, or other device or program as your needs might dictate. The previous examples should provide you with enough information to customize this powerful feature to your needs.

11

Configuring the vi/ex Editor

For most casual users, the default configuration of vi is quite adequate. However, you may have some special needs or preferences that make it advantageous to have certain editor operating characteristics and features changed to suit your situation. You have two choices:

- Use the :set command to immediately change the desired operating characteristic or feature.

- Store the desired characteristics and features in a default configuration file that vi/ex uses each time a new session begins.

The first part of this chapter explains how to use configuration commands to set up characteristics and features. The latter part of the chapter explains how to set up a configuration file so that your preferred characteristics are automatically configured every time you use vi.

Automating the Editor Configuration

There are three ways to configure the editor automatically each time you use it with the options, macro definitions, and other characteristics that you prefer:

- Define non-default values in your local environment variable EXINIT.

- Build an editor configuration file named *.exrc* in your home directory and/or in the current directory that contains a series of ex editor :set commands, macro definitions, and other desired characteristics.

- Embed ex editor commands in the first and/or last five lines of the file being edited.

Each time the UNIX command that starts the `vi/ex` editor is executed, the editor searches for the environment variable `$EXINIT` and uses its contents as configuration commands if it exists. If EXINIT is not defined, the editor then searches for the file *.exrc* in your home directory and uses its configuration commands if the file exists. If neither EXINIT nor *.exrc* exists, the default values discussed earlier in this chapter are used instead.

After processing the EXINIT variable and/or *.exrc* file in your home directory, the editor then searches the current directory for another file named *.exrc*. If the file exists, it is also processed. This provides a means to have various kinds of files in assorted directories and alter the editor configuration to meet the needs of each directory.

After completing the above tasks, the editor opens the file being edited, and then, if the `modelines` option is set, it scans the first and last five lines in the file to determine whether any `ex` commands have been placed there. If so, the commands are executed before editing control is transferred to the user. See the `modelines` option discussion later in this chapter for more information about the modelines option.

An example *.exrc* file follows below. Lines beginning with a double quote character are comments and are ignored by the editor during startup. Their presence slows the startup process somewhat, but they make the script easier to interpret.

```
"
" This .exrc file contains comments to tell you what each command
" does. Some commands may not be desirable in your case.  If so,
" comment them out by using the " character, or delete them.
"
" The actual names of special keys are in capital letters (like INSERT LINE).
" The exact names are not universally used, but you should have no trouble
" figuring out which keys they refer to.  Some may not be present on
" your terminal, depending on make and model.
"
" Caution: This file reflects characteristics of an HP2622 terminal
"          or terminal emulator (TERM=hp2622).  If you use other
"          terminals or other TERM values, changes may be needed.
"
" **************************************************************
" **************************************************************
"
```

```
" Set up automatic indenting and set right margin at column 72:
set autoindent wrapmargin=8
"
" Block any messages from other users to protect display:
set nomesg
"
" Change NEXT PAGE key to CTRL-F (ACK) command character:
" (Cannot be used in certain situations)
map   ^[U ^F
"
" Change INSERT CHAR key to vi insert (i) command:
map   ^[Q  i
"
" Change DELETE CHAR key to vi delete character (x) command:
map   ^[P  x
"
" Change DELETE LINE key to vi delete line (dd) command:
map   ^[M  dd
"
" Change INSERT LINE key to vi Open-new-line (O) command:
map   ^[L  O
"
" Change CTRL-X to "adjust both margins on current paragraph":
map ^X {!}adjust -j^M
"
" S = save current vi buffer contents and run spell on it, putting list of
"     misspelled words at the end of the vi buffer.
map   S G:w!^M:r!spell %^M
"
```

The last `map` command in the file shows how to use the ⓢ key in command mode to run the `spell` command automatically on the current buffer and append the output of *spell* to the buffer file. Here is how it works:

- When the ⓢ key is typed, the G command moves the cursor to the last line of the file.

- The `:w!` command then writes the buffer to the original file so that it is up-to-date.

- The `:r!spell %` command tells the editor to run *spell* on the current filename, then read the standard output from *spell* into the current buffer after the current (last) line in the file.

- The ^M characters are carriage-return characters that separate the commands in the mapping.

Baud Rate Versus Display Size

On most UNIX systems, terminals are wired directly to the computer and use high-speed modems or network connections. Such installations usually display a full screen on the terminal display, typically 23 lines plus a command line at the bottom of the screen. However, when a slower modem is used for connection over public telephone lines, the time required to draw the screen when opening a new session or redrawing after a jump to a new location in the file can become disconcerting.

To minimize delays in updating the display, `vi` displays fewer than 23 lines on baud rates of 1200 or less, then adds more lines as editing progresses in the new file area. To further conserve time and resources, `vi` always determines and uses screen updating methods that require the fewest possible characters to make the needed display changes. Partial screen displays are discussed in greater detail in this chapter under the `window`, `w300`, `w1200`, and `w9600` options. If you are using a slow modem connection, but still prefer a full screen, you can override the default values on these options by setting them to non-default values as explained in this chapter.

Configuration Options

The following operating options can be configured by use of the vi/ex :set command. The option listing shows typical default values for most releases of vi. To determine the current option settings for your session, use the :set all command. Commands are in (almost) alphabetical order if you ignore the no prefix on those options that are disabled.

Typical Default vi/ex **Option Settings**

noautoindent	nonovice	noshowmode
autoprint	nonumber	noslowopen
noautowrite	nooptimize	tabstop=8
nobeautify	paragraphs=IPLPPPQPP LIbp	taglength=0
directory=/tmp	prompt	tags=tags /usr/lib/tags
noedcompatible	noreadonly	term=hp
noerrorbells	redraw	noterse
flash	remap	timeout
hardtabs=8	report=5	ttytype=hp
noignorecase	scroll=11	warn
nolisp	sections=NHSHH HU	window=8
nolist	shell=/bin/sh	wrapscan
magic	shiftwidth=8h	wrapmargin=0
mesg	noshowmatch	nowriteany
nomodelines		

Enabling, Disabling, and Setting Options

To enable or disable an option, use the :set command followed by the option name, and then press (Return) as follows:

:set *option_name* (Return)   Enable the option.

:set no*option_name* (Return)   Disable the option.

:set *option_name=value* (Return)   Assign a value to the op-
                                                tion.

Some (but not all) commands can be abbreviated to save typing. The abbreviation for each option, if available, is listed with the command in the following list, which describes each option in greater detail. When typing a command, spell the option name in its entirety as shown above, or use the abbreviation shown in the paragraphs that follow. No other spellings are recognized and produce an error if used.

Option Descriptions

The following topics describe the options that are supported on vi and ex. Each option is recognized by one editor or the other, or both, as indicated between parentheses in the heading for that option. In general, vi options apply equally to view, and ex options apply to edit and vedit.

autoindent (vi/ex)

abbr: ai   Default: noai

To enable: :set autoindent   or   :set ai

To disable: :set noautoindent   or   :set noai

Automatic indenting is most commonly used when writing structured programs, as in C or Pascal. When this option is set and the editor is in insert mode, the editor determines the current indent (as it exists in the preceding line when a new line is started), then uses that indent on all subsequent lines until it is changed. Thus, when starting a new line, if the previous line starts with its first visible character in column 10 from the left side of the display screen, all subsequent lines will also start in column 10.

If disabled, (Return) moves the cursor to the extreme left margin of the next line, regardless of the indent of current or previous lines.

How vi/ex Determines Current Indent

The current indent is defined as the column position of the first visible character on the line where the cursor was located at the time insert mode is entered. If an Open command is used to open a new line before the current line, the current line indent, not the previous line, is used. Note that vi/ex uses a combination of tabs and spaces to set the indent of new lines being added. If your requirements are such that tabs are not acceptable, this option probably should not be used.

Changing Current Indent

To change `autoindent` on a given new line, space over to the desired column to increase the indent. To decrease the indent to the previous `shiftwidth` column, use (CTRL)-(D) (back-tab) as the first character in the line. To input a single line with no indent and return to the previous indent, use a circumflex (^) followed by (CTRL)-(D) at the beginning of the unindented line. If the first character pressed after (Return) is not a (CTRL)-(D) or (^) followed by (CTRL)-(D), no change in indent occurs. However, if you start a new line with one or more tabs or spaces, the next following line is started at the new indent determined by the position of the first visible character on the current line.

No Whitespace Added to Empty Lines

`autoindent` automatically adds indenting whitespace (space or tab) characters whenever text is added in the line. If an empty line (such as between paragraphs or blocks of program source code) is created, no whitespace characters are added to that line in the file (an empty line has zero length except for its terminating newline character).

When `autoindent` is disabled, (Return) moves the cursor to the left column of the next line, regardless of the indent in previous lines.

`autoindent` is inactive during `global` commands and when the keyboard input device is not a terminal.

autoprint (ex only)

abbr: ap   Default: ap

To enable:	`:set autoprint`	or	`:set ap`
To disable:	`:set noautoprint`	or	`:set noap`

The `autoprint` option prints the current line automatically after each of the following commands: `copy`, `delete`, `join`, `l`, `move`, `shift`, `substitute`, and undo. This command is essentially the same as adding p at the end of each of the above commands. In multiple commands typed on a single line, autoprint applies only to the last command in the line.. autoprint is not active in global operation.

autowrite (vi/ex)

abbr: aw   Default: noaw

To enable:	:set autowrite	or	:set aw
To disable:	:set noautowrite	or	:set noaw

With autowrite, buffer contents are written automatically to the current file if the vi or ex editor encounters a next, rewind, tag, or shell escape (!) command. In vi, a ^ (switch files) or ^| (tag goto) command will also trigger autowrite. The edit and ex commands do not force an autowrite.

Bypassing the Autowrite Feature

Occasionally, you may be editing a file and then decide to abandon the file without placing the modified text back in permanent storage. If the autowrite option is set (which means that if you try to quit the editor, it will write the file back anyway, which is not what you want), you can prevent autowriting when terminating or changing files by using alternate forms of standard editor commands:

- quit! instead of quit
- edit instead of next
- rewind! instead of rewind
- stop! followed by the tag! command instead of tag
- shell instead of ! (When you exit from the new shell, the edit resumes.)

From vi, use:

- :e# when switching between two files
- :ta! command when using tag files to find text segments

beautify (vi/ex)

abbr: `bf`   Default: `nobeautify`

To enable:	`:set beautify`	or	`:set bf`
To disable:	`:set nobeautify`	or	`:set nobf`

Using `beautify` allows you to eliminate all control characters except tab, newline, and form-feed when you enter text from the keyboard. The `beautify` option does not affect command input.

directory (vi/ex)

abbr: `dir`   Default: `directory=/tmp`

This option specifies which directory is to be used by `vi` or `ex` when you are creating the buffer file following an `edit` *file* command from within the editor. This option does not affect the buffer location if the option is set during the session. To control the location of the buffer at the opening of each session, you must set the option in the *.exrc* file in your home directory (`$HOME`) or you must open the session without specifying a filename. If you open the session without specifying a filename on the UNIX command line, set the option after the session is open, and then specify the name of the file to edit; the buffer location will be determined by the directory specified when this option was set.

If write permission is not available for the specified directory and the directory is specified by *.exrc,* the editor exits and terminates immediately. If write permission is not available for the specified directory when the file is specified interactively after the session is open, an error message is generated.

edcompatible (vi/ex)

abbr: `ed`   Default: `noedcompatible`

To enable:	`:set edcompatible`	or	`:set ed`
To disable:	`:set noedcompatible`	or	`:set noed`

When this option is enabled:

- If a **g** (global) or **c** (check) suffix is present on a `substitute` command, the **global** or **check** flag is toggled and the command is processed accordingly. If the suffix is absent on subsequent substitution commands, the toggled flag (unchanged from the previous substitution command) is used to determine how to process the command. When a new suffix appears on a `substitute` command, the flag is again toggled to its opposite state and processing is reversed accordingly.

- An **r** suffix on a substitution command recognizes the **ed** metacharacter **%** as the replacement string from the last preceding substitution instead of using the ~ metacharacter that is normally used in **vi/ex** for that purpose. As usual, the **&** metacharacter represents the text string that matched the search regular expression in the current substitution string.

errorbells (vi/ex)

abbr: `eb`   Default: `noerrorbells`

To enable:	`:set errorbells`	or	`:set eb`
To disable:	`:set noerrorbells`	or	`:set noeb`

When enabled, this option precedes error messages with a bell *only* on terminals that do not support a standout or highlighting mode, such as inverse video. If the terminal supports highlighting, the bell is never used prior to error messages and this option has no effect.

flash (vi/ex)

abbr: none   Default: `flash`

To enable:	`:set flash`	or	`:set fl`
To disable:	`:set noflash`	or	`:set nofl`

When enabled, this option causes the screen to flash instead of beeping, provided an appropriate *flash_screen* entry is present in the *terminfo* database for the terminal being used (for more information, use the **man** command to view the *terminfo*(4) entry).

hardtabs (vi/ex)

abbr: `ht`   Default: `hardtabs=8`

To enable:	`:set hardtabs`	or	`:set ht`
To disable:	`:set nohardtabs`	or	`:set noht`

This option defines the spacing between hardware tab settings and the number of spaces used by the system when expanding tab characters. Tab stops are placed in each column number (starting at the left edge of the screen) that corresponds to an integer multiple of the numeric value used when setting this option.

ignorecase (vi/ex)

abbr: `ic`   Default: `noignorecase`

To enable:	`:set ignorecase`	or	`:set ic`
To disable:	`:set noignorecase`	or	`:set noic`

When matching regular expressions, `ignorecase` maps all uppercase characters in text to lowercase. Uppercase characters inside regular expressions are also mapped to lowercase except for those characters which specify character class. (See the table titled "Classes of Single-Character Expressions" in Appendix A for more information on character classes.)

lisp (vi/ex)

(no abbr)   Default: `nolisp`

        To enable: `:set lisp`

        To disable: `:set nolisp`

This option sets `autoindent` so that the Lisp program code can be properly indented automatically. It also alters the meanings of ( ), { }, [[, and]] to match Lisp usage while you are in `open` or `vi`. For example, with `lisp` set, parentheses denote the beginnings and ends of lists.

list (vi/ex)

(no abbr)   Default: `nolist`

        To enable: `:set list`

        To disable: `:set nolist`

This option displays all printed lines and shows tabs and newlines in the same manner as the ex `:list` command.

magic (vi/ex)

(no abbr)   Default: `magic` for `ex` and `vi`

To enable:	`:set magic`
To disable:	`:set nomagic`

Since the default here is `magic`, setting `nomagic` reduces the number of regular expression metacharacters to only `^` and `$`. To re-enable disabled metacharacters while in `nomagic` mode, precede them with a `\`. For example, if the metacharacters `~` (text in the last previous replacement) and `&` (text matching the regular expression in the current replacement) are part of the replacement pattern, they must be preceded by a `\` to be used as special characters. The metacharacters `.`, `[ ]`, `&`, `~`, and `*` are the more significant characters affected by this option.

mesg (vi/ex)

(no abbr)   Default: `mesg`

To enable:	`:set mesg`
To disable:	`:set nomesg`

Setting `nomesg` blocks write permission to your terminal from other system users while you are using `vi` (equivalent to the UNIX command `mesg n` ⌈Return⌉). If `mesg` is set, other users can use the UNIX `write` command to send messages to your terminal, possibly disrupting the screen display unless you have disabled that ability from a `mesg n` command prior to starting the editor.

modelines (vi/ex)

abbr: `modeline`   Default: `nomodelines`

To enable:	`:set modelines`	or	`:set modeline`
To disable:	`:set modelines`	or	`:set nomodeline`

If `modelines` is set, the editor scans the first and last five lines in the file when a new file is opened, looking for any ex commands that might exist in those lines. After all *.exrc* and `$EXINIT` commands are processed, and before editing control is given to the user, the commands embedded in the first and last five lines of the file, if they exist, are executed.

Any commands that are placed in the file must lie within the first and/or last five lines of the file, must be prefixed by `ex:` or `vi:`, and must be terminated by a colon (`:`), all in a single line. The commands can be prefixed by `ex:` or `vi:`, but only valid `ex` editor commands can be used. For example, to set the list option, use this command anywhere in the first or last five lines:

    `ex: set list:` [Return]

or

    `vi: set list:` [Return]

There is no restriction on the length of the command except that it must fit on a single line, and it must not exceed approximately 1020 total characters. To separate multiple commands on a single modeline, use the vertical bar character (`|`).

When using this option, make sure that the first and last lines in a normal file cannot be incorrectly interpreted as commands. To be safe, your *.exrc* file should probably leave this option disabled unless you have a specific need that requires enabling modelines.

number (vi/ex)

abbr: `nu`   Default: `nonumber`

To enable:	`:set number`	or	`:set nu`
To disable:	`:set nonumber`	or	`:set nonu`

Setting this option causes the editor to precede all printed or displayed lines of text with a line number. In text input mode (insert, append, or open), a line number is provided and the cursor is advanced to the beginning text column whenever a new line is started. Line numbers are displayed on the terminal only; they are not included in the file when it is written back to permanent storage. To add line numbers to a file, use the UNIX `pr` command.

optimize (vi/ex)

abbr: `opt`   Default: `optimize`

To enable:	`: set optimize`	or	`: set opt`
To disable:	`: set nooptimize`	or	`: set noopt`

Setting this option suppresses automatic carriage returns by the terminal on terminals that do not support direct cursor addressing. This streamlines text output in certain situations, such as when you are printing multiple lines that contain leading whitespace.

paragraphs (vi/ex)

abbr: `para`   Default: `paragraphs=IPLPPPQPP LIbp`

This option specifies the one- or two-character macro[1] names that are to be recognized (in addition to empty lines) as paragraph boundaries in the interpretation of cursor movements related to the { and } commands in `vi` or in `ex` open mode. All macros defined by the `sections` option are also recognized as paragraph boundaries in addition to those defined by `paragraphs`.

If any macros have a single-character name, use a blank (space character) to substitute for the missing second character in the name. When typing

---

[1] A macro is a one- or two-character symbol following a period (.) at the beginning of a line of text that serves as a formatting command to a text formatting program such as `nroff`. The macro usually replaces a larger set of lower-level commands that would be necessary to, for example, clean up a paragraph, space down for the next paragraph, then continue with the next block of text, or perform some other comparable task.

a space character in such situations, you must precede the space with a backslash (\) to prevent the editor from interpreting it as a delimiter.

For example, to define recognized paragraph macros to include `.bullet`, `.item`, `.step`, and `.note` in addition to blank lines and the `mm` macros `.P` and `.PP`, use the command

> `set paragraphs=PPP\ buitstno` (Return)

after a colon (or colon prompt from `vi`) or in the *.exrc* file in your home directory `$HOME`. When the `:set all` command is used to list the current options, the backslash preceding the space is not shown because it is consumed during initial interpretation by the editor.

When the editor is scanning for paragraph boundaries, only the first two letters after the period at the beginning of the line are used by `vi` to recognize a macro. Any subsequent characters on a text line containing a defined macro character pair are ignored by `vi` and `ex`.

prompt (ex only)

(no abbr)   Default: `prompt`

To enable:	`:set prompt`
To disable:	`:set noprompt`

If this option is set, the editor prompts for a new command when in command mode by printing a colon.

readonly (vi/ex)

abbr: `ro`   Default: `noreadonly`

To enable:	`:set readonly`	or	`:set ro`
To disable:	`:set noreadonly`	or	`:set noro`

This option sets the read-only flag for the file being edited, thus preventing accidental overwriting at the end of the session. This option is equivalent to invoking `vi` or `ex` with the `-R` option or to using the UNIX `view` command. Setting this option in the *.exrc* file in your home directory or in the `$EXINIT` variable in your *.profile* file has the effect of making all files being edited read-only so that the edited result must be placed elsewhere. It does not, however, prevent overwriting the original file by using the `:w!` command.

redraw (vi/ex)

(no abbr)   Default: `noredraw`

To enable: `:set redraw`

To disable: `:set noredraw`

Use the `redraw` option to simulate an intelligent terminal on a dumb terminal. With this option set, the editor prints new characters on the current line to the right of the cursor and reprints lines as needed when inserting, deleting, or changing visible characters on the display. Since `redraw` transfers large amounts of data to the terminal, it is useful only when the data path from the terminal to the computer operates at high speed.

remap (vi/ex)

(no abbr)   Default: `remap`

To enable: `:set remap`

To disable: `:set noremap`

The `remap` option allows the editor to link a macro definition directly to the last definition found in a series of redefined macros. For example, if a is mapped to B, and B is mapped to c, `remap` will map a to c. The option `noremap` ignores the link between B and c and maps a to B.

report (vi/ex)

(no abbr)   Default: `report=5`

To enable:	`:set report`
To disable:	`:set noreport`

To help detect large changes in the editor buffer file, set a threshold of change (in number of lines) using the `report` option. Most commands that change the contents of the buffer will notify you when this threshold is exceeded. Commands that have the potential for greater change, such as `global`, `open`, and `visual`, will notify you of the net change in the number of lines in the buffer after the command is finished.

scroll (vi/ex)

(no abbr)   Default: `scroll=11`

To enable:	`:set scroll`
To disable:	`:set noscroll`

The `scroll` option sets the value for the number of logical lines scrolled when the editor receives an end-of-file character (typically (CTRL)-(D)) from the terminal keyboard while in command mode. The `scroll` option also sets the number of lines printed when you use a command-mode command (which is twice the value of `scroll`).

sections (vi/ex)

(no abbr)   Default: `sections=SHNHH HU`

The `sections` option specifies the one- or two-character macro[2] names that are recognized as section boundaries in the interpretation of cursor movements related to the `[[` and `]]` commands in `vi` or in `ex open` mode.

For macros with single-character names, substitute a blank (space character) for the missing second character in the name. When typing a space character in these macro names, precede the space with a backslash (\) to prevent the editor from interpreting it as a delimiter.

For example, suppose you are using a proprietary text-formatting program in which section heads are set by the section level macros *.1* through *.4*. To reconfigure the editor so it can recognize the macros *.1*, *.2*, *.3*, and *.4,* use the command

        set sections=1\ 2\ 3\ 4\ (Return)

after a colon (or the `ex` colon prompt) or in the *.exrc* file in your home directory `$HOME`.

shell (vi/ex)

abbr: `sh`   Default: `sh=/bin/sh`

Use this option to define the path and filename of the user SHELL environment variable if it is currently undefined. If the SHELL environment variable is defined, that value is used instead.

---

[2] A macro is a one- or two-character symbol following a period (.) at the beginning of a line of text that serves as a formatting command to a text-formatting program, such as `nroff`. The macro usually replaces a larger set of lower-level commands that would be necessary, for example, to clean up a paragraph, to set a new section head, and then continue with the next paragraph, or to perform some other comparable task.

shiftwidth (vi/ex)

abbr: sw   Default: `shiftwidth=8`

To enable:	`:set shiftwidth`	or	`:set sw`
To disable:	`:set noshiftwidth`	or	`:set nosw`

The `shiftwidth` option sets the spacing between tab stops. Use `shiftwidth` to reverse tabbing with `^D`, when using `autoindent` while appending text, and when using the right- and left-shift (`>>` and `<<`) commands.

showmatch (vi/ex)

abbr: sm   Default: `noshowmatch`

To enable:	`:set showmatch`	or	`:set sm`
To disable:	`:set noshowmatch`	or	`:set nosm`

This feature is especially useful when writing with the Lisp programming language. With `showmatch` in `vi` or `ex` open mode, the cursor moves to the matching (or { for one second when the closing) or } is typed and then returns to the closing character.

showmode (vi only)

(no abbr)   Default: `noshowmode`

To enable:	`:set showmode`
To disable:	`:set noshowmode`

If this option is set and you are in `vi`, the message INPUT MODE is displayed in the lower right-hand corner of the `vi` display area of the terminal screen whenever `vi` is operating in input mode, such as when inserting text. This feature is very helpful for beginning users who may experience difficulty in understanding the difference between command mode and input mode and knowing which mode is currently active.

The INPUT MODE message displayed by vi relates only to vi program operation. When vi is used on intelligent terminals, vi may overwrite the current screen or place the terminal in terminal screen input mode, whichever requires less communication overhead. When the terminal is placed in its own internal input mode, it may display a second INPUT MODE message, usually below the softkey labels. The terminal input-mode message has no direct relationship to the INPUT MODE message displayed by vi when the showmode option is enabled. This option is not available on all implementations.

slowopen (vi/ex)

abbr: slow   Default is terminal- and speed-dependent.

To enable:	`:set slowopen`	or	`:set slow`
To disable:	`:set noslowopen`	or	`:set noslow`

Setting this option alters the display algorithm used for vi editing to accommodate slow or unintelligent terminals by limiting the printing of input or new text in exchange for better operating speeds.

tabstop (vi/ex)

abbr: ts   Default: `tabstop=8`

This option defines the tab spacing used by the editor when it is expanding tabs in the input file being edited.

taglength (vi/ex)

abbr: `tl`   Default: `taglength=0`

This option specifies the maximum number of characters considered significant in a tag. Characters beyond the limit are ignored. Setting `taglength` to zero (which is the default) makes all characters in the tag significant.

tags (vi/ex)

(no abbr)   Default: `tags=tags /usr/lib/tags`

This option specifies pathnames and filenames to be used as tag files for the `tag` command or −t option when the editor is started. vi (or ex) sequentially searches the specified tag files for the tag name, then uses the tag file entry to open the file containing the tagged text and search for the tag in that file. With the default for this option, the editor searches first in the current directory for file *tags* and then searches the tags file in */usr/lib*, which holds the master (system-wide) tags. Tags are most commonly used to edit large complex program structures that involve a large number of files in multiple directories, although they are useful in much smaller structures.

term (vi/ex)

(no abbr)   Value is obtained from the environment variable, TERM.

This option defines the type of terminal being used with the editor. The value is obtained from the TERM user-environment variable and cannot be altered from within vi/ex.

terse (vi/ex)

(no abbr)   Default: `noterse`

To enable: `:set terse`

To disable: `:set noterse`

The `terse` option lets you obtain shorter error diagnostics. The experienced user will find this option more useful than the beginning user.

timeout (vi/ex)

(no abbr)   Default: `timeout`

To enable:	`:set timeout`
To disable:	`:set notimeout`

This option sets or disables the timer used to determine whether an escape character is the escape key (such as when ⎡ESC⎤ is used to terminate input mode in `vi`) or the first character in a two-character escape sequence representing arrow keys, function keys, and so on. If set, the `timeout` function is enabled, meaning that if an escape character is not followed within the time limit by another character, the escape is treated as a separate character rather than as part of a two-character sequence.

If this option is disabled (`:set notimeout`), the timeout counter is disabled and any escape character received is always treated as the first character in a two-character escape sequence. The default length of the timeout period is 500 ms. For information on how to change the length of the timeout, use the `man` command to view the `timeoutlen` entry.

ttytype (vi/ex)

(no abbr)   Value obtained from ttytype database

This option defines the ttytype for the terminal being used with the editor. The value is obtained from a database containing the tty port and the kind of terminal attached to that port. This value cannot be altered from within `vi` or `ex`.

warn (vi/ex)

(no abbr)   Default: `warn`

To enable:	`:set warn`
To disable:	`:set nowarn`

This option will cause the editor to send a warning message if no **no write since last change** message appears before a ! or **shell** command escape. To disable the message, use **nowarn**.

window (vi/ex)

(no abbr)   Default: `window=speed depen-`
                                                      `dent`

This option specifies the number of lines that are displayed in a **vi** text window when a file is opened or after a jump is made to another location in the file. This option is based on modem baud rate regardless of whether a modem is attached. The default values for this option are as follows:

- 8 lines at 600 baud or less
- 16 lines at 1200 baud
- the full screen minus 1 line at greater than 1200 baud

The limited number of lines applies only when the entire screen must be redrawn. If you are working in a limited area in the file, the number of lines displayed increases until the screen is full. The screen then remains full until an editor command creates a situation in which the entire screen must be redrawn.

This option is useful when a slow-speed modem is used to improve screen updating performance by restricting the amount of display area that must be altered during redraws, scrolls, and so on.

w300, w1200, w9600 (vi only)

(no abbr)   Default: `not invoked`

These are `window` settings that are useful as an `$EXINIT` variable or in an *.exrc* file. These settings make it easy to change the 8-line/16-line/full-screen rule, but they can be used only if the speed is slow (300), medium (1200), or high (9600).

wrapscan (vi/ex)

abbr: `ws`   Default: `wrapscan`

To enable: `:set wrapscan`   or   `:set ws`
To disable: `:set nowrapscan`   or   `:set nows`

When this option is set, pattern searches resulting from a /, ?, n, or N command automatically wrap around to the opposite end of the file and continue whenever the beginning or end of the file is reached.

wrapmargin (vi/ex)

abbr: `wm`   Default: `wrapmargin=0`

To enable: `:set wrapmargin`   or   `:set wm`
To disable: `:set nowrapmargin`   or   `:set nowm`

This option defines the position of the right margin with respect to the right-hand screen boundary that is to be used for automatically wrapping to a new line when the margin is exceeded during text input (automatic newline insertion) from `vi` or from open mode. The default setting (0) sets the editor so that there is no automatic newline insertion when the text reaches the margin. See the "Continuous Text Input" topic in Chapter 3 for more details.

writeany (vi/ex)

abbr: `wa`   Default: `nowriteany`

To enable:	`:set writeany`	or	`:set wa`
To disable:	`:set nowriteany`	or	`:set nowa`

Usually, checks are made before `write` commands to protect files. The `writeany` option inhibits these checks, so you can write to any file that the system's protection mechanism will allow.

Chapter Summary

The following configuration options used with `:set` were highlighted in this chapter:

Automatic indentation.	`autoindent` or `ai`
Automatic line printing.	`autoprint` or `ap`
Automatic write to buffer.	`autowrite` or `aw`
Discard control characters.	`beautify` or `bf`
Specify directory.	`directory` or `dir`
Set error bells.	`errorbells` or `eb`
Set flashing screen.	`flash` or `fl`
Define tabs.	`hardtabs` or `ht`
Ignore case.	`ignorecase` or `ic`
Set Lisp autoindent.	`lisp`
List printed lines.	`list`
Set metacharacters.	`magic`
Allow messages sent to terminal.	`mesg`

Look for ex commands in file.	`modelines` or `modeline`
Precede text lines with numbers.	`number` or `nu`
Suppress automatic carriage return.	`optimize` or `opt`
Set paragraph boundaries.	`paragraph` or `para`
Set colon prompt.	`prompt`
Set read-only flag.	`readonly` or `ro`
Simulate intelligent terminal.	`redraw`
Link macro definitions.	`remap`
Specify feedback threshold.	`report`
Set scroll value.	`scroll`
Set tab stop spacing.	`shiftwidth` or `sw`
Match () and {}.	`showmatch` or `sm`
Show mode.	`showmode`
Slow printing to screen.	`slowopen` or `slow`
Define tab spacing.	`tabstop` or `ts`
Define tag length.	`taglength` or `tl`
Specify tag path and filenames.	`tags`
Define terminal type.	`term`
Set short error diagnostics.	`terse`
Toggle timer for escape.	`timeout`
Define ttytype.	`ttytype`
Send "no write" warning message.	`warn`
Specify lines in window.	`window`
Set wraparound scan for searches.	`wrapscan` or `ws`
Define margin wrap.	`wrapmargin` or `wm`
Inhibit write checks.	`writeany` or `wa`

A

Regular Expressions

Introduction

Regular expressions are a simple pattern-matching language used by most major UNIX text-processing tools for locating desired text patterns in a file. They can be used to locate a misspelled word, to find all five-letter words in a file that begin with T or t, to locate lines in a file that contain a certain pattern of characters (or a given word) followed by an arbitrary string of text that is followed, in turn, by another specific pattern of text characters, or to find almost any other imaginable combination. Indeed, the usefulness of regular expressions is frequently limited only by your imaginative abilities, as will become evident through further study of the topics in this appendix.

This appendix explains how to define and use regular expressions to conduct pattern searches when using an editor or text processor. The subject matter presented here is somewhat tedious and usually of limited interest to beginning users. However, as you gain experience in using the commands presented in other parts of this book, you will frequently need to understand regular expressions at varying levels of complexity. We suggest that you peruse this topic only to the extent of your current interest but that you be familiar with its content so that you know what capabilities are available when you need them.

UNIX editors (such as `vi`, `ex`, `ed`, and `sed`), text processors (such as `awk` and `grep`), and other UNIX facilities use user-supplied character sequences called **regular expressions** (or **RE**s for short) to search text files for any character patterns that match the possible character sequences defined by the regular expression. Like the UNIX operating system itself, regular expressions tend to intimidate newcomers and inexperienced users who have not discovered their incredible ability to locate quickly both simple and tedious character sequences so that needed information or changes can be made with minimum effort.

Regular expressions are especially helpful when handling particularly complex operations commonly encountered in sophisticated text edits, such as search-and-replace or global changes or when using `ed` or `sed`. However, if you are willing to invest the necessary time to learn how to use REs, you will find the effort most rewarding. For example, a few hours spent learning how to use REs effectively in `sed` command scripts can save literally weeks of tedious interactive editing with `vi` when the task is large and complex but of such a nature that `sed` can handle most of the job in a few minutes.

Why Use Regular Expressions?

One of the most common tasks for a text editor or text-processing program is to scan a file or block of text for a certain sequence of characters prior to performing an insert, append, delete, copy, or replace operation. The character sequences can vary from very simple to extremely complex.

For example, suppose a file contains the word `cjt`, which happens to be a typographical error that should have been `cat`. Searching the file for a character sequence that matches the regular expression `cjt` quickly locates the misspelled word, and a simple substitution of `ca` for `cj` solves the problem quite easily.

On the other hand, consider this problem: A source file contains the `nroff/troff` font-change commands `\fI` (change to italic font) and `\fR` (change back to Roman font) throughout the text. You want to change the file to a format that uses the standard `mm` (memorandum macros) macros `.I` and `.IR`. This situation poses several problems. First, you have no control over what characters lie between the `\fI` and `\fR`. You know that there is usually only one word between each pair of font changes and that both the `\fI` and `\fR` nearly always appear in pairs on the same line. In addition, the `\fR` may or may not be followed by a punctuation character, such as a period, comma, or semicolon. A sequence like this

```
... running text \fIword\fR more running text ...
```

must be changed to

```
... running text
.I word
more running text ...
```

and this sequence

```
... running text \fIword\fR.  More running text ...
```

must be changed to

```
... running text
.IR word .
More running text ...
```

Several characteristics soon become apparent in this problem:

- The \fI is nearly always preceded by a space or appears at the beginning of a line.

- The \fR occurs in several positions:

  □ At the end of a word before a space character

  □ Between the word and a period, comma, colon, or semicolon

  □ Between the word and the end of the line

  □ Between the word and one or more spaces or tabs at the end of the line

One solution to this problem using the **sed** editor is to create a file (called, for example, *sdreplace*) containing a series of commands which will make the corrections to the text file (called, for example, *textfile*). *sdreplace* might appear as follows:

```
#search for " \fI" and replace with "newline.IR "
s/ \\fI/\
.IR /g

#search for "\fI" and replace with ".IR "
s/\\fI/.IR /g

#search for "/fRend-of-line" and delete
s/\\fR$//g

#search for "\fR " and replace with "newline"
s/\\fR /\
/g

#search for "\fR" and replace with " "
s/\\fR/ /g
```

Typing

```
sed -f sdreplace textfile > new.text
```

makes the changes specified in *sdreplace* to the file named *textfile*. The
resulting changed text is placed in the file called *new.text*.

Although we used the sed editor to automate the solution to this problem,
it is also possible to make these corrections from within vi. First type Q to
switch to ex mode and then type each of the commands listed above one at
a time.

Here is another problem: Suppose you want to use an editor such as vi or
ex (or sed if you are performing the operation on several files in a single
batch) to remove all whitespace at the end of every line in a file (or files) if
it exists. If you tell the editor to remove all spaces and tabs, the file would
probably become unusable. You need some way to tell the editor to look for
only spaces and/or tabs at the end of the line after the last visible character.

Regular expressions provide an easy-to-use and easy-to-understand (once it
is clearly explained) method for describing any type of character sequence or
pattern so that it can be correctly identified by the text editor or processor
before a specified action is taken. Of course, when multiple successive
operations must be performed in a given area of text, care must be exercised

A-4   Regular Expressions

in choosing the sequence of operations. The pattern recognition and text alteration performed by one operation must not sabotage the success of a subsequent operation by altering or destroying a pattern that the next operation must be able to recognize in order to perform its work correctly.

Where Are REs Used?

Regular expressions are used by several popular UNIX commands/programs:

- `vi` and its related editors `edit`, `ex`, `vedit`, and `view`

- The `ed` editor and its restricted-access counterpart `red`; also `bfs`, a close relative of `ed`, that is used for searching (scanning) unusually large files for an expression

- `sed`, the streaming editor, which is used to edit (non-interactively) files according to a script of commands

- `grep` and its relatives `egrep` and `fgrep`, which are commands used to search input files for lines that match a given pattern

- `more`, a command that is used to view continuous text, one screen at a time

- `awk`, a language for scanning and processing text patterns

- `expr`

- `lex`, a command used to generate programs that can do simple lexical analysis of text

- `nl`, a command that reads lines from an input file and reproduces the lines and line numbers as output

- The `-n` option of the `acctcom` command, which can be used to search and print process-accounting information that matches a pattern.

- `bs`, a compiler/interpreter created for programming where development time is as important as execution time

Regular expressions are also used in connection with the system subroutines `regcmp` and `regex` and in the compile and match routines discussed on the *regexp*(3) manual page (use the command `man regexp` to view this manual page).

When Are Regular Expressions Not?

This heading is intentionally confusing. The software that makes up the UNIX operating system and other similar systems has come from many sources and many authors. How each program handles regular expressions varies somewhat, depending on the program and the operating environment. As some programs from one vendor (University of California, Berkeley, for example) have been merged into the AT&T System V UNIX package, as in the case of `vi/ex`, a few minor changes have been made in some instances for various reasons. This factor, combined with the natural evolution of programs between releases, has led to differences in minor details even though the programs appear largely unchanged to the non-expert user.

As a direct consequence of this confusion amid standardization, the various ways in which regular expressions are handled by various programs has led to attempts by various standards bodies, such as the IEEE POSIX committees and the X/OPEN internationalization committee, to resolve the matter more fully. At the time of this writing, there were three general categories of interpretation of regular expressions, with most of the differences largely of little interest to the non-expert user. As the standards issue reaches a fuller resolution, it will be easier to include a complete set of information in future editions of this book.

Defining the Search Area

Some UNIX commands, such as `grep`, search entire files for a regular expression, while others, such as most editors, can limit searches to as little as one line or can search the entire file, depending on the specified address range and nature of the command that includes the regular expression. In this appendix, searches are usually referred to as extending throughout the file because that is how they are most commonly used. However, the same principles apply whether the search is throughout a long file, through many lines in a file, through a few lines, or for only one line.

Simple Matches

In their simplest form, regular expressions define a character sequence, character by character, exactly as it is expected to look in the text being searched for a matching string. Thus, the regular expression

```
Now is the time
```

tells the search program to scan its input text for the text pattern Now is the time on a single line with or without additional text. On the other hand, if a period and asterisk character pair is introduced between Now and time in this manner

```
Now.*time
```

where the period represents any arbitrary character except newline (end-of-line) and the asterisk represents zero or more of the preceding character (this combination is often called dot-star), the expression can then match any of the following text patterns, provided each pattern appears on a single line, with or without other text:

```
Nowtime
Now's the time
Now is not the best time
Now is not any time
Now is the worst time
```

In this example, the period tells the text scanner to look for any character except newline (end-of-line) in the position represented by its placement in the regular expression. The asterisk tells the scanner to accept any number in succession (zero or more) of the immediately preceding character (or single-character expression as described later). Thus, the two together match zero or more successive arbitrary characters except end-of line. The use of the .* combination is shown in several later examples along with other uses of the period in the same editor command.

Note that a regular expression will match the largest matching string. For example:

```
Now.*time
```

would also find the phrase

```
Now is the best time of all times
```

However, it would not find the phrase:

```
Now is the best
time
```

Regular expression searches cannot span lines.

Shell Metacharacters

It is important at this point that you clearly understand that the use of characters in regular expressions to represent other characters in text is not related to the shell interpreting special characters as representations of something else. For example, in a regular expression, $ represents end-of-line, whereas the shell interprets it as a command to substitute the contents of a variable in place of the present parameter in the command (parameter substitution), as in $HOME, which tells the shell to use the contents of the shell variable named HOME. Likewise, the asterisk in a regular expression indicates zero or more of the previous character or single-character expression in succession, whereas the shell interprets the asterisk to mean zero or more arbitrary characters, such as when identifying a file name.

These two examples show extreme difference and some similarity. Some characters have nearly the same meaning when interpreted by the shell as when they are processed in a regular expression. However, if you clearly establish in your mind that shell special characters are interpreted in a completely different environment (much like a foreign language in a foreign country) and have nothing to do with regular expressions (despite some similarities), learning how to use them will be much easier.

Regular Expressions Versus Editor Commands

Another area of common confusion lies in the use of certain characters in regular expressions and using the same characters in other parts of an editor command. For example, the period (.) character represents any arbitrary character except newline when it appears in a regular expression, but it represents the current line when it appears in a line address. Some learners become confused when they see an editor command such as the following ex editor command:

```
.,.+3s/^.*[0-9]//
```

where:

- The first dot represents the current line (first address).

- `.+3` represents the third line following the current line (second address).

- `s` is the abbreviated form of the `ex` editor's `substitute` command.

- The first `/` character separates the regular expression from the command. The second separates the regular expression from the replacement text. The third terminates the replacement text and also separates any command options and/or flags that may follow the replacement text string.

- The complete regular expression used for the pattern search is `^.*[0-9]`, and it is interpreted as follows:

  □ The `^` symbol specifies that any matching text pattern must start at the beginning of the line.

  □ `.*` represents an arbitrary number (zero or more) of arbitrary characters lying between the beginning of the line (represented by the circumflex) and the last occurrence in the line of any numbers lying in the range 0 through 9 (defined by the character sequence `[0-9]`).

  □ `[0-9]` is a single-character regular expression that specifies a match for any single character in the numeric range of 0 through 9.

In spoken language, a literal interpretation of this command is, in essence, "Starting with the current line and continuing through the third line after the current line, search each line starting at the beginning of the line and, if you find an arbitrary number of arbitrary characters followed by a numeric character before the end of the line, replace those characters (including the last numeric character on the line) with nothing." In other words, delete the characters identified by the regular expression.

A more straightforward way of saying the same thing is, "If the line contains one or more numeric characters, delete all characters from the beginning of the line through the last numeric character on the line, but don't disturb any subsequent non-numeric characters through the end of the line."

Here is another example, where a second character ($ this time) has a dual meaning and the period (.) is used three ways:

```
.,$s/^.*[0-9].*$/This line contained a number in the range 0-9./
```

Here:

- As before, the first dot represents the current line (first address).

- **$** represents the last line in the file (second address).

- **s** is the abbreviated form of the **ex** editor's **substitute** command.

- The regular expression is the same as before, except that a sequence `.*$` has been added at the end.

  □ The `.*` sequence means, as before, an arbitrary number of arbitrary characters.

  □ The **$** represents the end of the line, meaning an arbitrary number of characters up to the end of the line.

- Any text pattern that matches the regular expression is replaced with the replacement text between the last two slash characters in the line.

Note the use of the period as an address, then as an arbitrary character twice in the regular expression, and then as a replacement character at the end of the replacement sentence. In the regular expression, the period represents an arbitrary character. If you were searching for a text pattern containing a period in a specific position, such as a period at the start of a text formatting macro at the start of a line, the period would have to be **escaped** by a backslash character to protect the period from being interpreted by the regular expression compile-and-match operations associated with the editor. For example, to form a regular expression to match a **tbl** table-start macro `.TS` where the period is always in the first column in the line, construct a regular expression as follows:

    ^\.TS

Failure to use the backslash causes the interpreter to also match such occurrences as **ATS**, **oTS**, and **?TS** since the period can represent any character except end-of-line (also called newline).

The previous example is equivalent to saying, "Replace any line containing a digit in the range of 0 through 9 with the replacement text."

Constructing Regular Expressions

As indicated in the earlier topic on simple matches, the most elementary form of regular expression is a series of common typing characters that restrict matching to an identical character in an identical sequence in the file being searched. Thus, `cjt` in a regular expression matches `cjt` occurring anywhere in the specified region in the file. However, there are other times when text can be classified into general patterns that do not have identical contents. For example, consider the following series of lines that result from execution of a UNIX `ls -l` command:

```
drwxrwxrwx   2 hank      projA      1024 Dec 29  1987 proj_mail
drwxr-x---   2 hank      projA      1024 Oct 25  1987 proj_status
-rwxr-----   2 hank      projA      1024 Jan 24  1988 do_today
drwxr-x---   2 hank      projA      1024 Oct 20  1987 master_files
drwxrwxrwx   2 hank      projA      1024 Dec 20  1987 prod_input
drwx------   2 hank      projA        64 Nov 15  1987 personal
```

Each line is arranged in a columnar format. Some columns have identical text on every line, while others vary greatly. Suppose you needed to modify lines that describe directories. It is easy to identify lines that are directories because a `d` is present in the first column. However, if you needed to list directories that included write permission for users outside of the group named `projA`, the task would become somewhat more complex. How each situation can be handled in an expression is described below.

To identify a character at the beginning of a line, it must be preceded by a circumflex character (^) like this:

    ^d

This expression tells the search algorithm to look for the letter `d` immediately following an imaginary zerowidth character at the beginning of each line (represented by the circumflex character) in the text being searched. Since this expression looks at only the first visible character on the line, no other information is available for additional scrutiny.

To find the directories that have write permission enabled for users outside of the group named `projA`, the letter `w` must be present in column 9. Since we do not know or care what other permissions are set for the directory, we can look at column 1 to find the directory (must match `d` as before) and at column 9 for a `w`. We can use the period character to represent arbitrary text for other characters in columns 2 through 8, thus forming the expression:

```
^d....  ... w
```

Finding Long Lines

You can find the lines in a file that contain, for example, more than 50 characters by searching for a pattern matching a regular expression composed of 51 dots. If 51 (or more) arbitrary characters are present in the line, a match occurs. However, if you are using **sed**, which can have multiple lines in the pattern space at the same time, a match occurs if 51 or more characters occur between the beginning of the pattern space and the first embedded newline, between the last embedded newline and the end of the pattern space, or between two embedded newlines.

There are many more possibilities, but first, let's introduce the other characters used in constructing regular expressions.

Single-Character Expressions

All regular expressions are constructed from a series of one or more single-character expressions. Single-character expressions can take several forms as indicated in Table A-1:

Table A-1. Classes of Single-Character Expressions

Character Class	Characters in Class	Description and Use
Typing characters	A-Z, a-z, 0-9, !, @, #, %, <, >, (,), {, }, ,, ~, |, :, ;, ? +, =, -, _, (Tab), (Space), control characters	Any alphanumeric or symbol character that can be typed on a standard terminal keyboard except characters used in substitutions. These characters match only identical characters in the text scanned. Note that you must precede a ? with a backslash (\) if ? is used as the first character in a backwards search in vi where the search command character is also a ?.
Substitution or search control characters	., ^, $, /, [,], \, *, and -.	These characters represent another character or the beginning or the end of the line or serve as delimiters, range identifiers, or escape characters in regular expressions. However, under certain conditions, - and] are interpreted directly as explained below.
Sets or ranges of characters	[set_of_characters] or [range_of_characters] or [combination_of_both]	A group of single characters or range of characters enclosed within a pair of square brackets (such as [actz58&] or [3-7]) where a match is accepted if any of the characters between the brackets or in the specified range appears in the position defined by the position of the single-character expression in a larger expression. The second form example shown accepts a match if 3, 4, 5, 6, or 7 appears in the position indicated.

The hyphen is interpreted as a range specifier when defining sets of characters, as in the single-character expression [a-z], unless it is the first character in a set of characters, as in the expression [-abdfh12], which matches any one of the characters -, a, b, d, f, h, 1, or 2. Likewise, the right square bracket (]) terminates the expression unless it is the first character in the set, as in the group [ ]=+rt12], which matches any one of the characters], =, +, r, t, 1, or 2.

Using Typing Characters as Single-Character Expressions

The simplest form of regular expression is a series of one or more typing characters in succession, as in a word of text. For example, the regular expression copiler, which consists of seven single-character expressions, can be combined with an editor search command to locate a misspelling of the word *compiler* in a file. In general, this form of regular expression is constructed by simply typing a pattern, usually preceded and followed by a slash character (/) to delimit it from other parts of the editor or text processor command.

While quite useful and frequently employed, this form of regular expression has many limitations, especially where multiple patterns having related characteristics need to be located as described in the topics that follow.

Using Beginning- and End-of-Line Anchors in Regular Expressions

It is one thing to locate the word **The** anywhere in a text file. It is quite another thing to locate the word **The** when and only when it is the first (or the last) word on a line, especially if, in addition, you don't want the search to match the word **There** or **Then** at the beginning of a line.

Two characters are reserved for use in regular expressions to represent the beginning and the end of a line. The circumflex (^), sometimes called "hat" or (incorrectly) "caret," represents a zerowidth imaginary character at the beginning of the line, provided it is the first character in the expression. The dollar sign ($) likewise represents a zerowidth imaginary character at the end of a line, provided it is the last character in the expression. When constructing a regular expression, the ^ or $ is typed as a single-character expression just as any normal character, except that it must be the first or last character, respectively, in the expression. In a nutshell,

^*expression* searches for *expression* at the beginning of the line, whereas *expression*$ searches for *expression* at the end of the line.

Both ˆ and $ must appear as the first or last character, respectively, in an expression in order to be interpreted as beginning- or end-of-line substitution characters. If they appear elsewhere in the regular expression, they are interpreted literally as ordinary typing characters. Thus, the expression $The causes a search routine to search for a four-character sequence consisting of the four visible characters $The followed by any arbitrary combination of characters and/or end-of-line.

For example, to find the three letters The at the beginning of a line, the correct regular expression would be ˆThe. In this example, the circumflex tells the search algorithm to look at the beginning of each line for the character T followed immediately by the characters h and e (if no match occurs, the search routine immediately skips to the next line). To prevent matching other words, such as Then or There, add a space after the e in The (assuming that The is always followed by a space character when it appears at the beginning of a line in the file). This forces the search routine to look for a space after the word before it accepts the match.

Likewise, to locate the same word at the end of a line, use the expression The$. This tells the search routine to look for The followed immediately by end-of-line. In this instance, unless there is an unusual condition in your text file, it should be unnecessary to begin the expression with a space character because the word is probably preceded by a space since the initial T is uppercase.

Suppose you used an expression such as $The or end$$. What then? In the first case, the search routine looks for the characters $The anywhere on any line being searched. In the second case, the search is for end$ at the end of any line in the search area. Similarly, Theˆ causes a search for Theˆ anywhere on any line in the file, while ˆThe searches for The at the beginning of each line.

Representing Arbitrary Characters

If you are a frequent user of text processors, you commonly need to search for a group of text objects that closely resemble each other but that also have important differences. A simple example might be a search for these and those where only one letter is different. A search for the picks up many unwanted words, but by using the dot (.) character (period) to represent any arbitrary character except newline (end-of-line), the regular expression `th.se` matches both words. However, it also matches `th se` in `both secondary [schools ... ]`.

This problem is easily overcome by using control characters in the search. For example, `/th[oe]se` would find only `those` and `these`. Control characters in expressions are discussed in more detail later in this appendix.

Another challenge is finding all occurrences of a word regardless of its position in a line. This can be done by using word delimiters if they are available (`vi` only). To find the word `the` when using `vi`, simply surround the word with the character pairs `\<` and `\>` as in `\<the\>`. This matches the conditions `^the` (`the` at the beginning of the line and followed by a blank), `the$` (`the` at the end of the line preceded by a blank), and `the` preceded and followed by blanks elsewhere in the line where blank is a space or a tab character. Unfortunately, only the `vi` editor is able to identify words by this method. Other editors require tests for each of the three conditions.

Note   Three terms are used when discussing whitespace. [Space] refers to the ASCII space character; [Tab] refers to the ASCII horizontal tab character. The term **blank** refers to either a tab or a space.

Using Substitution Characters in Expressions

The most commonly used substitution character is the period and a combination of the period and asterisk as described earlier. Other combinations of substitution and typing characters make up the great majority of regular expressions in most operations. Other examples are included in the previous chapters of this book.

Using Control Characters in Expressions

Characters in this group add dramatic flexibility to your collection of available text-processing capabilities. Two very useful character groups are the right and left brackets used to define ranges of characters and character sets to match a given character position and the left and right parentheses, each preceded by a backslash, to construct subexpressions.

Let's talk about the right and left brackets. Suppose you need to isolate a pattern, such as the filename that contains [DEF] in a long list of filenames, as well as any other information regarding the [DEF] characters. Assuming the names all start at the beginning of the line and end with whitespace, the regular expression looks like this:

```
.*\[DEF\]
```

Note the use of backslashes before square brackets to force interpretation as text characters instead of control characters.

Now let's change the rules so that any filename that has three uppercase letters between square brackets is matched. Here is the expression:

```
.*\[[A-Z][A-Z][A-Z]\]
```

This expression matches a square bracket followed by a letter in the range A through Z, followed by another, and followed, in turn, by another. A closing square bracket finishes the expression matching.

Suppose you want to match the words **that**, **they**, **thou**, and **thee**, but not **them**. You can specify certain characters that can be accepted as a match in each position by placing the characters between square brackets as follows:

```
th[aeo][tyue]
```

However, this expression also matches the words **thay**, **thau**, **thae**, **thet**, **theu**, **thot**, and so on. These examples show the need for judgment in setting up regular expression groups and ranges to obtain correct results.

Excluding Characters from a Set

You can also specify that any character is to be accepted as a match *except* those specified by starting the series with a circumflex and placing the series between square brackets. For example:

```
[^aslm]
```

in a given position tells the matching routines to accept any character in the position represented by this single-character expression except **a**, **s**, **l**, and **m**.

Other combinations are possible. For additional information, refer to the examples in the previous chapters and to the *ed*(1) manual page entry (use the command **man ed** to view this manual page).

Index

Beginning-of-word, move cursor to, 4-21

Bill Joy, 2-1

Blank, 7-13

Blanks at end-of-line, remove, 7-14

Boundary
text object, 4-25

Boundary commands, sentence, section, or paragraph, 4-23

Buffer
append to file, 9-56

default buffer, 6-1

execute contents of as an ex command, 9-64

force write buffer to existing file, 9-56

named buffers, 6-1, 9-11

placing text in named/unnamed for move/copy, 6-2

retrieving text from, 6-3

used to copy or move text, 6-1

write as standard input to UNIX command, 9-57

write to file, 9-55

Buffer as standard input/output in shell operations, 10-1

Buffer, executing as a command, 7-14

Buffer file description, 3-2

Buffer file, recover after crash, 9-45

Buffer file, use by ex, 9-67

Buffer, pipe to a UNIX command, 9-62

Building ex commands, 9-9

C

Change
all or part of sentence, paragraph, or section, 5-26

change current automatic indent, 5-47

multiple lines of text, 5-41

repeat last change or deletion, 5-29

replace or overwrite characters, 5-23

replace or retype lines, 5-24

swapping characters, 5-35

swapping lines, 5-42

swapping words within a line, 5-39

text between boundaries in line, 5-27

text blocks using text pattern search, 5-28, 5-41

uppercase to lowercase, 5-35

word or part of word, 5-26, 5-39

Change current directory (ex command), 9-20

Change current workfile name, 8-12

Change files without reloading editor program, 3-8

Change files without restarting editor, 9-24

Change from ex to vi, 7-11

Change from vi to ex, 7-10

Change line or lines to new text and toggle autoindent (ex command), 9-19

change line or lines to new text (ex command), 9-18

Change to open mode (ex command), 9-38

Changing current file list for editing, 9-68

Changing files in multi-file edit, 8-3

Changing from vi to ex and vice versa, 9-53

Changing lines to single-column text, 7-12

Changing text
command format, 5-12

overview, 5-12

Character on current line, delete through, 5-19

Character on current line, delete up to, 5-19

Characters and lines, delete, 5-15

F

File
   append workfile to existing, 8-11
   automatic configuration, 11-2
   backup before ex command, 7-4
   change current workfile name, 8-12
   change files without reloading editor
      program, 3-8
   current position in, 4-12
   determining size of, 4-4
   edit existing, 3-4
   .exrc files, 11-2
   merge external file into text, 8-6
   merge external file into text buffer
      (ex command), 9-43
   modify current workfile name before
      write operation, 8-11
   pipe workfile to a command, 8-12
   protect from editor overwrite, 3-4
   save all or part of current workfile,
      8-9
   search for pattern, then merge exter-
      nal file, 8-7
   write all or part to UNIX command,
      10-19
File list, defining new list for editing,
   9-68
File marker, set (ex command), 9-35
File markers used to save part of
   workfile, 8-10
Filename expansion in commands, 9-68
Filename length, 2-13
Filenames
   metacharacters in, 8-4
Files
   changing in multi-file edit, 8-3
   copy or move text between, 8-3
   editing multiple, 8-1
   simultaneous edit of two, 8-4
   switching between two being edited,
      8-5

File size, 2-12
Find all lines containing *pattern*, 9-28
Finding tabs and control characters, 9-
   33
Fixing mistakes (undo), 5-3
Flags and options after ex commands,
   9-10
flash option, 11-11
Force write buffer to existing file, 9-56
Format
   text change commands, 5-12
Forward search
   on current line, 4-19
Function key, map macro to, 9-34

G

Get editor commands from script file
   (ex command), 9-48
Global command list size limit, 2-13
Globalization, 2-4
Global searches, 9-27
Global searches for a pattern, 7-7
Global search for lines containing *pat-
   tern*, 9-28

H

hardtabs option, 11-11

I

Identify editor software version/change
   date, 9-53
ignorecase option, 11-11
Indent, change current, 5-47
Indenting, automatic, 5-46
Input mode
   exit from, 3-9, 3-12
Input Mode, 2-6
Insert/delete buffer size, 2-13
Insert new line in file, 5-5
Insert new text and toggle autoindent
   (ex command), 9-30

Text pattern search to find text block change boundary, 5-28

Text patterns used to save part of workfile, 8-10

Tilde command (~), 9-65

Tildes (~) on side of screen, 2-10

timeout option, 11-23

Transposing characters xp, 5-22

ttytype option, 11-23

Two files, simultaneous edit of, 8-4

Typing ASCII control characters, 5-6

Typing errors in ex command line, 7-2

Typographical errors
using (BACKSPACE) key, 3-10

U

unabbreviate command, 9-15

Undo, 5-3

undo ex commands, 7-4

Undoing previous ex command, 9-14

Undo previous change (ex command), 9-52

Updating permanent storage, 3-12

Uppercase, change to lowercase, 5-35

Use of (ESC) key, 3-9, 3-12

User-defined text objects using markers, 6-9

Using ex commands, 9-1

Using tags to change editing location, 9-51

V

vedit editor, 2-2

version command, 9-53

vi, change from to ex, 7-10

vi, change to from ex, 7-11

view editor, 2-2

vi to ex, switching from, 2-3

W

w300, w1200, w9600 options, 11-25

warn option, 11-24

Wild-card characters in filenames, 8-4

Window containing *count* lines, print (ex command), 9-59

Window, display, 4-1

window option, 11-24

Word or part of word, change, 5-26

Word or part of word, delete, 5-16

Words, changing within a line, 5-39

Words, move cursor forward/backward by, 4-21

Words, swapping, 5-39

Words used as text objects, 6-7

Workfile, append to existing file, 8-11

Wrapmargin, 3-11

wrapmargin option, 11-25

wrapscan option, 11-25

Write all or part of file to UNIX command, 10-19

Write and quit, terminate session, 9-56

writeany option, 11-26

Write buffer as standard input to UNIX command, 9-57

Write buffer to file, 9-55

write command, 9-56

Write temporary file to file, 3-13

Write to existing file, 3-13

Writing read-only files, 9-68

Wrong filename specified when opening session, 3-7

Y

Yanked/deleted text, put back in file, 9-41

Yanked or deleted text, recovering, 5-22

Yank text into buffer (ex command), 9-58